Practical Business Continuity Exercises

How to test your organization's resilience

Charlie Maclean-Bristol

First published in Great Britain and the United States in 2026 by Kogan Page Limited

Kogan Page
Kogan Page Ltd, 2nd Floor, 45 Gee Street, London EC1V 3RS, United Kingdom
Kogan Page Inc, 8 W 38th Street, Suite 902, New York, NY 10018, USA
www.koganpage.com

EU Representative (GPSR)
eucomply OÜ, Pärnu mnt 139b–14 11317, Tallinn, Estonia
www.eucompliancepartner.com

Kogan Page books are printed on paper from sustainable forests.

ISBNs

Hardback	978 1 3986 2821 2
Paperback	978 1 3986 2823 6
Ebook	978 1 3986 2824 3

British Library Cataloguing-in-Publication Data
A CIP record for this book is available from the British Library.

Library of Cataloging-in-Publication Data
A CIP record for this book is available from the Library of Congress.

Typeset by Integra Software Services, Pondicherry
Printed and bound by CPI Group (UK) Ltd, Croydon CR0 4YY

To all those who plan, deliver and learn from exercises,
helping ensure organizations are better prepared when crises occur

CONTENTS

LIST OF FIGURES AND TABLES

ABOUT THE AUTHOR

Charlie Maclean-Bristol MA (Hons), PgD, FBCI, FEPS, CBCI, MCIPR is a leading resilience consultant specializing in crisis management exercising, cyber incident simulations and business continuity exercises. With over 30 years' experience, he has helped organizations around the world prepare for and respond to crises.

He was brought up on the small Isle of Coll in the Hebrides, a remote island of around 200 people, three hours by boat from the mainland. Living in such a remote community taught him the importance of self-reliance, preparedness and resilience from an early age.

Charlie began his career as a Captain in the King's Own Scottish Borderers, where he gained his first experience of contingency planning, training and incident management while conducting patrols and anti-terrorist operations on active service in Northern Ireland. After leaving the Army, he moved into the resilience profession, becoming Emergency Planning Manager at Anglian Water and later Business Continuity Manager at Scottish Power.

In 2007, he founded PlanB Consulting, an independent resilience consultancy, with his wife Kim. Over the following years the company grew into one of the UK's leading specialist consultancies, working with organizations across the public and private sectors around the world. In May 2024, PlanB Consulting was acquired by Databarracks, where Charlie continues to work as a Director, delivering consultancy, training and crisis exercises globally.

Charlie is also the co-founder of Business Continuity Training (BCT), a certified training services provider he established with his brother Lauchlan Maclean-Bristol, which delivers professional business continuity and resilience training courses.

Throughout his career he has designed, delivered and facilitated hundreds of crisis management, cyber incident and business continuity exercises for organizations across six continents, helping teams test plans, build confidence and learn from realistic scenarios.

Charlie is one of the few professionals who is a Fellow of both the Business Continuity Institute (BCI) and the Emergency Planning Society. He has received multiple industry awards including Business Continuity Consultant of the Year, and in 2023 he was awarded the BCI Global Award for Business Continuity and Resilience Volunteer and inducted into the BCI Hall of Fame in recognition of his contribution to the profession.

He holds a Postgraduate Diploma in Emergency Planning and Disaster Management and is a former Module Leader at Glasgow Caledonian University, where he taught resilience, continuity and crisis management to MSc and MBA students.

Charlie is a regular conference speaker and writer, publishes a weekly blog on resilience and business continuity, and has appeared on television and radio discussing crisis management and preparedness. He is also the author of *Business Continuity Exercises: Short Exercises to Validate Your Plan*.

ACKNOWLEDGEMENTS

I would like to thank all colleagues, past and present, at PlanB Consulting and Databarracks for their ideas, experience and support.

Thank you to Smrithi Luice for creating the figures for this book.

I am also grateful to the many clients and business continuity professionals who have shared ideas, case studies and lessons over the years. Their experience and learning have helped shape the thinking behind this book.

01

Introduction to business continuity exercises

In this chapter, you will learn about:

1 What an exercise is
2 The difference between exercise and training
3 Why we conduct exercises
4 What individuals gain from taking part in exercises
5 Ten core principles of effective exercising

What is an exercise?

An exercise is a controlled, objective-driven activity used to practise, test, evaluate or explore future plans, processes or capabilities within an organization or team. In this context, a capability refers to the ability to perform a task effectively. This includes skills, knowledge and behaviours, as well as infrastructure and equipment. **ISO 22300:2021** (**Security and resilience – Vocabulary**) describes an exercise as '*Process to train for, assess, practice and improve organizational performance*'.

To be effective, exercises must be tailored to an identified need, with a clear purpose and defined objectives. They can be conducted across all levels of the organization and may involve all relevant stakeholders. Exercises provide an opportunity to assess risks and consequences, validate response plans and improve preparedness.

Managing an incident is a practical endeavour. It requires not only technical knowledge but also the reflexes and decision-making speed that come from experience and repetition, similar to developing 'muscle memory' for sports people. Alongside this, effective incident management depends on a set of core skills, knowledge and competencies that can be taught and practised. For individuals with less experience, structured training builds understanding, while exercises help translate learning into action.

Exercises should have measurable or defined outcomes. These could include lessons learnt, actionable improvement plans and, in some cases, a formal assessment process or score.

There are different types of exercise, each offering different outcomes. They are typically tailored to participants' levels of experience. Exercises should follow a progressive approach, often described as 'crawl, walk, run', so that teams are not overwhelmed and can take part in an exercise appropriate to their skill level and experience. Each exercise should build on the last, supporting confidence and development over time.

Exercises are usually the final element in the business continuity or crisis management life cycle. They form part of an ongoing cycle of improvement. By conducting regular exercises, teams can test and refine their plans, improve their incident response capabilities, and develop familiarity with key roles and processes.

Exercises provide participants with a safe environment to apply their knowledge, build confidence and refine their responses. The skills taught and practised should align with best practices from emergency services, the military, academic research, and both the public and private sectors. The perceived wisdom is, 'a plan is not complete until it has been exercised'.

The difference between exercises and training

An exercise differs from a training session in its purpose, structure and expected outcomes. Training focuses on developing knowledge and skills, often using instructional methods such as presentations, workshops or hands-on practice. It is typically guided, with facilitators providing explanations, demonstrations and feedback to help participants build their capabilities. In contrast, an exercise is designed to test and validate an organization's plans, procedures and team performance in a simulated scenario.

Rather than teaching new skills, exercises challenge participants to apply their existing knowledge in a realistic and dynamic environment. Exercises may be discussion-based, such as tabletop exercises, or operational, involving live simulations and role-playing. Unlike training, where mistakes are part of the learning process, exercises assess decision-making, teamwork and response effectiveness under pressure. Additionally, exercises often conclude with a debrief, allowing participants to reflect on their performance and identify areas for improvement, ensuring continuous development and organizational resilience.

Although there is a difference between training and exercising, they exist on a continuum as part of the same journey. Training typically comes first, helping participants learn the basics of business continuity response. However, this learning must soon be validated through an exercise. It is important to recognize the connection between training and exercising, rather than treat them as entirely separate activities.

It is equally important to understand that exercises can be delivered as a blend of training and practical activity. The two should not be seen as mutually exclusive. Later in the book, we will discuss the importance of training before an exercise, as it enhances participants' learning during the session and improves knowledge retention.

A blended approach might involve, for example, an hour of training followed by a two-hour exercise. During the exercise, coaching can be provided to team members to remind them of key elements such as effective logging or to highlight skills that may be lacking. These identified gaps can then be addressed in follow-up training sessions, ensuring continuous improvement. So, when designing an exercise, don't feel constrained by the idea that every part of the session must consist solely of traditional exercise elements. It is entirely appropriate to mix and match training and exercise activities, depending on what you are trying to achieve and what the participants need.

Why do we conduct exercises?

Conducting exercises is fundamental to effective business continuity and crisis management planning. Here are the key reasons why exercises are important:

Validating plans, procedures and capabilities

Validation is a critical reason for conducting exercises. It ensures that business continuity, cyber and crisis management plans are not only theoretically sound but capable of performing effectively in real-world conditions. By simulating realistic scenarios, exercises test whether plans, procedures, roles and resources are practical and aligned with operational realities. Exercises identify gaps, inconsistencies and flawed assumptions before a real incident occurs. Responding to scenarios can expose unclear responsibilities, over-reliance on key individuals or suppliers, and assumptions that fail under pressure. They also reveal interdependencies between departments and external stakeholders that may not be visible during routine planning. By exploring these issues in a safe environment, organizations can update plans, improve training and strengthen systems before disruption materializes.

Strengthening organizational resilience through practised readiness

Exercises are one of the most effective ways to build resilience. They take the plan off the shelf and turn it into action. It is not enough to have a plan; people must understand it and be able to use it under pressure. Realistic scenarios test decision-making, speed of response and clarity of roles. Regular practice builds confidence, highlights areas for improvement and demonstrates to leadership and regulators that the organization is prepared. Resilience comes from people being ready to act, not from documents alone.

Enhancing team coordination

Effective crisis management depends on clear communication and coordination. Exercises provide a structured way for teams to practise working together internally and externally. By rehearsing together, teams improve information sharing, reduce misunderstandings and clarify responsibilities. It can also identify issues that fall between the responsibilities of teams. Regular exercises strengthen collaboration and trust, ensuring that when an incident occurs, teams understand their role and can work together effectively.

Complying with legal, contractual, regulatory and industry standards

Many industries mandate the regular testing of business continuity and crisis management plans to meet compliance requirements. Standards such as ISO 22301 (Business Continuity Management Systems) and ISO 22398 (Societal Security – Guidelines for Exercises) provide frameworks for best practices in exercising. Additionally, compliance with local regulations, such as the UK Civil Contingencies Act 2004, ensures that organizations meet statutory obligations and maintain operational readiness. For financial institutions in Europe, DORA (Digital Operational Resilience Act) has a requirement to exercise, as does the UK Operational Resilience regime in the UK.

Often organizations will have contractual requirements for their suppliers to exercise their plans.

In many cases, the need to exercise is explicitly stated in policies, contracts or service-level agreements, making it a formal obligation rather than a discretionary activity. Any organization may require business continuity in their supplier contacts, but the more regulated the sector, the more likely it is that there will be business continuity in the contract.

Improving stakeholder confidence

A robust crisis management exercise programme enhances confidence both internally and externally. Employees feel reassured knowing that their organization is well-prepared for potential disruptions, reducing anxiety during an actual crisis. Externally, clients, partners and regulators gain assurance that the organization prioritizes resilience and is committed to maintaining operational continuity.

Fostering a culture of learning

Exercises should form part of an ongoing learning cycle. Feedback from each session enables continuous improvement of individual learning, plans and response strategies. This approach encourages reflection, innovation and stronger resilience over time.

Practising tools and techniques

Exercises provide an opportunity to practise incident management tools and techniques. Communication channels, remote working arrangements and alternative locations can be assessed to confirm they function as intended.

Reducing incident impacts

Well-designed exercises can play a vital role in reducing the financial, operational and reputational impact of real-world incidents. By identifying weaknesses and gaps in advance, organizations can take proactive steps to strengthen their resilience before a crisis occurs. Practising recovery strategies in realistic, simulated environments enables teams to minimize downtime and accelerate the restoration of critical operations. A well-rehearsed response helps to reduce disruption, protect stakeholder confidence and preserve business continuity.

Managing expectations

Exercises help leaders and teams understand the practical realities of crisis response. They provide insights into what is realistically achievable during a crisis, highlight the limitations of available resources and offer a clearer understanding of how stakeholders, including customers and suppliers, might react under pressure. This realism is essential for setting appropriate expectations and making informed decisions.

Building relationships with external stakeholders

Joint exercises with emergency services, suppliers and regulators strengthen relationships and improve mutual understanding. Shared practice ensures alignment of response strategies and supports effective collaboration during real incidents.

What do individuals gain from taking part in exercises?

Developing personal capabilities

Exercises give individuals the opportunity to strengthen their incident management skills. Participants become more familiar with plans, procedures and responsibilities, and gain practical experience applying them in simulated conditions. Practising in a safe but pressured environment builds resilience and sharpens judgement. Over time, repeated participation improves response instincts and the ability to adapt to unfamiliar or escalating scenarios.

Enhancing teamwork and collaboration skills

Although exercises are team based, the learning is personal. Individuals understand how their role fits within the wider response and how to contribute effectively under stress. These experiences strengthen trust and mutual respect, particularly when working with colleagues they may not regularly engage with.

Practising crisis role responsibilities

Exercises give people the opportunity to test out their crisis role in a realistic setting. Individuals learn what their responsibilities look like in action, rather than just on paper. They experience how their decisions affect others, how escalation processes work and what actions are expected in the first minutes and hours of a disruption.

Often, individuals are assigned incident roles that go beyond their day-to-day responsibilities; for example, a people coordinator may be tasked with supporting staff affected by an incident, even though this may not be part of their usual job.

Improving personal communication under pressure

Exercises allow individuals to practise communicating during high-stress situations. This includes receiving and relaying information, providing updates to leadership, and interacting with internal or external stakeholders.

People learn how to express themselves clearly, concisely and appropriately under time pressure, especially when information is incomplete or the situation is evolving. For some roles, this may also include dealing with media or public messaging, helping individuals build confidence in representing their organization externally.

Understanding system and resource dependencies

Exercises highlight how individual roles depend on systems, tools and support services that may fail during a crisis. Experiencing simulated disruptions improves awareness of these dependencies and develops adaptive thinking when plans are disrupted.

Building individual confidence

Perhaps most importantly, exercises help individuals build confidence in themselves, in the plans and in the team around them. Through practice, people become more comfortable in their crisis role and more capable of handling the pressures of a real incident.

Confidence can be a specific learning outcome of an exercise. For some programmes, participants' self-assessed confidence is measured before and after the session to understand the impact of the exercise. In nearly all the exercises I have conducted, participants have stated that their confidence increased after participating in the exercise.

Ten core principles of effective exercising

The following are the ten principles of effective exercising. When exercises are being planned, they should be periodically reviewed against this list, and adjustments should be made if necessary.

1 **Simplicity**
Scenarios should be easy to understand while maintaining an appropriate level of internal complexity. The exercise should be accessible to all participants, ensuring engagement without overwhelming them with unnecessary detail.

2. **Appropriateness**
   Exercises must be tailored to the seniority of the team, the organization's risk profile and the participants' skill levels. A well-matched scenario ensures relevance and maximizes learning outcomes.
3. **Realism**
   Scenarios should be grounded in real events, likely risks and feasible situations. However, care should be taken to avoid debates over plausibility, as the focus should remain on response and decision-making.
4. **Learning**
   Every exercise should be designed to provide a meaningful learning experience that reinforces knowledge, develops skills and enhances overall preparedness.
5. **Clarity**
   Exercise objectives must be clearly defined and communicated, ensuring participants understand what the exercise is designed to achieve and how success will be measured.
6. **Surprise and challenge**
   Exercises should be sufficiently challenging to test participants' skills and decision-making under pressure. Incorporating unexpected elements ensures adaptability and engagement.
7. **Verisimilitude**
   The appearance of realism is often more important than absolute accuracy. Scenarios should feel credible and immersive, even if they do not perfectly replicate reality.
8. **Debrief**
   A structured debrief at the end of the exercise is essential to capture key learning points, review performance and identify areas for improvement.
9. **Well-planned**
   A significant investment of time, effort and resources goes into planning and delivering an exercise. To be effective, it must be well-executed, well-structured and deliver meaningful results.
10. **Supportive, psychological safety and encouraging mistakes**
    The exercise should complement and reinforce prior training, helping participants apply their knowledge in a practical setting and encouraging a supportive environment where mistakes are accepted as essential learning opportunities.

KEY LEARNINGS

- Exercises are structured activities used to practise, assess and improve organizational and individual performance.
- Training and exercises form a continuum; learning begins in training and is tested through exercising. Both elements can be present in an exercise.
- Repetition through exercises builds muscle memory, enabling instinctive crisis response under pressure.
- Effective exercises use realistic, challenging scenarios and can include extreme but plausible events.
- Exercises validate plans, roles, responsibilities and decision-making processes under real-time stress.
- Participants build personal confidence, communication skills and teamwork through realistic practice.
- Exercises should be matched to participant readiness using a 'crawl, walk, run' progression model.
- A psychologically safe environment encourages learning from mistakes and trying new approaches.
- Debriefs are essential for capturing lessons, identifying gaps and driving continuous improvement.
- Exercises demonstrate organizational resilience and support compliance with legal and contractual obligations.

02

The different types of business continuity exercises

In this chapter, you will learn about:

1 The different types of exercises

2 Which type of exercise is good for each level of participants

As well as many ways to conduct exercises, there are also various names for the same exercise. This is especially noticeable between the US and the UK. According to the Federal Emergency Management Agency (FEMA) in the US, '*A functional exercise examines and/or validates the coordination, command, and control between various multi-agency coordination centres (e.g., emergency operation centres) without the actual movement of personnel or equipment*'.[1] In the UK, we would call this a simulated exercise (SIMEX). The difference can become an issue when the sponsor commissioning the exercise uses a term in one way and the person designing and developing the exercise interprets it differently. It is therefore important to clarify exactly what type of exercise they want delivered and how it is to be carried out.

Exercises should not be viewed in isolation but as part of a broader, progressive training programme. They should ideally follow a structured path from simpler to more complex formats, often referred to as the 'crawl, walk, run' model. This approach allows participants to build their confidence and competence over time. You start with basic awareness training and discussion-based exercises, then move onto tabletop sessions, and finally into SIMEX. Each stage helps embed the learning from the previous one, while gradually exposing individuals and teams to greater pressure, complexity and realism. By adopting a progressive approach, organizations ensure their people are not overwhelmed too early and that they build up the readiness and resilience required to manage real incidents effectively.

Plan walkthrough

The main objective of a plan walkthrough is to review the plan with those who would implement it.

A plan walkthrough is a structured, conversation-led review of a business continuity or recovery plan. It is commonly used when a plan is new, recently updated, or when team members are unfamiliar with its contents. Walkthroughs are particularly valuable when knowledge is limited or confidence needs strengthening.

At its core, a walkthrough helps people understand what the plan is for, how to use it and where they fit in. It is not a simulation, but a guided discussion that works through the plan step by step, allowing time for questions and clarification. A well-run walkthrough builds understanding, ownership and confidence.

With larger groups, it can be helpful to begin with a quick poll on participants' confidence in the plan, their ability, and the organization's ability to manage an incident. This can reveal useful insights and highlight gaps between perception and preparedness.

PLAN CONFIDENCE

I ran a series of plan walkthroughs for a utility company on a Caribbean island. At the beginning of each exercise, I asked all participants to rate their confidence in the company's, their division's, and their individual department's ability to manage an incident. Across all five exercises, participants had the lowest confidence in the company's overall ability to manage an incident, while their highest confidence was in their own department. Perhaps the lesson here is that the closer you are to a plan, the more confident you are that it will work.

Next, move into the plan itself. Begin with a simple scenario and work through each stage of the response. Ask questions such as, 'What would you do if this happened tomorrow? What actions would you take?' This helps participants understand how the plan works in practice rather than just on paper.

I prefer to use a straightforward scenario; for example, the headquarters building has burnt down. A simple scenario keeps the focus on response. You may introduce a second scenario, such as the loss of all IT, to explore how the response would differ. Avoid too many scenarios, but using one or two helps keep the discussion relevant.

A walkthrough can also explore a specific emerging risk, such as public unrest during a major event near your offices. Working through how the organization would respond makes the discussion practical and current.

These discussions also reveal gaps in the plan, unclear wording or unrealistic assumptions. By reviewing the plan with those who would implement it, issues often emerge that would not surface in a more formal exercise. A walkthrough is therefore a simple but effective way to build understanding, clarify roles and strengthen resilience.

Good for

- Validation of plans and procedures
- Exploring scenarios
- Exploring the end-to-end management of an incident

Not so good for

- Teamworking and leadership
- Exploring communications
- Practising incident management skills

Tests and technical exercises

The main objective of tests and technical exercises is to check whether systems, applications or equipment can meet recovery requirements.

Technical exercises or tests assess the performance and resilience of specific systems, infrastructure or technical components that support an organization's ability to respond to and recover from disruptions. These exercises are often conducted by IT, cyber, facilities or engineering teams and may include activities such as failover testing, server recovery, backup verification and telecoms redundancy checks. Unlike tabletop or scenario-based exercises, which test human response and coordination, technical exercises aim to validate the recovery of systems under stress or failure conditions. Tests often result in a simple yes-or-no answer; for example, whether a system can be recovered within a specific time frame. This makes them different from most other types of business continuity exercises, which tend to focus more on process and decision-making than binary outcomes.

An IT disaster recovery test might simulate the loss of a primary data centre and evaluate how quickly systems can be restored from backups at an alternative location. These exercises are critical for identifying technical single points of failure (ensuring time to recover is realistic), configuration issues or a lack of knowledge or skills to implement the recovery. Integrating technical tests into the broader exercise programme ensures that both human and technological aspects of resilience are regularly validated and aligned.

Good for

- Validation of ability to recover and time taken for systems and processes

Not so good for

- Teamworking and leadership
- Exploring communications
- Practising incident management skills
- Exploring scenarios
- Exploring the full life cycle of incident management

Tabletop exercises

According to the Business Continuity Institute, '*Tabletop exercises are the most common type of exercise and are used to validate plans and rehearse team members in their roles*'.[2] They are one of the most widely used and effective formats for developing crisis response capability. As they take place in a safe, discussion-based environment, they allow teams to explore plans, make decisions and discuss their roles without the pressure of responding during a SIMEX. This makes them particularly useful for building confidence, improving coordination and testing how people think, not just what they know. They are also highly flexible: they can be tailored to any scenario or audience. Whether you are training a new crisis team, refreshing executive leadership or testing a specific issue like cyber or supply chain disruption, the format can be adapted to meet your objectives.

They are also relatively easy to plan and deliver, making them accessible for exercise beginners. The same exercise can be run multiple times for different parts of the organization, reducing the need for extensive planning each time.

> TABLETOP EXERCISE OR DESKTOP EXERCISE
>
> I have always used the term 'tabletop exercise', but it can be used interchangeably with 'desktop exercise'. *Tabletop* is more common in the US, whereas *desktop* is more common in the UK. For all intents and purposes, they are the same thing.

Single-entity tabletop

The main objective of a single-entity tabletop is for an incident management team to practise their response across a number of time frames or phases of an incident.

This is a tabletop exercise in which a single entity participates. It could be a department, a location or an incident management team. The scenario is presented using slides, followed by either a single question or a series of questions posed to the team. They discuss their answers and then provide feedback to the exercise director. The exercise is conducted through a series of these 'turns'.

Once the first question has been addressed, the scenario is updated to reflect a new event or a further unfolding of the situation. The simulated time is also advanced. These time jumps allow later stages of the response to be explored, which is not as easily done in a SIMEX, where the exercise is run in real time. A team leader should be designated to provide feedback on the team's behalf and a script should be designated to take notes.

Multi-agency / team tabletop

The main objective of a multi-agency or team tabletop is for multiple incident management teams or a number of organizations to coordinate their response.

This exercise involves multiple teams, groups or organizations participating in the same activity. It aims to coordinate plans and responses, examine interdependencies, identify unrealistic assumptions and ensure a joined-up approach to incident management. Participants might include several departments from the same organization, multiple incident management teams or different organizations working together. The exercise may test an existing plan or explore a new threat or event for which no plan has yet been developed. If there are several incident teams from within the same organization, the exercise could involve all operational teams or include a hierarchy of plans covering operational, tactical and strategic levels.

Usually, the different groups are seated at separate tables. If there are enough exercise staff, each table should have an umpire or facilitator, although this is not always possible. As with the single-entity tabletop exercise, one or more questions are posed to each team. They discuss the scenario and then provide feedback on their answers to the wider group in turn. The questions may be the same for all tables or specific to each team, depending on the exercise's aims.

Good for

- Validation of plans and procedures
- Exploring communications
- Exploring scenarios
- Exploring the full life cycle of incident management
- Coordinating responses

Not so good for

- Teamworking and leadership
- Practising incident management skills

Wargaming or stress test exercising

Wargaming or stress test exercising is used to challenge an incident management team's response. It is a structured decision-making exercise in which participants respond to unfolding events in a simulated environment. Unlike a typical tabletop or SIMEX, it is not just about validating plans, but also about exploring possibilities, assumptions and strategic 'what ifs'.

Wargames are particularly useful for testing unfamiliar scenarios or when teams are already confident in their existing plans. They challenge thinking, expose blind spots and test how decisions hold up under pressure.

In a business continuity or crisis management context, wargames explore strategic questions. For example, what if a critical supplier failed during a geopolitical event, or a cyber-attack escalated due to media reaction? These exercises push leaders to consider longer-term impacts, stakeholder expectations and difficult trade-offs such as reputation versus compliance. Decisions are examined and, where appropriate, challenged to explore alternative outcomes.

Wargames typically involve Red and Blue teams. The Blue team acts on behalf of the organization and responds in accordance with established plans. The Red team provides constructive challenge by introducing new information, questioning assumptions and reflecting stakeholder perspectives, such as those of regulators, customers and the media.

The format is similar to a tabletop, with an unfolding scenario delivered in stages. The Blue team responds, the Red team challenges, and facilitators guide the discussion before determining what carries forward into the next stage.

These exercises must be conducted in a positive environment where challenge is accepted as constructive. The aim is insight rather than simple validation. Wargaming is especially valuable for mature organizations, offering a different, more strategic way to exercise.

Good for

- Challenging assumption
- Validation of plans and procedures
- Exploring communications
- Exploring scenarios
- Exploring the full life cycle of incident management

Not so good for

- Teamworking and leadership
- Practising incident management skills

Simulated exercise (SIMEX)

A SIMEX is designed to feel as realistic as possible, allowing participants to experience the pressures, team dynamics and leadership challenges of a real incident. Unlike tabletop exercises, which follow structured discussion, a SIMEX is dynamic and fluid. It introduces time pressure, uncertainty and complex decision-making, requiring teams to respond in real time using their actual plans, tools and incident rooms. The environment should replicate real conditions, including logs, IT systems and administrative support (see Figure 2.1).

Ideally, the team should be co-located in an incident room, though hybrid arrangements can be used if they reflect normal operations. One team may participate, or multiple teams from the same or different organizations. Within one organization, this may include strategic and tactical teams working together. Multi-agency SIMEX exercises can simulate sector-wide or government responses to major incidents such as cyber-attacks or public health emergencies.

The exercise usually begins with an incident in progress. Injects are delivered as events unfold and may come from various stakeholders. The most realistic method is for role-players to deliver emails, calls or face-to-face interactions. A simpler but less realistic option is delivering injects by slide. Another approach is giving participants different information at the outset, requiring them to share it to build situational awareness. Reports, briefing papers and simulated media coverage can also be used.

Media and social media engagement can be practised in real time through calls, simulated press releases or live feedback from role-players acting as journalists or members of the public.

Scenarios may be fully scripted or adapted dynamically in response to participant decisions. SIMEX exercises typically run continuously, although a final time jump may be used to explore longer-term implications.

A dedicated role-player cell delivers injects and simulates external stakeholders. The role-player coordinator manages inject flow and may adjust the scenario in consultation with the exercise director. The exercise director maintains overall control, manages pace and intervenes if the scenario drifts off course.

Successful delivery requires balance: providing meaningful content, allowing time to absorb information and maintaining engagement without overwhelming the team. Umpires should assess performance, with at least one focused on the organization being exercised.

FIGURE 2.1 SIMEX configuration

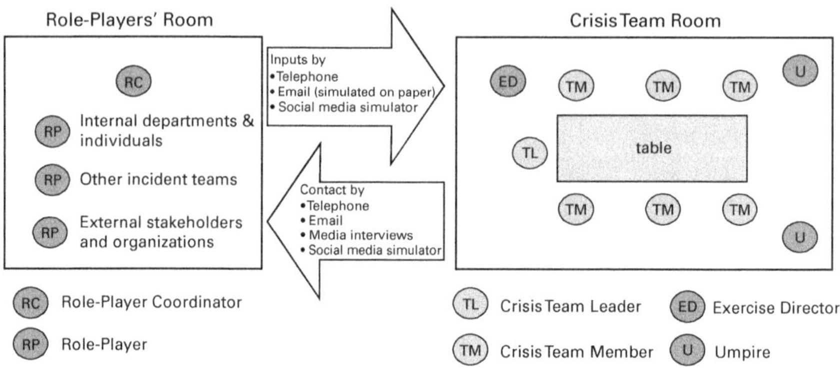

Participants often report that a SIMEX feels like managing a real incident and provides insights directly applicable to future events. Further discussion of SIMEX exercises follows in Chapter 3.

Good for

- Validation of plans and procedures
- Exploring communications
- Exploring scenarios
- Teamworking and leadership
- Practising incident management decision-making, incident team meetings, information management and administrative support to the team
- Practising situational awareness and sense-making
- Sharing information

Not so good for

- Inexperienced incident management teams

Live exercises (LIVEX) and drills

The main objective of live exercises and drills is for teams to practise their response in the location and using the equipment they would rely on during a real incident.

These exercises are practical activities designed to test individuals and teams in real time, replicating events as closely as possible. They range from fire evacuation drills to the response to simulated aircraft or train crashes with actors playing casualties.

At a basic level, there may be regulatory requirements to conduct drills, such as fire evacuations or practising responses to hazardous materials. Under the UK's COMAH regulations, operators must test on-site plans and involve external responders in exercising off-site plans. In airports, multi-agency live exercises for major incidents are standard and often required by national or ICAO guidance.

Larger exercises can have a live operational element supported by tactical and strategic teams, allowing practice of information flow and decision-making from the scene to incident rooms. In the UK this is known as a LIVEX, while in the US it is referred to as a full-scale exercise. These are operations-based exercises involving multiple agencies and real-time resource deployment.

A LIVEX may include scene management, triage, casualty evacuation and coordination between agencies. Additional complexity may involve CBRN scenarios or the establishment of rest centres and temporary mortuaries. The focus is coordination, command and control, and effective communication between on-site responders and senior teams.

However, live exercises can be costly and resource intensive. Responding organizations may charge for participation, and extensive planning is required to ensure safety and value. Many operational tasks, such as treating and transporting casualties, are routine activities, so the real learning often lies in command, coordination and inter-agency working. In some cases, similar learning can be achieved through lower-cost simulation methods. Health and safety risks must also be considered.

Despite these challenges, both small drills and large live exercises contribute significantly to preparedness. For many responders, exercises provide rare opportunities to practise specialist roles and equipment. A well-designed LIVEX should balance realism and learning against cost, complexity and risk, ensuring that the benefits justify the investment in preparedness and performance.

Good for

- Validation of plans and procedures
- Exploring communications
- Exploring scenarios
- Teamworking and leadership
- Practising situational awareness and sense-making
- Sharing information

Not so good for

- Inexperienced incident management teams
- Practising incident management decision-making, incident team meetings, information management and administrative support to the team

Blended incident management training and workshops

Often, especially if the incident management team is new to exercising, or if you want to introduce general staff to incident response and exercising, a workshop approach can be used. This would consist of formal classroom training followed by a number of short exercises. It could be delivered to a specific group of staff or to a group of managers, using incident management as a group activity. Further information, including elements that could be included in a workshop, can be found in Chapter 10.

FOOD MANUFACTURING LIVE EXERCISE

PlanB Consulting was asked by a food manufacturer to put together some training for their shift managers in responding to incidents. They could be on shift in the middle of the night and be the most senior person in the factory, so they would have to manage an incident until the plant management could attend the incident, which could take up to a couple of hours.

The training was to give them the tools, procedures and the confidence to fulfil this role. A full day programme was devised. It started with general classroom training about incidents and some of the issues they would face. Training was also delivered around the mnemonic RECAP[3] which gave them a framework for managing their response.

After the classroom training, there were a number of practical training sessions where those attending practised their initial response. This included an exercise based on the 'Outside Now' exercise format (see Chapter 13). They practised reporting an incident from the site using the mnemonic METHANE[4] and then did a series of mini live exercises where they had to respond to a set-up scenario. The training was a mixture of classroom training, practising the application of that training, and a number of short live exercises.

Good for

- Inexperienced incident management teams
- Exploring communications
- Exploring scenarios
- Validation of plans and procedures

Not so good for

- Teamworking and leadership
- Practising situational awareness and sense-making
- Sharing information
- Practising incident management decision-making, incident team meetings, information management and administrative support to the team

Which type of exercise is good for each level of participants?

Although most exercise formats could be used for any level of participants, some exercises lend themselves to different levels of staff, as shown in Table 2.1.

TABLE 2.1 Which exercise type is helpful for each level of participants?

Exercise type	Senior Managers	Middle Managers	Junior Staff / Team Leads
Plan walkthrough	●●	●●●	●●●
Tests and technical exercises	●	●●	●●●
Tabletop	●●●	●●●	●●●
Wargaming / Stress testing	●●●	●●	●

(continued)

TABLE 2.1 (Continued)

Exercise type	Senior Managers	Middle Managers	Junior Staff / Team Leads
SIMEX	●●●	●●	●●
LIVEX / drills	●	●	●●●
Blended incident management and workshops	●●●	●●●	●●●

Key
●●●= Highly suitable
●● = Moderately suitable
● = Less suitable

KEY LEARNINGS

- There are many ways to conduct exercises, and terminology varies between countries, so it is important to clarify exactly what type of exercise is being requested and delivered.
- Exercises should be designed as part of a progressive programme using a 'crawl, walk, run' model, where complexity increases gradually as teams gain confidence.
- Plan walkthroughs are effective for reviewing new or updated plans and building understanding of roles and responsibilities.
- Tests and technical exercises validate the functionality of systems and equipment and focus on achieving measurable recovery outcomes.
- Tabletop exercises are discussion-based and excellent for exploring scenarios, validating plans and improving coordination in a low-pressure setting.
- Multi-agency and single-entity tabletop exercises test coordination between teams and ensure alignment of plans and responsibilities.
- Wargaming or stress testing helps challenge assumptions, test decision-making and explore complex 'what if' scenarios in a strategic environment.
- SIMEX exercises provide a realistic, time-pressured environment to test plans, communications and decision-making under authentic conditions.
- Live exercises and drills replicate real-world operations, testing people, equipment and coordination across multiple agencies in real time.
- Blended training and workshops combine classroom learning with short, practical exercises, ideal for new teams or organizations starting their exercise journey.

Notes

1 FEMA (n.d.) Types of training and exercises, EMI LMS (IS-559). https://emilms.fema.gov/is_0559/groups/155.html

2 Business Continuity Institute (2023) Good Practice Guidelines Edition 7.0: Business Continuity Management Lifecycle. Caversham: BCI, p 223

3 Risk assessment, Essential tasks, Communications required, Actions to be carried out, Preserve evidence

4 Joint Emergency Services Interoperability Principles (JESIP) (n.d.) *M/ETHANE*. www.jesip.org.uk/joint-doctrine/m-ethane/

03

Guidance for designing and developing SIMEXs

In this chapter, you will learn about:

1. The meetings to develop a SIMEX
2. How to use different channels for delivering injects
3. Running online SIMEXs
4. Developing a role-player's guide
5. Writing an exercise telephone directory

A SIMEX is a more immersive and complex type of exercise that requires additional planning elements not typically found in other formats. These exercises usually involve more planning meetings than other formats to ensure the scenario is tailored, realistic and detailed. While a SIMEX follows the same overall process of design and development as outlined in other chapters of this book, there are several specific components unique to its delivery. This chapter gives some of the unique planning elements for developing and delivering a SIMEX.

Meetings to develop a SIMEX

As a minimum, four meetings are required to plan a SIMEX, plus a rehearsal (see Figure 3.1). However, a complex SIMEX, especially one involving several different teams, may require additional meetings. It should be noted that documents will need to be produced between meetings and sent to those involved in planning the exercise so they can review and provide feedback before the next meeting.

FIGURE 3.1 Meetings required for SIMEX planning

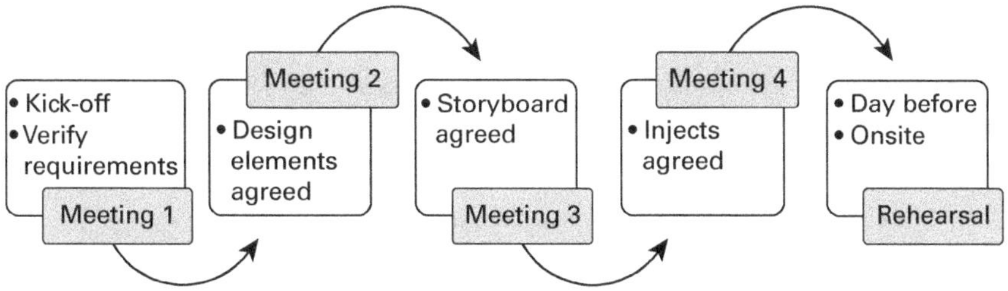

Meeting 1: Kick-off

The initial meeting launches the exercise planning process. At this meeting, all elements of the design phase should be discussed and, if possible, agreed. Some of these elements may have been agreed prior to the exercise being commissioned, while others are decided as the exercise details are discussed.

A key output of the meeting is to agree on is the delivery date for the exercise. If the exercise involves senior managers, this can be the most challenging thing to tie down. We often agree the date of the exercise almost as soon as the exercise is agreed and then the exercise planning process works backwards from it.

Another output of the exercise, which should be agreed early, is if there is a need for a design team to help plan the exercise, as once this team is agreed, they should attend all planning exercises, especially if they are likely to be role-players on the day of the exercise. A subject matter expert may just attend one meeting to provide expert advice into the development of the scenario or injects.

It is important that the role-player coordinator and exercise director remain the same throughout the exercise's development to ensure continuity of thought and that they are aware of why the exercise has been planned the way it is. Umpires can attend the exercise development meetings, but their presence is optional rather than mandatory.

When multiple people are involved in developing an exercise, it can be difficult to create materials collaboratively during meetings. In my experience, the most effective approach is to discuss the broad outlines and themes as a group but then have the exercise director and role-player coordinator develop the detailed materials outside of the meeting. These materials can then be brought back to the design team for review and refinement. This streamlines the process and makes the best use of the design team's expertise alongside the planning skills of the exercise director and role-player coordinator.

Before the next meeting, the first draft of the exercise instruction should be developed and sent to the sponsor and any others involved in the planning of the exercise before Meeting 2, with sufficient time for them to read the document. This should include the first draft of the purpose, objectives and scenario overview.

Meeting 1 attendees should include an exercise director, a role-player coordinator, a sponsor and a design team.

Meeting 2: Agree on design phase and scenario discussions

The design phase should be signed off on, including the purpose and objectives. The second part of the planning meeting then focuses on reviewing the details of the scenario and how the exercise will develop over time, with a view to developing the exercise storyboard.

Exercise storyboard development involves creating a structured narrative that outlines the progression of an exercise scenario, including key events, injects and decision points. It helps ensure the exercise flows logically, meets its objectives and keeps participants engaged. The group will agree on the full storyboard, including the events that will take place during the exercise, how the media and social media stories will develop, and how the different stakeholders, both internal and external, will react during the exercise.

Before the next meeting, the storyboard is written up and sent to the sponsor for review and comment.

Meeting 2 attendees should be the exercise director, role-player coordinator and design team.

Meeting 3: Agree storyboard and discuss injects

This session focuses on finalizing the storyboard and then developing the individual injects which will drive the exercise play. This will also look at who the injects should go to, what channel will be used for the delivery and what the expected response to the inject will be.

Before the next meeting, the injects are developed and sent to the client.

Meeting 3 attendees should be the exercise director, role-player coordinator and design team.

Meeting 4: Agree on the injects

In this meeting, the injects are reviewed and agreed. This may involve ensuring the persons submitting the injects are appropriate, confirming that the injects align with the exercise's objectives, and agreeing on the method of input for the exercise. The expected answer for each inject should be reviewed and signed off. Ensuring there are injects for all players is important for keeping all participants engaged in the response.

Meeting 4 attendees should be the exercise director, role-player coordinator and design team.

Rehearsal: Getting ready for the big day

This is typically held the day before the exercise, when the delivery team meets on-site to ensure all participants are briefed and prepared. Further information on the activities to be conducted at the rehearsal is contained in Chapter 18.

Rehearsal attendees should include the exercise director, role-player coordinator, umpires and role-players / design team.

How to use different channels for delivering the SIMEX injects

PowerPoint

I would avoid using PowerPoint slides for delivering injects in SIMEX. This approach is unrealistic, as in real-life incidents, communications do not arrive neatly packaged on slides. Even during the initial briefing, I try to avoid using slides, as they tend to disrupt the atmosphere of the exercise and make it feel more like a training session than an immersive simulation.

Face-to-face

People come into the incident room to brief the team. These may include subject matter experts, members of the board or parent company, or representatives from other teams, such as the team leader of a silver team or computer incident response team (CIRT), or someone coming from the scene of the incident to brief what happened first-hand on-site.

These exercises are particularly effective when real personnel deliver the briefings in their actual roles within the organization. They use appropriate language, share relevant organizational details and present the information as they would in a real incident, which adds to the realism and overall impact of the scenario.

It is essential that those presenting the information have an agreed script and rehearse their roles to ensure they stay on message, avoid delivering incorrect information, and do not omit crucial details needed to shape the scenario. Encourage them to practise the delivery so they are not just reading the information on a piece of paper.

You might have external people come into the incident room, such as emergency services, government officials or suppliers, but it is unlikely that they would actually turn up at the incident room. Interaction with them could be carried out by a telephone call.

Telephone call

The exercise should be organized so that participants do not need to use their own mobile phones for receiving and making exercise calls, as real calls could be confused with exercise calls. Once participants start using their phones, they usually use it as an excuse to start looking at their emails or their social media and their attention is lost from the exercise.

One of two mobile phones should be in the centre of the incident room table, with the participants told to answer if it goes off. Sometimes, if the person answers, it goes on speaker so all team members can hear the information. This phone can also be used to call externally to the team to the role-player's cell.

Calls from the site of the incident, made by a relevant role-player to update the team on unfolding events, can be a highly effective way of driving the scenario. It also feels much more realistic to participants, helping them to immerse in the exercise environment. However, it is unrealistic for people, especially external parties, to be phoning directly into the incident room's number. In the initial briefing, you may say that although this is unrealistic, it may be done for exercise purposes.

Instead of having a phone in the middle of the table, you may decide to use written telephone injects. This can be simulated where a receptionist or PA receives the call, writes it into a memo, and delivers it to the relevant person in the incident room. This can cut down on the number of role-players needed as the telephone calls can be prewritten as paper memos.

Emails

Emails can be an effective way to convey detailed information during an exercise. As the information is provided in a fixed, written format, there is less risk of miscommunication, which can happen through verbal delivery, such as messages being misheard, altered or misunderstood.

This helps keep the exercise on track and ensures that all participants are working from the same accurate information. We also tend to use paper emails to keep participants off their computers, where they can be distracted by real work and encouraged to focus on teamwork and leadership.

Incoming paper emails can be pre-printed with the other exercise injects. Outgoing emails must be handwritten by participants, and there must be a system in place for a runner to collect them and deliver to the role-player cell.

If the exercise involves sending actual emails, then an exercise@.... email address can be set up to receive all incoming messages. Return emails can use this address or paper mails can be used. Where a real email may have to be used is when press statements or other communications need to be drafted and reviewed by the incident team for approval, or when an external stakeholder requires text to be sent to them. It is more realistic to draft text on a computer and send it than to handwrite it.

Internal communications

Internal communications can, in some cases, be difficult to simulate, depending on the usual method of communication within the organization. If an email distribution list is used, a paper email from those in the incident room can easily simulate this.

If 'town hall' meetings are typically conducted, these can be simulated by having the person who would usually deliver the briefing leave the incident room, brief a role-player acting as staff and then return to the incident room.

Intranets can be simulated using a social media simulation tool, or alternatively, text can be handwritten or typed, then emailed or handed to the role-players, who will acknowledge it as if it were posted to the organization's intranet.

Calls to regulators, customers, parent companies, boards or other external stakeholders

These calls can be an excellent way of practising speaking to third parties and making sure those tasked with the role think through what they are going to say. Although it is unrealistic for regulators, customers and external stakeholders to call directly into the incident room, they can email or telephone and then give a time when they would like a call.

Media and social media

Chapter 15 details how the media and social media may be simulated.

Using a script instead of individual injects

Instead of delivering multiple injects from different external sources, each exercise participant should be provided with a script or briefing sheet summarizing what they know. This allows them to contribute to the SIMEX by simulating a scenario in which they've gathered information from on-site staff, internal colleagues or external stakeholders, and are now presenting their understanding to the team. This method provides a quicker, more efficient way to feed information to participants than issuing separate injects from various organizations. In real-life situations, it is common for members of the incident team to arrive at meetings with pre-existing knowledge they have already gathered before the formal team discussions begin.

Running online SIMEXs

If the exercise is to be conducted in a hybrid format or fully online, careful planning is essential to ensure that in-person interactions are effectively conveyed to remote participants. Injects can be shared via the video conference chat function or by email. If the team needs to split into functional groups for separate discussions, breakout rooms should be utilized. The exercise delivery team must ensure that there are enough umpires available, ideally one per breakout room. When an umpire joins a breakout room, they should switch off their camera and avoid participants wanting to include them in the discussion. It should also be agreed in advance how breakout rooms will be managed, including who is responsible for moving participants in and out of them.

Developing a role-player's guide

All those in the role-player cell will require copies of the inject list plus the exercise telephone guide. Depending on the complexity of the exercise, a role-players' guide may need to be developed, especially if the role-players are not familiar with the stakeholders' roles, or the exercise director wants them to behave in a certain way.

I do not personally often produce a role-players' guide, as the level of detail is not usually necessary. They are mainly used in multi-day exercises, such as in the oil industry, where they involve numerous stakeholders to be role-played. They can be used to designate the attitude or point of view for stakeholder organizations to adopt towards the organization being exercised. This could include a role-player playing a particular protest group, or to have particular character types portrayed.

The front page of the role-players' guide should detail some 'dos and don'ts' for role-players. Each call / email must start with 'FOR EXERCISE' to ensure no one is misled into thinking an incident is actually happening. Role-players should be instructed to log their calls, including incoming and outgoing calls, and to fill in the actual response to injects.

Unless role-players are playing themselves in their own day job, a separate contact name should be created for each role they undertake, and this should be detailed in the guide. These names should not be celebrities or silly names.

It is important to make clear that role-players have a certain amount of scope to ad-lib when delivering inputs / speaking with responders so long as they do not fundamentally change the message or direction of the response.

The following information may be included in the role-players' guide.

1. **Who they are playing:** A clear description of the individual or stakeholder they are representing (e.g. concerned member of the public, protester, journalist, regulator, site manager, emergency services contact). Include their name, job title, role, organization and any relevant background.
2. **Relationship to the organization:** If they are external to the organization, clarify their relationship with the organization and how familiar they are with its operations.
3. **What they know:** Provide a script, bullet points or a briefing sheet of what they know about the incident at that point in the scenario. This should reflect what someone in their role would realistically be aware of.
4. **Tone and behaviour:** Guidance on how to act: are they angry, confused, professional, emotional, demanding, calm or urgent? This helps bring realism and appropriate pressure to the exercise.
5. **How to respond to questions:** Guidance on what they can and cannot say. They should be encouraged to ad-lib where appropriate, but also know when to say, 'I'll check and call you back', if participants ask for information not in their brief.

6 **Escalation instructions:** If a participant reacts unexpectedly or takes the conversation off-script, role-players should know when to pause, escalate to the role-player leader or exercise director, or create a follow-up inject.

Role-player log sheet

Role-players should be issued with log sheets, which can be used to record the timing and content of each incoming and outgoing interaction with the exercise participants. These can be used to assess the actual response to an inject, provide a timeline for the response and measure how long requests for information took to be complied with.

The exercise director should collect the log sheets after the exercise, as they can serve as useful inputs for the post-exercise report and may also support any cold debrief. The log sheet could be the organization's standard incident response log or a simple spreadsheet used to capture interactions with the exercise participants. The content of the sheet should include the name of the exercise, the name of the person completing the sheet, the time of the interaction, sender and recipient, details of the call or interaction and any relevant comments.

Development of an exercise telephone directory

If the exercise involves responders calling real individuals or role-players, then an exercise telephone directory must be available for reference. The directory should list the roles or individuals that responders may want to contact to support the response along with the relevant phone number. It should also include some direction on how to manage calls and list each role that it is anticipated they need to contact with the associated number.

If contacts are playing for real, state USE REAL NUMBER which will direct responders to their documentation to source contact details. If the number is role-played, then put the contact details for the person undertaking the role. Sometimes, real players prefer to use a different number from their usual contact; include this in the directory as required.

Always include an ANY OTHER CONTACT option. There will be contacts that are not listed on the directory. Responders should use this number, tell the role-player who they want them to play and then the role-player will take on that role. ANY OTHER CONTACT should be assigned to a role-player who is likely to be less busy than the others.

Provide information about how media and social media will be simulated (including details of any URLs and how to log onto and simulation platforms), and the details of who to call if you want to speak to those running the exercise (exercise control).

Communications among those running the exercise

During the exercise, role-players may be located in a separate room, while the exercise director may move between the incident room and the role-player room. Umpires are typically based in the incident room to observe the participants. There may also be additional personnel involved in managing the exercise. It is important to establish a clear and reliable communications channel between those running the exercise to track which injects have been delivered and to share other important information, such as requests for additional injects or changes to the scenario.

WhatsApp, or a messaging platform such as Slack or Microsoft Teams, can be used effectively for this purpose. A dedicated group or channel should be created solely for exercise coordination to avoid confusion. While email can be used, it is not ideal, as messages may be delayed or overlooked amid other routine communications. A real-time messaging system ensures that exercise control remains tightly coordinated and responsive throughout the event.

KEY LEARNINGS

- SIMEX exercises require additional planning effort compared to other formats, including more detailed scenario development, more coordination meetings, and greater preparation of supporting materials.
- Every inject should be clearly linked to a learning objective or testing requirement and integrated logically into the scenario, with agreed delivery methods and expected outcomes.
- Role-players must be properly briefed, scripted and supported with tools such as role instructions and telephone directories to maintain realism and consistency.
- Exercise materials are best developed outside planning meetings by the exercise director and role-player coordinator, then reviewed and refined collaboratively to streamline the process.

- A minimum of four structured planning meetings plus a rehearsal is normally required to design, refine and prepare a SIMEX effectively.
- Injects can be delivered through multiple channels – face-to-face, telephone, email, scripted briefings or written notes – and the chosen method should balance realism, control and practicality.
- Online and hybrid SIMEX delivery requires additional planning to manage inject flow, breakout rooms, observation by umpires and participant engagement.
- Role-player guides and briefing materials improve consistency and realism, particularly in complex exercises or where role-players are unfamiliar with the stakeholders they represent.
- Role-player log sheets enhance control, traceability and post-exercise evaluation.
- Strong internal communications among the exercise delivery team, using real-time messaging platforms, are essential to coordinate inject delivery and adapt dynamically during the exercise.

04

Building a multi-year strategic exercise roadmap

In this chapter, you will learn about:

1. Why exercise programmes are important
2. How to document a multi-year strategy
3. End-to-end validation of a recovery strategy

'The organization shall implement and maintain a programme of exercising and testing to validate over time the effectiveness of its business continuity strategies and solutions'.[1]

Organizations should have an exercise programme that plans activities as part of a multi-year approach, rather than a one-year programme, which is often the default for many organizations. A well-structured multi-year exercise programme helps organizations move beyond ad hoc or compliance-driven testing to a more strategic, systematic approach. By planning exercises across several years, organizations can ensure that over time critical risks are addressed, key teams are prepared and business continuity capabilities are continuously improved.

Why are exercise programmes important?

The following reasons are why a programme of exercises is important:

Risks are addressed systematically

The risk to the organization is approached methodically rather than at the whim of the business continuity manager, sponsor or consultant. The business continuity manager may have their own devious scenario which they will use to catch out the team they are exercising, or the consultant may have a scenario that has worked for other clients and is easy to reproduce. In developing your programme, you should identify the organization's top three to five business continuity risks, ensuring they have not been previously exercised, and then develop them as exercise scenarios. This way, you will know that the most likely risks or those with the biggest impact have been practised, and that your incident management team is prepared to handle them.

Strategies and solutions are reviewed and checked

When reviewing a strategy, solution or multiple solutions, they need to be validated to ensure that timing can be met, that resources to recover are adequate and that they would work if implemented. This could include not only testing the incident management team responsible for coordinating the response, but also verifying the technical elements that support the risk. This may involve technical tests, plan walkthroughs, tabletop exercises or SIMEX tests.

Agreed dates for exercises

Many times, I have been called into an organization to run an exercise that their standard requires every 12 months, but for various reasons, they have waited 15 months or longer to run the next one. I have then observed gaps of a year or two since their last exercise, with the longest being seven years. Having an annual programme provides a set date for conducting your exercise.

Participants' skills and knowledge build over time

In common with the crawl, walk, run methodology, especially if you have a new team which has not got much experience in exercising, you build their skills over time and then build on what they learnt in the last exercise. As will be outlined in Chapter 6, having an exercise programme provides an opportunity to identify the competencies required for all those in incident management teams and to ensure they are built over time throughout the programme. If the participants' first exercise is a SIMEX, it may discourage them from taking part in further exercises, as they may feel they lack the skills or knowledge to respond effectively.

Experiencing different types of exercises

As we have seen earlier in Chapter 2, different types of exercise offer distinct benefits and teach various skills. By engaging in a programme of different exercises, members of the incident management team are exposed to diverse perspectives on an incident and can develop a range of skills, knowledge and capabilities.

Demonstrate commitment to exercising

As seen in the quote at the beginning of the chapter, ISO 22301 requires organizations to have a programme of exercises. Where there are regulatory or contractual requirements for exercises, showing your exercise programme and progress against what has been agreed is a good way to demonstrate commitment to business continuity.

Slot in shorter exercises

Having a 12-month gap between exercises can be a long time, and people often forget what they have learnt. Shorter exercises, even for just 45 minutes or an hour, are an effective way to keep the team's skills alive without requiring a half-day commitment.

EXAMPLE

End-to-end validation of a call centre recovery strategy

This is an example of a programme of exercises for a call centre to validate their recovery strategy. For IT security reasons, the call centre staff cannot work from home and are therefore all located in the same building. They provide a critical service to the organization, so it is very important they recover the next working day.

The business continuity manager has a recovery strategy in place, under which they will move to another building 10 miles away, and then provide their service from there. There are a number of component parts which make their strategy work, and they all should be tested as part of a full end-to-end recovery test.

An important element of the plan to check is whether staff are willing to work from an alternative location. This involves considering the length and complexity of their commute, whether they can reach the site within a reasonable time, and whether they are comfortable with the working environment provided.

There then needs to be a programme for validating their strategy and verifying the solutions within it. The following are the different elements that should be exercised to validate the plan.

1 **Recovery PC check**: A member of staff visits the recovery site once a quarter to verify that they can log in to the computer they would use during recovery, access all the applications they expect and log in easily. The exercise could involve only one or two people and be completed in a couple of hours within office hours.

2. **Telephony switching**: Every six months, staff responsible for their call centre telephony practise switching the telephony from the main site to the recovery site. This could involve routing calls from the main call centre to the backup over a weekend when they don't usually take calls. The lines could be open; a few staff could make 'customer' calls, and several could practise receiving them, validating the strategy of re-routing calls and confirming they have the IT functionality to make adjustments in line with the calls.
3. **Business continuity team exercise**: The call centre's business continuity team could hold an annual exercise to practise decision-making and logistics for relocating the call centre to the recovery location. They may not always practise the call centre recovery scenario and could only do this once every three years, with different scenarios in between. Other scenarios could include loss of staff, IT functionality or a bomb threat.
4. **Awareness training**: Staff could take part in annual awareness training, reminding them of the strategy and verifying that they can relocate sustainably to the recovery call centre for several months while the primary call centre is being restored.
5. **Full 'dress rehearsal'**: Every three years, a full 'dress rehearsal' could be carried out. This could involve the incident management team deciding to invoke the plan, planning and then informing staff of their move to the new site. They could plan transport, tell staff where to assemble, move staff to the recovery locations and then get them up and operating at the new site. This would involve taking live customer calls. This would then prove that the recovery strategy is valid and would work if implemented.

It is worth noting that some technical exercises practising recovery involve a small number of staff, allowing them to be practised frequently, as they cause minimal disruption yet provide important validation of the strategy.

How to document a multi-year strategy

Let's continue with the example of a company that provides call centre services. It has three call centres, in Glasgow, Newcastle and Bristol, and a headquarters in London. It has a business continuity plan for each call centre, one for the head office functions, and tactical and strategic plans. This requires a three-year programme of exercises, as shown in Table 4.1.

TABLE 4.1 Exercise programme overview example

Ex No	Plan/item	Type/ description of the exercise	Responsible for Ex	Standard	Planning date
1.1	Call centre staff awareness for each call centre	Awareness training for the call centre staff on the recovery plan and recovery strategy	Call centre BC coordinator	Awareness training should take place once a year	By Apr 2026/7/8
1.2	Call centre BCP	Annual BCP exercise (tabletop or plan walkthrough)	Head of each call centre	One exercise a year	By Apr 2026/7/8
1.3	Headquarters BCP	Annual BCP exercise (tabletop or plan walkthrough)	Business continuity manager	One exercise a year	By Apr 2026/7/8
1.4	IT recovery	Check that call centre staff can log on to the recovery location's IT	Head of each call centre	Four times a year	By Jan 2026/7/8
1.5	IT recovery	Check that the telephony can be switched to recovery centre and that customer calls can be taken	IT manager	Twice a year	By Feb 2026/7/8
1.6	Call centre BCP	Full recovery rehearsal with a move of all staff to recovery centre	Business continuity manager	Once every three years	By 2028

(continued)

TABLE 4.1 (Continued)

Ex No	Plan/item	Type/ description of the exercise	Responsible for Ex	Standard	Planning date
1.7	Tactical plan	Annual team exercise	Business continuity manager	Year 1 Plan walkthrough Year 2 Tabletop exercise Year 3 SIMEX or tabletop with strategic team	By Apr 2026/7/8
1.8	Strategic plan	Annual team exercise	Business continuity manager with external support	Year 1 Plan walkthrough Year 2 Tabletop exercise Year 3 SIMEX or Tabletop with tactical team	By Apr 2026/7/8
1.9	DR test	Practice of recovery to standby data centre	IT manager	Annual test	By Apr 2026/7/8

Once the programme has been agreed and signed off, then each exercise can be planned. This could be done on a three-year basis or annually, at the beginning of each year. All exercises should be documented in this way so the business continuity manager can demonstrate progress against their programme of work.

Once you have your multi-year programme in place, you want to make sure you can show progress over time. The easiest way to do this is to keep a simple log of all exercises, including when they were held, who attended and the key outcomes. You should also document any lessons learnt and ensure a process is in place to follow up on them.

It's also useful to keep track of things like how many of your plans have been exercised, how many people have taken part and how many lessons have been closed out. This helps demonstrate improvement over time and shows auditors, regulators or senior managers that the organization is taking its business continuity seriously.

Documenting the requirements of each individual exercise

Tables 4.2 and 4.3 are examples of the details required for each individual exercise.

By documenting a multi-year programme, you are much more likely to validate all your solutions and have a strategic view of your readiness, rather than having an ad hoc training programme that does not build readiness across the whole organization. Of course, any programme may be open to change if new threats materialize and they need to be exercised. In my experience, most organizations do not have programmes of exercises, but they would greatly benefit if they did.

TABLE 4.2 Exercise 1.1 Call centre staff awareness

No	Item	Details
1.	Exercise number	1.1
2.	Plan or solution exercised	Call centre staff awareness
3.	Exercise name	Exercise Neptune
4.	Style of exercise	Awareness training
5.	Responsible for planning	Call centre BC coordinator for each site
6.	Purpose	The purpose is to ensure as part of the yearly requirements that all staff are trained on the business continuity solution
7.	Objectives	Ensure the following from the training: • How to contact the company to find out if the plan has been activated or not • Where their role will recover to • In what circumstances will the plan be activated? • How will recovery differ from their existing work
8.	Attendees	All call centre staff
9.	Resources	Training room
10.	Risks	Difficulty of getting all staff at one time; may need to run a series of sessions
11.	Duration	45 minutes to one hour
12.	Planning date	23 January 2026
13.	Status	Planned / in progress / on hold / completed

TABLE 4.3 Exercise 1.2 Call centre BCP

No	Item	Details
1.	Exercise number	1.2
2.	Plan or solution exercised	Call centre BCP
3.	Exercise name	Exercise Phoenix
4.	Style of exercise	Plan walkthrough
5.	Responsible for planning	Head of the call centre
6.	Purpose	Get the incident management team together and walk through the plan
7.	Objectives	• Familiarize new members of the team with the plan • Identify any changes or updates to the plan • Refresh the knowledge of the existing plan for existing members of the team
8.	Attendees	All members of the call centre incident management team including deputies
9.	Resources	Training room
10.	Risks	Ensuring that deputies are available for the exercise as well
11.	Duration	1 to 1.5 hours
12.	Planning date	23 Mar 2026
13.	Status	Planned / in progress / on hold / completed

KEY LEARNINGS

- A multi-year exercise programme supports a more strategic, structured approach than ad hoc or one-off exercises.
- Planning exercises across several years ensures that key risks are addressed and critical capabilities are validated over time.
- A systematic programme prevents exercises from being shaped by the personal preferences or limited experiences of the person designing them.
- Exercises help test not just incident response but also the viability of business continuity strategies and solutions.

- Regular scheduling of exercises helps ensure compliance with standards, avoids long gaps and builds organizational discipline.
- Progressive exercising builds team confidence and capability, especially important for less experienced teams.
- Using a mix of exercise types allows teams to learn a range of skills and validate different aspects of the plan.
- A documented programme helps demonstrate commitment to exercising and meets statutory, contractual or regulatory requirements.
- Shorter exercises can be used between major sessions to maintain awareness and refresh skills.
- Keeping good records of exercises, lessons and improvements provides valuable evidence of organizational learning and readiness.

Note

1 International Organization for Standardization (ISO), 2019. ISO 22301:2019: Security and resilience: Business continuity management systems: Requirements. Geneva: ISO

05

Making exercises educational by design

In this chapter, you will learn about:

1. Three levels of learning: visual, verbal and kinaesthetic
2. Experiential learning (Kolb)
3. Honey and Mumford's learning styles
4. Situated learning theory (Lave and Wenger)
5. Behaviourist learning theory
6. Single and double-loop learning
7. Cognitive learning theory
8. Problem-based learning

Until writing this book I never really paid much attention to different academic theories when designing my exercises. I often found that different tools and techniques worked, but I was unsure of the theory behind why they worked. By writing this, I have learnt that people learn in different ways, which is reflected in how they engage in an exercise. While we may already include elements outlined in this chapter in our exercises that suit a range of learning styles, it is worth taking time to understand how individuals learn. By doing so, we can deliberately design exercises that cater to varied preferences. Even small, simple adjustments can help participants with different learning styles get the most value from the session.

Three levels of learning

When designing learning objectives for an exercise, it is important to recognize that learning occurs at three levels. At the individual level, participants build skills, knowledge and confidence to manage incidents effectively. At the team level, the focus is on collaboration, leadership and working towards shared goals. At the organizational level, the exercise reinforces how teams and roles coordinate within their responsibilities to achieve a common aim.

The exercise should be designed with clarity about which levels of learning are intended. Objectives, scenario and exercise development must support those outcomes. Training and workshops may focus on individual learning, sometimes with mixed groups. Team learning should involve established teams and may require a different exercise style. Organizational learning may involve multiple teams in the same exercise or injects that reference decisions and actions from other teams to reflect the wider response structure.

Learning styles: visual, verbal and kinaesthetic

Having an understanding of different learning styles can help those designing and developing the exercise create more engaging and inclusive learning experiences by appealing to a number of different learning styles. While everyone can learn through multiple styles, most individuals have a preferred style that helps them learn more effectively.

Visual learners

Visual learners prefer to receive information through images, diagrams, charts and written instructions. They understand content more effectively when it is presented visually, such as via flow charts, mind maps and visual timelines. To support visual learners, the following could be incorporated into the exercises:

- Ensure copies of the plan are available. This can be especially important when the plan contains diagrams and tables that make it easy for visual learners to absorb information.
- If appropriate for the type of exercise, use written injects. These could be on screen or on paper.
- Utilize wall boards to display information, risk, events, timings and actions.
- Ensure that logs and meeting notes are available.

Verbal (auditory) learners

Verbal (auditory) learners learn best through spoken or written words. They benefit from discussions, explanations, briefings and reading materials. To support verbal learners, the following could be incorporated into the exercises:

- During the exercise, there are likely to be extensive discussion and team meetings about incident response, which will suit verbal learners.
- Ensure that at team meetings, the agreed actions and decisions made are read out and confirmed, as this will help verbal learners.
- Include a selection of verbal inputs, such as telephone conversations or briefings, to input information.
- Conduct a verbal debriefing at the end of the exercise.

Kinaesthetic learners

Kinaesthetic learners learn by doing, touching and experiencing. They retain knowledge more effectively through physical involvement and hands-on activities. In one exercise, I asked a normally quiet team member to manage the flip chart and log action and decisions. They were far more engaged once they were physically involved. To support kinaesthetic learners, the following could be incorporated into the exercises:

- Involve them in logging and assuming the role of administration support in team meetings, where they record information.
- Having plans, forms to fill out and documents can help with their learning.
- Setting up the incident room or performing practical tasks, such as using the contents of a grab bag.
- Practise using the actual technology or tools they would use during a real incident, such as telephony, radios and communications platforms.
- For IT-focused exercises, simulate tasks like server switchovers or logging into alternative systems

Through minor tweaks, planning and recognizing the different types, we can make sure our exercises cater to all types of learners.

Theoretical foundations of learning

Just as we consider visual, verbal and kinaesthetic preferences, we can also design exercises around specific learning theories to shape their format and outcomes. If we apply these theories deliberately, we can shape the entire exercise, from the briefing through to the debrief, to reinforce the kind of learning we want.

Experiential learning (Kolb)

Experiential learning theory (Kolb)[1] outlines that learning is most effective when grounded in direct experience. SIMEXs are an excellent way to practise experiential learning. Developed by David Kolb, the model presents learning as a four-stage cycle: concrete experience, reflective observation, abstract conceptualization and active experimentation.

1. **Concrete experience:** Learning begins with concrete experience, in which participants engage directly in an activity. Exercises should therefore be designed as realistic and immersive scenarios that provide meaningful experience aligned with participants' roles and organizational risks. Experience can be increased by encouraging participants to undertake different roles across successive exercises; for example, moving from team leader to communications coordinator.
2. **Reflective observation:** Requires time and space for participants to examine what occurred. There is always a temptation to reduce the time allocated to exercise debriefing, especially when participants are enjoying the exercise, making it difficult to bring it to a close. Without reflection, most of the learning evaporates. Debriefs should always combine participant self-reflection with structured feedback from umpires and organizers, addressing both strengths and areas for improvement. Encouraging each participant to share at least one personal learning point deepens engagement with the reflective process. Reflection may be supported by written feedback forms, personal logs and notes. Additionally, incorporating brief 'pause and reflect' moments during the exercise can facilitate immediate learning and reinforce situational awareness.
3. **Abstract conceptualization:** This is where participants make sense of what happened and decide what they will do differently next time. A follow-up cold debrief conducted several days after the exercise can enhance this stage by allowing participants time to process events and

consider how learning should inform future practice. Capturing individual and collective lessons within the post-exercise report ensures that insights are preserved and translated into improvement.

4 **Active experimentation:** Requires participants to apply new understanding in subsequent exercises or real-world incidents to test and refine their learning. Running further exercises within a relatively short timeframe reinforces improvements while insights remain fresh. This may be good in theory, but you may find it difficult to get incident teams to exercise again soon after the last exercise. Revisiting previously identified lessons and action plans before future exercises strengthens learning and continuous development and should always be carried out as part of the planning process.

Honey and Mumford's learning styles

Another way to think about how people learn is through the lens of Honey and Mumford's learning styles, which build on Kolb's experiential learning theory. Honey and Mumford identified four distinct preferences that people may lean towards when learning from experience: activist, reflector, theorist and pragmatist. In my experience, no one fits neatly into a single category, but I have definitely observed these different tendencies. Recognizing them can help in shaping exercises that better support how individuals take in and apply learning.

1 **Activists** are open-minded and enthusiastic about new experiences. They learn best through direct engagement and thrive in immersive exercises that fully involve them in the action. For these learners, include dynamic team tasks such as those found in a SIMEX, like incident team meetings, decision-making, or developing communications.

2 **Reflectors** prefer to step back, observe and take time before acting. They benefit from opportunities to watch others, gather information and reflect. They could take on the role of observers during exercises or be involved in a plan walkthrough or tabletop exercises, where they have time to reflect on the response, ask questions and think through how they would respond during the exercise.

3 **Theorists** value structure and clarity. They prefer to understand the underlying rationale and learn through models, principles and logic. They appreciate training before exercises and then have the opportunity to practise the skills and knowledge learned during tabletop exercises or

SIMEXs. Ensure that there is a direct connection between the training and the tasks required to be carried out during the exercise.

4 **Pragmatists** focus on applying learning directly to real-world tasks. They want practical outcomes and learning that can be implemented. Use realistic scenarios which have occurred to other organizations and give them the opportunity to use tools such as checklists, agendas and practise their documented role.

Designing exercises that blend activities creates a more inclusive environment and provides content for all four learning preferences. By understanding the motivations and preferences of different learners, you can adjust exercise play, exercise styles and conduct debriefs to bring out the best in each participant.

Honey and Mumford's model is not a scientifically prescriptive system; it remains widely used in professional learning contexts for its practical application. When used as a flexible design tool rather than a rigid rule, it can greatly enhance the quality and inclusivity of your business continuity exercises.

Situated learning theory (Lave and Wenger)

Situated learning theory, developed by Jean Lave and Etienne Wenger, proposes that learning occurs most effectively within its real context, through active participation in social situations. Rather than being abstract or classroom-based, learning is embedded in the activity, culture and environment in which it takes place.

A key concept is legitimate peripheral participation, where newcomers begin with lower-risk tasks and gradually take on greater responsibility as they become part of a community of practice. This reflects how incident response skills are often developed, by observing experienced colleagues and progressively assuming more responsibility through exercises and real events.

In exercises, this theory supports immersive, team-based SIMEX exercises. Participants learn through the roles they perform, the tools they use and the interactions they have with others. Role-play becomes central, turning the exercise into a shared learning space where knowledge is developed through participation.

To apply situated learning theory in exercises:

1 Design exercises that simulate real-world working environments, including team dynamics, decision-making and communication processes.

2. Ensure that participants respond within the designated incident roles and responsibilities, encouraging them to act as they would in a real incident.
3. Consider assigning new or less experienced staff as observers or in minor roles initially, allowing them to learn through observation and gradual engagement.
4. Encourage peer-to-peer interaction and mentorship during exercises to foster social learning.
5. Set up communities of practice, such as regular incident responder meetings or post-exercise discussions, to continue learning beyond the exercise.
6. Consider involving multiple incident teams or stakeholder organizations in the exercise, either playing themselves or using a knowledgeable role-player to represent them, to reflect the collaborative nature of incident response.
7. Ensure the exercise environment supports realistic use of tools, documents and processes.
8. Recognize that learning continues after the exercise and encourage participants to share their insights and lessons with others in their organization.

By framing exercises as opportunities for realistic participation, learning becomes more meaningful, relevant and likely to transfer into actual incident response.

Behaviourist learning theory

Behaviourist learning theory focuses on learning as a change in observable behaviour shaped by external stimuli. Learners respond to stimuli, and behaviours are reinforced through repetition, rewards and consequences. Pioneered by theorists such as B F Skinner and Ivan Pavlov, the theory suggests that with appropriate conditioning, desired behaviours can be developed and sustained.

This approach aligns well with structured, skills-based training. In exercises, behaviourism is evident when teams practise using checklists, log sheets and communication lists until responses become routine. Repetition embeds actions so they can be performed consistently, particularly under stress. Feedback during and after exercises reinforces correct behaviour and corrects errors.

> TIP
>
> There is always the risk that there is not enough time to practise standard operating procedures and the ways of working required under behaviourist learning theory. This is where short, focused exercises, conducted in 30–45 minutes, can be particularly valuable. Elements such as running an incident team meeting, logging actions properly, working to an agenda and ensuring all roles are fulfilled can be practised in isolation without the need for a full three-hour exercise. Even if the scenario is simple and the set-up is purely for practice, repeating these core skills helps ensure that, during a real incident, they become instinctive.

In military training, behaviourism is widely applied to develop discipline and automatic responses under pressure. Drill-based instruction and repeated practice ensure critical actions become instinctive. Immediate feedback and reinforcement shapes behaviour to meet operational situations.

To apply behaviourist principles in crisis exercises:

1. Repeatedly expose participants to the same types of injects to reinforce correct actions.
2. Provide consistent feedback on performance during simulations.
3. Practical training in real-world situations and practise skills such as logging, situational awareness and information management.
4. Include consequences in the scenario (e.g. media backlash) for poor decisions to reinforce preferred behaviours.
5. Encourage rote learning (learning by repetition) for essential procedures that must be followed in sequence.

By embedding these approaches, exercises can help teams internalize the 'muscle memory' of critical incident responses.

Cognitive learning theory

Cognitive learning theory focuses on the mental processes involved in learning, including thinking, memory and problem-solving. It views learners as active participants who interpret and organize information to build understanding. Theorists such as Jean Piaget and Jerome Bruner emphasized that internal thinking processes, not just external inputs drive learning.

This theory aligns well with exercises that require analysis and decision-making. Tabletop exercises, I find, are effective at fostering teamwork, as participants learn by interpreting complex instructions, organizing information and applying reasoning to resolve problems. By using complex scenarios, searching questions and allowing time for reflection and deeper consideration this allows for deeper cognitive engagement.

During exercises this approach develops higher-order thinking skills. Debriefs, reflective questions and the use of frameworks or checklists help participants structure, retain and apply new knowledge in future situations.

In practice, this means you should:

1. Use realistic, information-rich scenarios that require participants to organize and prioritize information.
2. Introduce injects that challenge assumptions and prompt analytical thinking.
3. Give instructions that contain contradictory information, then have the team recognize it and clarify the situation.
4. Have the team develop their strategic intent or prepare a briefing for a regulator or senior manager to ensure they review the situation and prepare an appropriate brief.
5. Encourage participants to articulate their reasoning during decision-making discussions.
6. Facilitate reflective debriefs that help embed learning and link theory to practice.

By supporting cognitive engagement, exercises not only improve technical knowledge but also enhance participants' ability to adapt and think critically under pressure.

Problem-based learning

Problem-based learning is an approach in which learners develop knowledge and skills by working through complex, real-world problems. It shifts the focus from rote learning to active exploration, with learners identifying what they need to know and how to obtain it. Originally developed in medical education, it can be applied to business continuity exercises.

This approach aligns well with exercises where the scenario drives learning. Rather than providing predefined solutions, participants face evolving challenges that require investigation, collaboration and judgement.

Working through ambiguity helps teams prioritize effectively and build confidence for real incidents. In cyber exercises, some of the critical decisions such as whether to disconnect systems or pay a ransom, are good examples of this type of learning.

In crisis exercises, participants apply situational awareness to understand the situation they are facing, explore response options and then make and justify decisions. The exercise is designed to elicit discussion rather than provide answers, encouraging reflection and therefore a deeper understanding of the issues involved. This develops independent thinking, adaptability and resilience; essential qualities in incident management.

To apply problem-based learning principles in crisis exercises:

1. Use scenarios that are deliberately open-ended or ambiguous, requiring analysis and prioritization.
2. Encourage teams to identify the information they need and formulate their own response strategy.
3. Limit direct guidance to promote independent problem-solving and decision ownership.
4. Include group reflection sessions to review how the problem was approached and what was learnt.
5. Design follow-up tasks that apply lessons learnt to new or escalating challenges.

By embedding problem-based learning into exercises, organizations can help teams think more clearly under pressure, practise the team working together and develop a problem-solving mindset that extends beyond the scenario and into real-life incident response.

Single-and double-loop learning

Single-and double-loop learning, introduced by Chris Argyris and Donald Schön, describe how individuals and organizations learn from feedback. These concepts help explain how teams adapt during exercises and real incidents.

Single-loop learning occurs when mistakes are corrected without questioning the underlying assumptions. It's like tweaking performance without altering the strategy. Double-loop learning goes further by challenging the assumptions and policies behind actions. A team may realize that its communications team's configuration and way of working are slowing responses and choose to redesign them. This deeper reflection leads to meaningful change and enhances long-term adaptability in incident management.

To encourage double-loop learning in exercises:

1. During debriefs, explore not just what happened, but why it happened, and whether the underlying assumptions or processes should be challenged.
2. Encourage reflection on broader organizational behaviours, not just immediate actions taken during the scenario.
3. Use 'what if' questions to prompt critical thinking about whether alternative approaches might have worked better.
4. Facilitate open discussion about decision-making frameworks and whether they are still fit for purpose.
5. Document insights and link them back to policy, plan or incident hierarchy changes, not just process improvements.
6. Include senior stakeholders in the learning process to ensure that double-loop learning feeds into organizational change.

Exercises often default to single-loop learning, refining processes without altering underlying beliefs. However, well-designed exercises that foster a reflective culture can drive double-loop learning, leading to more resilient, adaptive organizations.

Most exercise practitioners already use elements of these theories without realizing it. The difference comes when you apply them deliberately. If you think about how people learn while designing the exercise, you will increase its impact. That extra thought during planning often makes the difference between a good exercise and a genuinely educational one.

KEY LEARNINGS

- People learn in different ways, so exercises should be designed to accommodate a range of learning styles to maximize engagement and benefit.
- Exercises serve multiple purposes including developing personal capabilities, strengthening teamwork, validating plans and supporting organizational learning.
- Learning happens at three levels, individual, team and organizational, and exercises should be tailored to target one or more of these intentionally.

- Visual learners benefit from diagrams, written injects, wall boards and clear documentation throughout the exercise.
- Verbal learners respond well to discussion, briefings, spoken decisions and verbal debriefs.
- Kinaesthetic learners gain most from hands-on tasks like logging, using plans and equipment, or setting up the incident room.
- Kolb's experiential learning cycle shows that learning is most effective when participants reflect on their experiences and apply them in future situations.
- Situated learning theory encourages learning through active participation and teamwork in realistic, role-based simulations.
- Behaviourist learning theory reinforces learning through repetition, feedback and consequence-based scenarios to embed behaviours.
- Single loop learning helps refine actions, while double-loop learning encourages reflection on underlying assumptions and drives deeper organizational change.
- Cognitive learning theory supports exercises that challenge teams to think critically, analyse information and develop decision-making skills.
- Problem-based learning uses open-ended scenarios to promote exploration, problem-solving and autonomy in learners.
- Choosing and integrating appropriate learning theories during design helps create more impactful and educational exercises.

Note

1 Kolb, D A (1984) *Experiential Learning: Experience as the source of learning and development*, Englewood Cliffs, NJ, Prentice-Hall

06

Defining individual and team capabilities to build organizational response capability

In this chapter, you will learn about:

1. Identifying individual knowledge
2. Decision-making models
3. Individual incident management skills
4. Incident management behaviours
5. How to measure individual competency
6. Assessing team capabilities
7. Assessing organizational capability

In many of the organizations I've worked with, capability-building often starts with good intentions: individuals and teams receive training, participate in exercises, and run multi-team simulations to demonstrate how the organization would respond. While these activities are valuable, they are often approached in isolation. The individual elements are rarely broken down into their component parts, and very few organizations have clearly defined the specific knowledge, skills and behaviours (KS&B) that individuals need to demonstrate in their roles.

I'm often asked to deliver incident or crisis management training, but the expectation is usually that I, as the consultant, will determine what the team needs to learn. In most cases, there is no agreed KS&B framework in place. Without this foundation, each consultant or internal trainer interprets what 'good' looks like and decides which aspects of crisis management to teach, resulting in inconsistent training, differing expectations and a lack of clarity in team performance.

By clearly defining the KS&B for each role, organizations create a benchmark against which individuals can be assessed. This enables them to identify knowledge, experience or behaviour gaps and address them with targeted training or additional exercises. Assessments should occur when someone new joins the team, before a major exercise or after a poor performance in an exercise or actual incident, so that gaps can be addressed. Through annual assessments, organizations can monitor each team member's competence and ensure they maintain the required standard. Those who meet the agreed criteria can be formally recognized as proficient in their incident management role.

However, a capable team isn't just a collection of competent individuals. To function effectively under pressure, a team must operate as a cohesive unit. This means having clear roles, strong internal communication, shared situational awareness and the ability to make decisions collaboratively and in alignment with the organization's strategic intent. Teams also need defined escalation routes, accountability, the ability to adjust to changing circumstances and the ability to work with agreed behaviours.

Yet, capability is about more than just individuals or even teams; it is the organization's ability to respond effectively. It reflects how well people, processes, systems and structures come together in a real-world environment (see Figure 6.1). A competent organization doesn't just have plans on paper or a list of completed training sessions; it has proven its ability to perform under stress, during both exercises and actual incidents, and has the evidence to back it up through reviews, debriefs and observed outcomes.

Identifying individual knowledge

When developing individual knowledge, it is essential to identify what each person needs to learn and understand, and then document this clearly within a structured framework. The following presents a framework for outlining what an individual needs to acquire.

1 **Role clarity**: All members of the incident management team should be clear about their roles during an incident, including their responsibilities, authority and any specialist tasks they may be expected to undertake.

FIGURE 6.1 How skills, knowledge, behaviour, competency and capability fit together

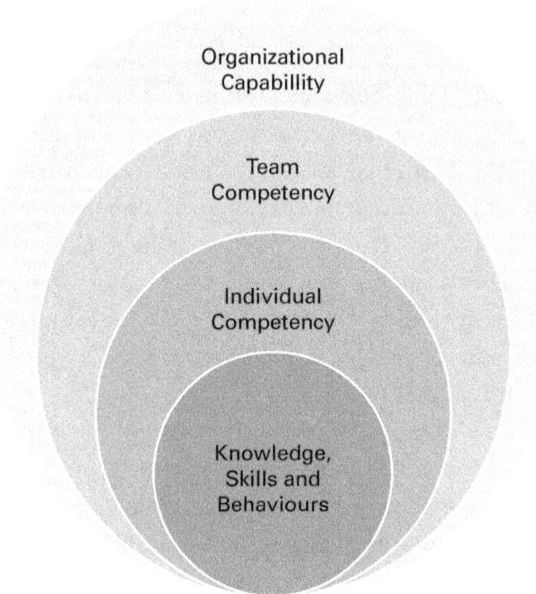

These responsibilities may differ from their normal day-to-day duties, so individuals need clarity, preparation and understanding of any additional expectations placed upon them.

2 **Applicable plans:** Incident responders must understand which plans and procedures apply to their roles. This includes knowing which teams they belong to, where to find relevant documentation and which additional materials provide context to their responsibilities. They should know where plans are stored, how updates are communicated and be aware of any allied contingency plans and procedures, such as communications plans.

3 **Management structure:** A sound understanding of the organization's incident management structure is essential. Individuals should know how the hierarchy operates, what each team is responsible for and how coordination is managed across response levels. This includes recognizing the role of external partners and how the organization works with them during an incident.

4 **Operational process:** Understanding how incidents are managed in practice is equally important. This includes how situations are assessed, activation criteria, team mobilization, meeting formats and coordination processes. Team members should also be familiar with any decision-making models used and understand how communications, debriefs and post-incident reviews are handled.

5 **Risk awareness:** Finally, it's important to have awareness of the key risks facing the organization, whether they relate to location, industry or findings from formal risk assessments and continuity planning. People should understand how these risks might play out in real situations, how they could impact the organization and what contingency plans are in place to deal with them.

EXAMPLE

Decision-making models

A decision-making model is a structured framework that helps incident teams assess evolving situations and make timely, consistent and defensible decisions under pressure. These models provide a step-by-step process for identifying the issues, weighing options, assessing risks and selecting a course of action, ensuring that decisions are informed, transparent and aligned with the overall strategy. They provide a handrail for decision-making in high-stress environments where time is limited and information may be incomplete. A decision-making model helps teams stay focused, avoid common cognitive biases and maintain accountability for their actions.

There are a number of different models in use in different industries. The Joint Decision Model[1] is used by the UK emergency services to support decision-making during complex and multi-agency incidents. It is designed as a continuous cycle, enabling teams to reassess information, risks and priorities as situations evolve. Key elements include developing shared situational awareness, assessing threats and risks, considering legal powers and policies, making proportionate and ethical decisions, and continuously reviewing outcomes. Its collaborative nature supports alignment across organizations and provides a transparent audit trail for defensible decision-making.

Another model is TDODAR,[2] a mnemonic used by airline pilots and engineers to structure decision-making during an emergency. It stands for T: Time, D: Diagnose, O: Options, D: Decide, A: Act or Assign, and R: Review. The model prompts the crew to clearly define the problem, consider the available options, decide on the best course of action, assign responsibilities and review the outcome. In practice, this provides a simple but disciplined way for flight crews to slow down their thinking under pressure and to give them a framework for decision-making.

PlanB Consulting uses a simple circular decision-making model called **Situation – Decision – Action**. In the **Situation** phase, the team members work to understand what is happening and whether any new information or circumstances require a change in response. During the **Decision** phase, the incident team comes together to share information, discuss the current state and agree on actions and communications. Finally, in the **Action** phase, the team members carry out the agreed actions and communications.

Individual incident management skills

The following list presents the basic skills each member of an incident team should possess:

1. **Incident recognition:** The individual should be able to recognize indicators that an incident has occurred, assess its nature and scale, evaluate it against established criteria, and determine whether to invoke the appropriate response plan.
2. **Situational awareness:** The individual should be able to gather information from internal and external sources, interpret it in context, identify gaps or inconsistencies, anticipate potential developments and share a coherent picture to support coordinated action.
3. **Response pace:** The individual should be able to manage the tempo of the response, judging when rapid action is required and when a measured approach is appropriate, and deciding when to communicate, escalate or intervene.
4. **Information management:** The individual should be able to identify essential information for team sharing, ensure incident information is recorded and stored in agreed systems, and present key priorities, risks and actions clearly, including through shared documents or visual boards.
5. **Accurate logging:** The individual should be able to maintain clear, timely and structured records in line with organizational standards, documenting decisions, discussions, actions and rationale throughout the incident.

6 **Decision-making:** The individual should be able to apply an agreed decision-making model under pressure, recognize the influence of stress, bias and group dynamics, evaluate options systematically and clearly document the reasoning behind decisions.

7 **Risk assessment:** The individual should be able to conduct dynamic risk assessments, identify emerging threats, evaluate potential consequences, escalate issues appropriately and record risk-related decisions and controls.

8 **Strategic intent:** The individual should be able to define and articulate a clear overarching aim, align tactical actions with organizational priorities and consider available resources, contingency plans and business impacts.

9 **Crisis communication:** The individual should be able to identify and prioritize stakeholders, tailor messages appropriately, follow agreed approval processes and apply relevant regulatory requirements and communication templates.

10 **Human factors:** The individual should be able to monitor fatigue and performance, support team well-being, maintain personnel continuity and foster a psychologically safe environment that enables effective contribution.

11 **Effective handover:** The individual should be able to provide and receive structured handovers that clearly transfer current facts, risks, decisions, rationale and outstanding actions to preserve continuity and situational awareness.

Incident management behaviours

To function effectively in high-pressure situations, individuals must possess not only the necessary knowledge and skills but also behaviours that support team cohesion, ethical conduct and sound decision-making. The behaviours listed should be consistently demonstrated by all team members, including leaders, during a crisis response. While different commentators and researchers define effective incident management behaviours in varying ways, this list reflects my own research and professional experience rather than any single published framework.

1 **Clear communication:** The individual should be able to communicate honestly and accurately, provide timely updates, listen actively to others and ensure that key messages are understood to maintain a shared understanding of the situation.

2. **Collaborative teamwork:** The individual should be able to work effectively across functions, support the roles and contributions of others, share information openly and avoid operating in isolation during the response.
3. **Situational awareness:** The individual should be able to monitor the evolving situation continuously, recognize emerging risks and early warning signs, assess whether actions are achieving the intended effect and contribute observations to the team's collective understanding.
4. **Decisiveness and judgement:** The individual should be able to make informed decisions in a timely manner using available information, apply sound judgement under pressure and take responsibility for the outcomes of those decisions.
5. **Adaptability and flexibility:** The individual should be able to adjust roles, priorities and strategies as circumstances change, remain effective under pressure and respond constructively to uncertainty or disruption.
6. **Integrity and accountability:** The individual should be able to act consistently with organizational values, demonstrate honesty and fairness in decision-making, take ownership of actions and decisions and acknowledge limitations or mistakes openly.
7. **Empathy and emotional intelligence:** The individual should be able to recognize and respond appropriately to the emotional impact of incidents on others, demonstrate compassion, support colleagues and remain sensitive to the needs of those affected.
8. **Psychological safety:** The individual should be able to encourage open dialogue, invite challenge and alternative perspectives, respond constructively to concerns and create an environment where team members feel safe to speak up.
9. **Empowerment and shared leadership:** The individual should be able to take initiative within their area of expertise, support others in doing the same, avoid unnecessary control and allow leadership to emerge appropriately within the team.
10. **Continuous learning:** The individual should be able to reflect on performance, identify lessons, seek and provide constructive feedback and apply learning to improve future incident and exercise responses.

A summary of the necessary knowledge, skills and behaviours is provided in Table 6.1.

TABLE 6.1 Summary of individual knowledge, skills and behaviours

Knowledge	Incident Management Skills	Behaviours
Role-specific responsibilities	Invocation of the plan	Clear and transparent communication
Plans and procedures relevant to their role	Situational awareness	Collaborative teamwork
Incident management structure	Cadence and pace of response	Situational awareness
How the organization manages an incident	Information management	Decisiveness and judgement
Risks and responses	Logging	Adaptability and flexibility
	Decision-making	Integrity and accountability
	Risk	Empathy and emotional intelligence
	Strategic intent	Psychological safety
	Developing a working strategy	Empowerment and shared leadership
	Communications	Continuous learning and improvement
	Managing human factors	
	Handover and transition	

How to measure individual competency

Individual competency during an exercise or incident response is a person's ability to apply the KS&B required to carry out their specific role effectively under pressure. This needs to be defined bespoke to the organization before any assessment takes place.

These competencies can first be baselined before the individual participates in an exercise or training and then tracked throughout the time they are assigned to a particular incident team role. Over time, you should be able to monitor how an individual's KS&B have improved and aligned with those agreed by the organization. Where there are gaps, new team members or fading skills and knowledge, these can be identified, and then training or additional exercises can be conducted to bring them up to the required standard.

Assessing knowledge

There are a number of ways to assess an individual's knowledge. Tests and quizzes can be delivered either online or in-person as part of training sessions, helping to confirm the required understanding. Self-assessment questionnaires may be completed when someone joins the incident team or before an exercise, allowing individuals to reflect on their own knowledge and identify areas for further training.

Scenario-based questions can also be useful, as they present individuals with scenarios and ask how they would respond. These could take the form of interviews or multiple-choice questions. Individuals can be assessed during tabletop exercises or SIMEX by observing how they apply their knowledge in practice. For larger teams with more than five or six people, additional umpires may be needed to ensure everyone is observed. If skill observation is a key objective, it should be built into the exercise design from the outset. Finally, attendance at relevant training courses can also be used to demonstrate knowledge acquisition.

Assessing skills

There are several different ways to assess individual skills in an incident management context. Observation during tabletop exercises is a useful method that allows facilitators to assess how someone structures a response, sets priorities and makes decisions under pressure. For instance, observers might watch how a participant handles the first team meeting or develops a strategy as new information emerges. SIMEXs offer another opportunity to assess skills in a more dynamic setting, where participants can be evaluated on how effectively they adapt, communicate and maintain situational awareness under real-time pressure. Self-assessment and peer feedback can also be valuable, with team members reflecting on their own performance and providing feedback to one another. This approach works best when agreed in advance and delivered in a constructive, supportive environment.

Assessing behaviours

There are several effective methods for assessing behaviours for individuals within incident management teams. Observation during SIMEX exercises offers the best opportunity to observe behaviours in a realistic environment, where pressure brings out participants' natural tendencies and interpersonal dynamics. Even during tabletop discussions, valuable insights can be gained about team interactions, such as who takes the lead, who provides support and how the group works together under pressure.

Self-assessment questionnaires can include behavioural prompts to encourage reflection, though it's important to note that individuals may not always evaluate themselves objectively. Peer review can also be used after exercises, where team members assess each other's behaviours. This approach should be handled sensitively and only used if the group is comfortable with it, as it can generate valuable insights when done well. Psychometric testing is another method that uses behavioural profiling tools to help determine whether individuals possess the attributes needed for effective crisis team membership.

Assessing team capabilities

When assessing a team's capabilities, it is important, as with defining individual knowledge, skills and behaviours, that these are clearly outlined in advance. This ensures they can be routinely used during team assessments and that there is consistency in what umpires and the exercise director expect to see demonstrated across all teams in the organization. Having clearly defined team capabilities offers a common reference point and guarantees that all teams are assessed consistently. Performance can be compared, and when gaps are identified, additional training or exercises can be organized. Personally, I tend to assess team capabilities more often than individuals.

This approach differs from more general observation of performance during an exercise, such as using tools like the PICTS mnemonic (see Chapter 17), or from developing performance indicators that are specific to a particular team or scenario. While these approaches focus primarily on how the response unfolds during the exercise, capability assessment systematically assesses whether the team consistently demonstrates the required competencies. Both types of assessment can be conducted simultaneously; however, in addition to observing the response, umpires should use a separate assessment sheet to evaluate the team's capability in a structured, consistent way.

The following is a list of possible criteria for assessing the capability of a team:

1. **Plans and response:** Ability as a team to implement the relevant plans, ensuring those with more knowledge of how to respond to the incident are listened to and that knowledge is shared across the team. Is an effective working strategy implemented?

2 **Clear team structure and role clarity:** The team must operate within its documented roles and responsibilities, and be clear about its authority and decision-making powers. It should also be able to escalate decisions to a higher-level team and delegate tasks to a lower-level team.
3 **Shared situational awareness:** The team must be able to build and maintain a common, up-to-date understanding of the incident that is shared across all team members.
4 **Aligned and coordinated decision-making:** The team should be able to make timely, clear decisions that align with the organization's strategic intent and consider cross-functional impacts. Decisions should involve a defined process, take into account the organization's culture and values, and be appropriately documented.
5 **Effective internal communication and coordination:** The team must communicate efficiently under pressure, sharing updates, assigning tasks, identifying relevant stakeholders for the incident, communicating appropriately at the right level and avoiding duplication or silos.
6 **Team resilience and adaptability:** The team should function effectively under pressure, adapt to changing demands and support one another through uncertainty or stress.
7 **Performance reflection and learning:** The team must be able to assess its own performance, capture lessons and adjust practices during and after exercises or incidents.

To conduct a formal team capability assessment, there are various methods available, though it is typically performed during an exercise. While a SIMEX is probably the most effective way to evaluate all aspects of a team's capability, a tabletop exercise involving significant interaction among team members can also serve as an assessment tool. If a formal evaluation is to be undertaken, a set of team capability criteria should be established, based on the examples outlined earlier.

Umpires can be briefed by the exercise director on what they should look for and then assess the team during the exercise. Umpires brought in from outside the organization may also be utilized to provide external scrutiny of the process. If there are multiple umpires and the exercise director also completes an assessment, it creates a broader pool of assessors and helps ensure the assessment appears more objective. Team members can self-assess at the end of the exercise, although in my experience, they often rate themselves higher than an umpire would.

Assessing organizational capability

To demonstrate organizational capability, there must be clear alignment between people, plans, processes, systems and structures, all working together to enable an effective response. This begins with defined individual competencies and extends to established team capabilities that show how groups operate cohesively.

The organization requires documented response plans, trained personnel, validated procedures and mechanisms for continuous improvement. Capability is demonstrated through consistent performance in exercises and real incidents, supported by a cycle of planning, training, exercising, assessment and improvement.

The following should be considered as ways to assess an organization's capability.

1. **Set clear standards and criteria:** The organization should be able to define explicit success criteria by identifying required individual knowledge, skills and behaviours, clarifying core team capabilities and establishing the structures and processes that enable effective response.
2. **Use exercises as structured assessment opportunities:** The organization should be able to design and deliver exercises that enable systematic observation of capability, using trained umpires and predefined indicators to assess decision-making, communication, escalation, handover and alignment with response requirements.
3. **Gather multiple perspectives:** The organization should be able to collect and integrate evidence from umpire observations, participant self-assessments, peer feedback and exercise outputs, such as situation reports and logs, to form a balanced evaluation of performance.
4. **Assess over time:** The organization should be able to monitor performance consistently across exercises and real incidents, identify trends, track improvements and recognize emerging or recurring capability gaps.
5. **Identify gaps and drive improvement:** The organization should be able to translate assessment findings into targeted development actions, including revised training, procedural updates and future exercise design, to strengthen overall response capability.

Although defining individual KS&B is not yet standard practice in many organizations, it is vital for clearly outlining what each person needs to do in their role. It offers a structured foundation for delivering targeted training and enables the organization to evaluate its staff and identify any gaps in KS&B. Teams should also be assessed against an established criteria to ensure they operate effectively. With both individual and team assessments in place, an organization can convincingly demonstrate its ability to manage incidents with confidence and consistency.

KEY LEARNINGS

- Training and exercising alone do not demonstrate capability unless the underlying knowledge, skills and behaviours required for each role are clearly defined.
- Many organizations build exercises without first agreeing what 'good' looks like, leading to inconsistent training, unclear expectations and variable performance.
- Defining individual knowledge, skills and behaviours (KS&B) provides a clear benchmark against which competence can be assessed and developed.
- Without a defined KS&B framework, different consultants and trainers will teach different things, resulting in fragmented capability across teams or the organization.
- Individual competence should be assessed regularly, not assumed, and gaps should be addressed through targeted training and further exercising.
- A capable team is more than a collection of competent individuals; it must operate as a coordinated unit with shared situational awareness and clear decision-making.
- Effective incident management depends on teams being able to communicate, escalate, hand over and work across operational, tactical and strategic levels.
- Team capability must be explicitly defined and assessed, rather than inferred from general exercise performance or informal observation.
- Organizational capability emerges when people, plans, processes, systems and structures are aligned and proven to work together under pressure.
- True capability is demonstrated through repeatable performance in exercises and real incidents, supported by evidence from assessments, debriefs and continuous improvement activities.

Notes

1. JESIP (n.d.) Joint Doctrine: The Interoperability Framework. www.jesip.org.uk/downloads/joint-doctrine-guide/
2. Moriarty, C D (2014) *Practical Human Factors for Pilots*, Academic Press

07

The 4D's: a four-phase framework for designing and delivering effective exercises

In this chapter, you will learn about:

1. The 4D's framework
2. Phase 1: Design
3. Phase 2: Development
4. Phase 3: Delivery
5. Phase 4: Debrief and evaluation

Exercises don't happen by magic. Even the most experienced incident response teams need structure, clarity and planning to maximize their effectiveness. I developed the 4D's framework – design, develop, deliver and debrief – to make it easier to remember the component parts of the exercise and as a marketing tool (see Figure 7.1). It's a practical and repeatable process I've used for years with clients at PlanB Consulting. These phases might not be entirely new, but they help bring structure and clarity to what can often feel like a complex and disjointed process. In this chapter, I outline the 4D's structure as an overview.

It should be noted that the design and development of an exercise is not always linear. Elements such as 'understanding the organization' and the structure of the exercise may need to be revisited and revised several times as the exercise planning evolves.

FIGURE 7.1 The 4D's

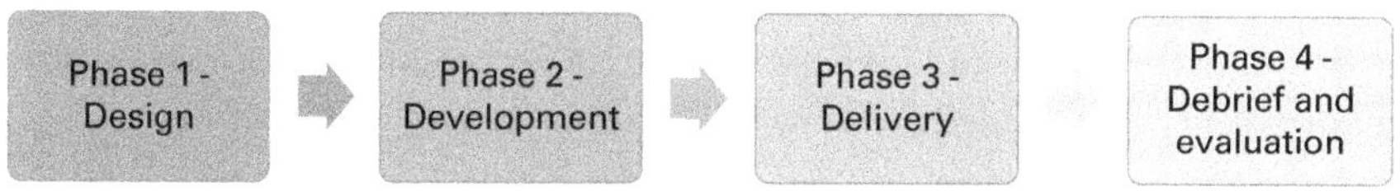

Phase 1: Design

The design phase focuses on defining the scope of the exercise and ensuring it meets the organization's requirements. Most exercises will have an internal sponsor who agrees on all elements during the design stage. Some sponsors may have very clear ideas about how they want the exercise designed, while others may not have strong opinions and will rely on those planning the exercise to guide them on various aspects of the exercise. If an exercise programme is already in place, this work should have been decided during the programme's development, and during this phase, only logistical details are typically discussed.

There are six elements which go into the design phase:

1 Exercise logistics – when, where, who and how long
2 Purpose
3 Objectives
4 Scope
5 Scenario
6 Type and structure of the exercise

Designing an exercise might be relatively straightforward for a simple desktop exercise, but more complex ones usually require several discussions to agree on the details. As with most things in life, the more thought and effort you put into planning, the smoother and more effective the delivery will be on the day. By the end of the design phase, the sponsor, the exercise director and the design team should have a clear understanding of how the exercise will run. This should all be captured in an exercise instruction.

The process usually begins with initial discussions with the sponsor. These help to agree on key points such as where and when the exercise will take place, its duration and its objectives. It's also important to determine the participants' level of experience and whether they will need any training before or after the exercise. During this discussion, you can define the type of exercise, whether it's a tabletop, simulation or live event, while considering any budget or time constraints. It's also the moment to understand what the sponsor expects from the scenario, how they want performance evaluated and whether there are any compliance or regulatory requirements to consider.

Once the initial discussions are complete, you'll need to define the scope of the exercise: who will be involved. The time allocated for the exercise should be sufficient to achieve the objectives, but realistic regarding who is participating and how much time and resources the organization is prepared to dedicate. At this stage, the exercise outline begins to take shape, detailing the scenario, the number and type of participants and the logistical support needed. Further meetings may follow to identify suitable subject matter experts, as well as to agree on who will act as umpires.

The exercise instruction becomes your main document for the exercise. It's a living document, updated throughout the planning process, ensuring all details for conducting the exercise are included to prevent last-minute surprises. It is also advisable to assess the team's capability to tailor the exercise to their experience. This could involve informal conversations, questionnaires or even a formal capability assessment.

Phase 2: Development

The development phase is where the exercise really starts to take shape. During the design phase, you will have confirmed the basics, such as the exercise date, who's attending, the type of exercise and its purpose and objectives. You'll also have an outline scenario, but the next step is to start building out the details.

These are the four activities within development:

1. Developing the storyboard
2. Developing injects or tabletop questions
3. Agreeing the exercise assessment and performance indicators
4. Agreeing on the post-exercise report

In developing the storyboard, one of the first tasks is to understand the organization in more depth, how it manages incidents, what the response structure looks like and what the actual impact of the scenario would be if it happened in real life. You also need to understand who the key stakeholders are and how the media and social media might perceive and react to the incident. Some research will be needed to make sure the scenario is both realistic and credible when delivered to participants. The impact described in the scenario should be plausible and align with the organization's operations and risks.

Once the research is complete, the next step is to develop the storyboard. This could be relatively straightforward; for example, a fire at the headquarters with casualties, one of whom later dies. Or it might be more complex, involving multiple stakeholders, cascading impacts and evolving events throughout the exercise. The detail required for the storyboard will depend on the type and length of the exercise.

After the main story is agreed, you'll need to develop the injects for the SIMEX or the questions for the tabletop exercise. This is where the really detailed work begins. The storyboard outlines what happens, but each inject needs to be carefully written, with appropriate text for each stakeholder involved. You'll also need to agree on how the exercise will be assessed, how feedback will be gathered, and start outlining the post-exercise report. This should all be shared with the sponsor and signed off in advance.

Throughout the development phase, everything that's agreed should be documented in the exercise instruction. This document should be regularly circulated to everyone involved in planning the exercise to ensure alignment. You may also want to decide at this point whether to produce a joining instruction for participants, so they're aware of the exercise logistics and any preparation they need to do in advance.

Phase 3: Delivery

In this phase, the exercise is prepared to be delivered, is delivered, and then the hot debrief is conducted.

It consists of four elements:

1. Exercise set-up
2. Exercise briefing
3. Conducting the exercise
4. Hot debrief and feedback

Preparation for delivery begins well before the day of the exercise. This includes decisions around room set-up, whether the room should be fully prepared in advance or whether set-up will form part of the exercise objectives. It also covers logistical planning, communications between the exercise team and the management of observers, PPE (if relevant), and security/confidentiality considerations. The week before, final checks are essential: confirming participant attendance, reviewing any impact from real events and adapting for any last-minute changes, such as remote participation. If required, a full dress rehearsal with the role-players – testing technology, confirming roles and running through injects – is strongly recommended. This ensures all parties are aligned and ready for live play.

The briefing is a critical moment that sets the tone and provides clarity for participants. It typically takes place immediately before the exercise begins, although it can be delivered earlier, or in alternative formats if necessary. The briefing covers everything from practicalities (timings, safety, housekeeping) to purpose, objectives, exercise scope, participant roles and the unfolding of the scenario. Participants are reminded not to 'fight the scenario' and respond to the scenario as it is presented to them. Briefings are also an opportunity to manage expectations, reinforce the learning focus and ensure everyone understands the format, especially if the exercise includes media simulation, remote participants or a hybrid set-up.

Once the exercise begins, the exercise director is responsible for overall delivery, supported by umpires and role-players. Their role is to ensure the scenario progresses smoothly, injects are delivered on time and that participants stay engaged and on track. Observers monitor activity without interfering, while umpires maintain close proximity to their teams to watch, listen and collect evidence for feedback. Exercise staff must remain fully focused, monitoring for off-script moments or disengagement, and ready to intervene if necessary. Emphasis is placed on encouraging real actions, not just verbal responses, and maintaining momentum until a natural end-point is reached.

The hot debrief takes place immediately after the exercise and is a crucial part of the learning process. Participants reflect on what went well, areas for improvement and how effectively the objectives were achieved. Different debrief formats can be employed based on the team's experience, dynamics and the time available. Exercise staff should also hold their own internal debrief to gather delivery insights. The outcomes of this session form the foundation of the post-exercise report and aid in the ongoing enhancement of team capability and future exercises.

Phase 4: Debrief and evaluation

Capturing lessons learnt and documenting them are perhaps among the most important parts of the exercise.

The four elements within this phase are:

1 Cold debrief
2 Post-exercise report
3 Next steps and follow-up
4 Reflect

A cold debrief is sometimes used, only after larger or more complex exercises, particularly when participants would benefit from time to reflect on their performance and learning. Unlike the immediate hot debrief, a cold debrief is held days or a week or two later, offering a more reflective and considered perspective. This format enables individuals to reflect on their experience, revisit their plans and actions, and come prepared with insights they might not have shared immediately after the event. They can be especially useful as emotional distance is required before discussing sensitive topics or decisions.

The post-exercise report is the official record of the exercise. It details key aspects, including who attended, what happened, how the scenario unfolded and how the team responded. It also includes key learning points, umpires' or facilitators' observations and recommendations for improvement. The report should be shared with the sponsor and shared internally. A well-written post-exercise report not only documents the exercise but also acts as a learning tool for future training, planning and response enhancement.

Following the exercise and debrief, a clear plan should be developed to address the lessons identified. This involves reviewing all observations and recommendations, agreeing on which actions will be taken forward, assigning ownership and determining how and when these will be implemented. Accountability is essential here; without follow-up, the benefits of the exercise may be lost. These steps ensure the exercise drives continuous improvement and helps the organization move from learning to action.

Finally, the design and delivery teams should step back and reflect on how the exercise was conducted. This internal review examines what went well in the preparation and delivery process, what could be improved for next time and any unexpected challenges encountered. It also provides an opportunity to gather learning around exercise logistics, team coordination and scenario design. These reflections can contribute to team development and inform the planning of future exercises, thereby enhancing both capability and confidence in exercise delivery.

KEY LEARNINGS

- A structured framework helps bring consistency and clarity to the planning and delivery of exercises.
- Careful design ensures the exercise aligns with organizational needs, objectives and expectations.
- The development phase translates the concept into practical detail through storyboarding, injects and assessment planning.
- Strong preparation and rehearsal help avoid disruption and ensure smooth delivery on the day.
- A clear and confident briefing sets the tone and enables participants to engage fully in the exercise.
- During delivery, the focus should be on observing real behaviours, decision-making and teamwork.
- The hot debrief captures immediate learning while the cold debrief allows for reflection after the event.
- The post-exercise report documents what happened, what was learnt and what should change.
- Follow-up actions must be assigned, owned and tracked to ensure real improvement occurs.
- Reflecting on the exercise delivery process helps improve future exercises and strengthens the organization's learning culture.

08

From umpires to participants: understanding exercise roles

In this chapter, you will learn about a number of different roles:

1. Sponsor
2. Participants
3. Exercise director
4. Design team
5. Umpires
6. Role-play coordinator and role-players
7. Observers and safety officers
8. Skills and attributes required for running an exercise
9. Use of consultants

When delivering training or a straightforward plan walkthrough, a single person is often sufficient to run the session. However, as exercises grow in complexity, particularly in live or SIMEX formats, a team is needed to plan and deliver the exercise effectively. For the exercise to run smoothly, roles must be clearly defined, documented and understood by everyone involved.

Everyone taking part in planning, delivery or reporting should be properly briefed on their role and what is expected of them. These briefs should make it clear what individuals should and should not do. It is especially important that during an exercise people remain within their designated responsibilities. If, for instance, an umpire starts advising the team or joining in the response, it can mislead participants, disrupt the scenario and ultimately undermine the objectives of the exercise. In smaller exercises, roles may be combined, but in larger or more complex scenarios, distinct and dedicated roles are usually required to ensure success.

The following section will discuss roles and responsibilities and the terms which should be used as part of the development of an exercise.

Roles and responsibilities

Sponsor

The sponsor's role is to commission the exercise, be responsible for the budget (or be responsible for finding or applying for the money to run it) and ensure that it meets any set requirements.

This could be a passive role in which the sponsor oversees an annual programme of exercises and engages consultants or internal resources to deliver it. The sponsor may be a committee, such as a risk committee, or an individual responsible for exercising within the organization, such as the chief risk officer or chief resilience officer. They may be quite specific about the requirements for the exercise, such as who will be exercised, the duration, scenario, style, objectives and timing, or they could be responsible for ensuring that the annual exercise is carried out and then discuss with the team who will design, develop and deliver it.

The sponsor may be involved in the planning of the exercise, but more commonly they will be kept informed of the progress of the planning process. They may have a role in the team being exercised so will participate in the exercise and they may review and sign off the post-exercise report. It is important that the sponsor's role is clear and that they agree on how much input they want to have and how much they want to be informed about the planning of the exercise. If a consultancy is used to deliver the exercise, the sponsor may designate one or more persons to work with the consultants to plan the exercise. If the exercise is planned in-house, the sponsor should designate who will be the exercise director and may also wish to appoint the exercise umpires.

Participants

These are the individuals taking part in the exercise. In most cases, participants are identified in advance and formally invited. However, in a no-notice exercise, anyone may be asked to step into a role, or there might be a pre-identified pool of potential participants. On the day, the response lead selects the most appropriate individuals to take part, depending on the scenario and the nature of the incident being exercised.

It is common practice to inform participants of the date, time and location of the exercise, and confirm whether they are required to attend, but not to disclose the detailed scenario in advance. Sometimes, they may be told that an exercise might take place within a certain time frame, and then they will need to wait to see if they are called to be part of the response team. Participants might be informed about the overall theme, such as it being a cyber exercise, but no information beyond this.

In some exercises, those involved in planning may also need to take part in the response and carry out their designated incident management team role. This may include members of the business continuity team who planned the exercise and then act in their assigned incident roles, sometimes as advisers. There may also be role-players involved. These individuals help to design the exercise and then participate in delivering or revealing the scenario. For example, during a cyber exercise we asked the chief information security officer to brief the team as though he were working with his technical team to manage the incident. He provided updates to the incident management team on actions taken and the current status of the response. As he had helped to develop the scenario, he was able to answer technical questions confidently and ensure that his responses remained aligned with the agreed scenario.

Exercise director

In most exercises, the exercise director is responsible for the end-to-end planning, delivery and reporting. Their responsibility is to ensure the exercise runs according to plan and delivers the intended outcomes. In simple exercises, they may also take on the role of umpire, although ideally, they should focus on running the exercise while the umpire observes and assesses participants.

In more complex exercises, such as SIMEXs, the exercise director's role is to ensure the exercise stays on track and achieves its objectives. They must rely on umpires to assess the performance of participating teams, as their full attention is needed on overseeing the exercise itself. It is important that the person directing the exercise and controlling the injects on the day is the same person who planned the exercise, as they will have a clear understanding of the rationale behind each inject and how the scenario was developed.

During the exercise, the exercise director is responsible for ensuring everything runs smoothly and objectives are met. This includes starting and stopping the exercise, managing time skips, steering the scenario and leading the debrief at the end. They also make sure all supporting elements contribute effectively. The exercise director may take notes during the exercise to support the debrief and contribute to the post-exercise report, but they are often so focused on managing the delivery that they don't have the capacity to conduct a full assessment of team performance.

I have witnessed the person who planned the exercise step aside on the day of the exercise, allowing a more experienced colleague to serve as exercise director. In my experience, this didn't work well. Without intimate knowledge of the scenario and injects, they couldn't deliver the exercise as effectively as the original planner, even if they were more senior and more experienced at running exercises.

Design team

All but the most straightforward exercises should have a design team responsible for planning the exercise and developing the details of any injects or questions. Their role is also to ensure that the scenario is realistic and feasible, and that the injects or questions are appropriate for the organization being exercised. The team may include subject-matter experts, representatives from the business areas participating in the exercise or specialists with expertise in the chosen scenario. Their input ensures the exercise is relevant, tailored to the organization and aligned with its objectives. Design team members should be involved throughout the planning process, rather than attending just a single meeting.

During the exercise, they may act as role-players. This requires only minimal briefing, as they already understand the wider context of the exercise. It also allows them to respond intelligently to participant queries or to ad lib additional injects where appropriate.

Exercise umpire

The role of the umpire is to observe the exercise and record objective assessment criteria and feedback to support the debrief and provide input to the post-exercise report. During exercise play, participants can agree with an umpire that a request has been actioned or that an action has been completed. Umpires should not participate in delivering the exercise, and they should avoid interfering with the response. Exceptions to this include situations where participants stray outside the scope of the exercise, are unsure how to carry out an action or have veered so far off track that the exercise objectives may not be met. In such cases, umpires should first discuss any necessary intervention with the exercise director.

There are broadly two areas the umpire should observe: participants' scenario management and whether their response is appropriate for their organization. This means umpires need a good understanding of how incidents should be managed, as well as knowledge of the organization and its expected practices.

When I deliver exercises, I typically aim to have two umpires per incident team taking part in the exercise. One umpire focuses on the participants' incident management skills, and could be from the consultant teams delivering the exercise, a member of the exercise design team or from the internal business continuity team. The other is an internal umpire who can assess whether the response aligns with the organization's specific expectations, requirements and procedures. The internal umpire can spot issues unique to the organization that an external umpire might miss.

Umpires and exercise staff should be easily identifiable to avoid confusion with participants. When appropriate, they should wear clearly marked tabards or badges. They must also be introduced at the start of the exercise, so everyone understands their role, who is observing and who is responding.

The ideal umpire is someone with a solid understanding of incident management principles and a good grasp of the organization's structure, culture and plans. They should be confident, observant and able to give clear, objective feedback without becoming involved in the response. When selecting an umpire, look for individuals who are respected by the team being exercised, understand the purpose of the exercise and can remain neutral throughout. Someone who has been in the organization a long time and brings a wealth of experience in incident management and a strong overview of how the organization operates is often a good choice. It's important they are well-briefed on the scenario, the exercise objectives and what they are specifically expected to observe and report.

Role-player coordinator

This role is usually only needed for a SIMEX or a live exercise. The role-player coordinator is responsible for ensuring that injects and any live elements of the exercise are input in accordance with the agreed schedule.

They will supervise the work of the role-players and ensure they are playing their allocated roles. They may also advise role-players on how to respond to an incoming inject if they are unsure how to reply. They will liaise with the exercise director on an almost minute-by-minute basis to insert injects. They may advise the exercise director if the response cell is being overwhelmed and that injects should be slowed down. They may also inform the exercise director if multiple injects have been sent to participants that require answers that have not yet been given. This, again, may be another reason to slow the input of injects.

Immediately after the exercise has finished, they should consult all role-players on any learning points; first on the participants' performance and then on the planning and delivery of the exercise. They may or may not be invited to take part in the hot debrief but should be consulted for points to include in the post-exercise report. They should be involved in developing the exercise, but on occasions, they may also join the process later as long as they understand the exercise, its objectives and the nature and importance of each objective; they can still perform their role effectively.

Role-players

This role is usually only needed during a SIMEX or a live exercise. Role-players are often drawn from the design team. They can have a number of different roles, such as briefing the team on the unfolding scenario, acting as someone who has attended the scene of an incident, serving as a subject-matter expert or portraying emergency services personnel or a team leader from a lower-tier incident management team. They might also take on the role of a senior manager, board member or regulator, and the incident team must report to them and inform them of the situation.

They could, in live exercises, play the role of casualties, members of the public or staff, witnesses or perpetrators of the incident, such as protestors. All role-players must be clear about their roles, why they are performing them and, when asked, what information they can release. They should also know when to consult the exercise director for clarification. Role-players with strong acting skills can significantly enhance the realism and impact of the exercise. They should remain in role throughout, but care must be taken to ensure they do not introduce any element of silliness into the scenario.

In a SIMEX, role-players are usually co-located with the role-player coordinator, who oversees their activity. They are responsible for managing communications with the team being exercised and for representing relevant stakeholders throughout the scenario. They will prepare for each call and log all interactions, including participants' reactions. Role-players will usually provide feedback to the role-player coordinator rather than to the exercise participants during the hot debrief.

Software operator

When software is used to support the delivery of exercise injects, a dedicated software operator should be considered. They are responsible for managing the technical aspects of the platform, inputting injects in line with the master events list and, where appropriate, responding to participant actions or queries within the system in consultation with the exercise director. The software operator ensures the scenario plays out smoothly through the platform, coordinating the timing and flow of media, social media or other digital injects. They may also monitor and log participant interactions and responses in real time, providing valuable input for the debrief and post-exercise report.

Observers

Observers should have no role in participating in the scenario or in the delivery of the exercise and are purely there to observe. They may include VIP visitors, members of the business continuity team, new starters, external parties or internal auditors. Observers should be properly briefed in advance, particularly on whether they are permitted to move between rooms if the exercise spans multiple locations. In some cases, observers may be situated in the role-players' room, allowing them to monitor the exercise without being visible to participants. Care should be taken not to have too many observers present, as this can make participants feel overwatched or uncomfortable. While observers typically do not take part in the formal debrief, they may be invited to submit any observations or feedback to be considered for inclusion in the post-exercise report.

Safety officer

A safety officer is only required for live exercises where there is a potential risk to exercise participants or role-players. This includes the possibility of physical injury during simulated activities or health concerns such as dehydration in hot weather. The safety officer may also form part of the design team, helping to shape the exercise play to ensure all activities are carried out safely. They should brief the role-players beforehand and may be present at the scene of the live exercise to monitor safety in real time. Safety protocols should be agreed in advance with the exercise director, including a clear mechanism that allows the safety officer to pause or stop the exercise immediately if any dangerous situation arises or appears imminent.

What are the skills and attributes required for running an exercise?

The following skills and attributes should be considered when identifying people to take the main roles in planning and delivering an exercise.

1. **Organizational and project management skills:** Essential for coordinating logistics, developing realistic scenarios and managing stakeholder expectations.
2. **Attention to detail:** Crucial in scenario design to ensure realism, coherence and alignment with learning objectives.
3. **Analytical and problem-solving abilities:** Enable those planning the exercise to anticipate challenges and adapt it dynamically as it unfolds.
4. **Facilitation and leadership skills:** Key for maintaining engagement, guiding participants and ensuring exercise objectives are met.
5. **Communication and interpersonal skills:** Necessary for clear briefings, managing team dynamics and fostering a constructive learning environment.
6. **Critical thinking and emotional intelligence:** Important for conducting thorough debriefs, extracting key lessons and managing participant feedback. They may also require emotional intelligence to decide the level of pressure they can put the participants under.
7. **Strong report-writing skills:** Essential for documenting findings, recommendations and lessons learnt post-exercise.
8. **Balance of structure and flexibility:** Ensures the exercise remains rigorous while being responsive to real-time developments.

EXAMPLE

Flexibility in mid-exercise delivery

A colleague of mine was involved in planning and delivering a SIMEX for an insurance company. On the design team was an external PR consultant who had contributed to planning the exercise and was due to take part, along with a colleague. The media response was a key element of the exercise. He was very insistent that there should be a 48-hour time jump midway through the SIMEX. From experience, we know that time jumps in SIMEXs can be problematic. You have to make assumptions about what the participants would have done during that time, which often leads participants to say, 'I wouldn't have done that', disrupting the exercise and damaging its credibility.

Despite our efforts, he couldn't be persuaded that the 48-hour jump was a bad idea. On the day of the exercise, we were informed that he was unavailable and would not be attending. As we approached the planned time jump, all the exercise staff agreed to scrap the 48-hour leap and instead opted for a shorter jump of a couple of hours. The injects were adjusted, and the exercise continued successfully.

Because we were an experienced team, the role-player coordinator and role-players weren't fazed by the mid-exercise change; they adapted the injects and carried on. Flexibility is a key skill and attribute for anyone delivering exercises.

Using consultants to plan and deliver your exercise

The first thing to note is that you don't need a consultant to plan and deliver your exercise. There are plenty of organizations that use internal staff to run their exercise, from the lowest-level operational plan walkthrough to highly complex SIMEXs involving the top management of an organization.

The advantages of using a consultant are as follows:

1. They may have more experience in running exercises than internal personnel and so can ensure greater benefit for the team being exercised.
2. They may have a great understanding of the scenario and its impact.
3. External third-party consultants are, on the whole, able to be franker about the performance of senior managers participating in the exercise than in-house staff.
4. They are likely to have seen many other organizations take part in exercises and can compare the organization's performance with other similar organizations.

5 The business continuity staff can take part in the exercise, even if they helped plan it, and can play their role in the response, as they would in a real incident.
6 Consultants can bring in subject-matter experts, such as communications specialists, to assess a particular element of the response.
7 Internal staff may be 'marking their own homework', as they are likely to have written the plan being exercised, set up the organization's incident management structure and have trained the participants. Therefore, they may not be entirely objective when assessing their own work.
8 Consultants can often work more quickly due to their experience, freeing up internal staff for other duties.
9 An external consultant can offer new ideas or approaches that internal teams may not have considered.

The disadvantages of consultants are:

1 They can be expensive.
2 They don't have an intimate knowledge of the organization being exercised, its processes and ways of working. Therefore, they might encounter a learning curve as they familiarize themselves with the organization's culture, systems and terminology.
3 They may not be cost-effective for short, low-level exercises, especially if a large programme of exercises is to be delivered.
4 Over-reliance on consultants can limit the development of internal capability in exercise planning and delivery.
5 Without clear communication, consultants may design an exercise that does not fully meet the organization's needs or culture.

A hybrid approach to using a consultant and cutting the exercise's cost is to plan the exercise in-house, then use consultants as umpires to assess the team being exercised. They may also be asked to write the post-exercise report. This provides an external, impartial view of a consultant without the cost of engaging them to plan, design and develop the exercise.

How to choose your consultancy

There are three things you should consider when choosing a consultancy to deliver your exercise: experience, credibility and chemistry. If you are commissioning anything more than a simple exercise, you are likely to require several consultants. They should either come from the same consultancy or be individuals who regularly work together, so they can operate as a cohesive team.

When it comes to experience, you should ask the consultancy what their expertise is in delivering the type of exercise you want, whether they have worked at the level of participants, whether they have run multi-team exercises and whether they or their organization hold any relevant certifications. There is plenty of training available on planning and delivering exercises but, apart from university degrees, where exercising is included in the curriculum, there are few formal personal qualifications. For organizations, the UK's National Cyber Security Centre's 'Cyber Incident Exercising' scheme (CIE) is one of the few certifications. Organizations seeking this certification must undergo a rigorous process to demonstrate their ability to deliver exercises.

It is not essential for consultants to have worked in the specific industry before, but it can help them understand the context and shorten the time needed to learn about the organization. It is important that consultants have experience working at the level at which the exercise will be run. If top management is being exercised, you want consultants who regularly operate and deliver exercises at that level. Similarly, if you are planning a SIMEX, and the consultancy has only delivered tabletop exercises, they may not be the best fit. If your exercise involves multiple teams or is multinational, you should check that they have experience in that context.

When assessing a consultancy, it is also important to check who will actually plan and deliver the exercise. Be wary of the 'bait and switch' in which a senior, highly competent consultant attends the initial meeting, but you are later handed over to less-experienced junior staff who are actually going to be planning and delivering the exercise. Ideally, the person planning the exercise should also deliver it on the day and provide feedback. You should feel confident that they are someone you would be happy to put in front of your CEO and that they have the gravitas and credibility to deliver robust, honest feedback.

Last, consider whether you have good chemistry with those delivering the exercise. You may be working with them quite intensively over a period of six to nine months to plan the exercise. Ask yourself: do you trust them? Will they listen to your views or bulldoze you with a 'consultant knows best' attitude? Insist on meeting the team or at least the one or two leaders who will be responsible for the design and development. While there may be additional people brought in for the exercise delivery whom you won't meet until shortly before the event, it is important to meet those doing the main planning work.

How to work with the consultant

Working effectively with a consultant requires a collaborative approach, as both you and the consultant share an interest in ensuring the exercise's success. Begin by clearly documenting all agreed design elements in the exercise instruction, so that all parties have a shared understanding of how the exercise will run. Active input from the design team is essential, particularly in helping the consultant understand the organization's structure, culture and terminology. This ensures, for example, that the correct names are used for teams, such as referring to the major incident strategy team by its actual title, rather than using a generic label like the crisis team.

It is equally important that the consultants are not left to work in isolation; successful delivery depends on active engagement and guidance from the organization being exercised. To support this, communication expectations should be set early, with regular progress meetings agreed upon and preferred communication channels and frequency established. Consultants should also be provided with contextual briefings, such as past exercise reports, audit findings or real incident reviews, to help them create scenarios that are realistic and relevant to the organization's current priorities.

Last, clarity around confidentiality and sensitivities is critical, especially where exercises touch on politically or reputationally delicate issues. Expectations regarding data handling, who will review the outputs and who will receive the final report should all be agreed in advance.

KEY LEARNINGS

- Complex exercises require clearly defined roles, responsibilities and boundaries to run effectively.
- Sponsors must provide strategic direction, resources and oversight without interfering in exercise delivery.
- Participants should be selected, briefed appropriately and kept unaware of scenario details to ensure realism.

- The exercise director oversees planning and delivery, ensuring the scenario stays on track and meets its objectives.
- A dedicated design team ensures the scenario is realistic, relevant and aligned with organizational needs.
- Umpires provide objective, structured assessment and must avoid influencing the team's response.
- Role-players add realism by portraying stakeholders and delivering injects in a controlled, coordinated way.
- A role-player coordinator is essential in SIMEXs to manage inject flow and support real-time scenario adjustments.
- Additional roles, such as software operators, observers and safety officers, enhance exercise effectiveness and safety.
- Delivering high-quality exercises requires skills such as facilitation, analysis, flexibility, communication and strong project management.

09

Agreeing on the exercise logistics: when, where, who and how long

In this chapter, you will learn about:

1 Questions for the kick-off meeting

2 Use of software for delivering the exercise

3 Choosing the right date and time of day

4 How long you should run an exercise for

5 Location of the exercise

6 Naming your exercises

7 'Who': understanding the organization being exercised

8 Reviewing the organization's documentation and use of social media

Typically, agreeing on the exercise logistics marks the start of exercise planning. Some of these logistics items may have already been determined before the exercise is formally proposed, while others are confirmed through discussion between the exercise sponsor and the planning team. Every exercise has to start somewhere, and it usually begins with an initial or 'kick-off' meeting.

Questions for the kick-off meeting

Depending on how the exercise was conceived, the organization of the kick-off meeting could either be with the sponsor, where they provide their guidance on the exercise and what they want out of it, or it could be the first meeting of the design team, if most of the design elements have already been decided. This meeting is to begin planning for the exercise. Only when all the elements of the exercise logistics are agreed upon should the design team proceed to development activities.

The following questions could be used as an agenda for the kick-off meeting to ascertain what needs to be agreed or what has already been agreed:

LOGISTICS

1. What is the date of the exercise?
2. Where will the exercise take place: in a physical location or online?
3. How much time can be allocated to the exercise?
4. Have timings for the exercise been agreed?
5. Is a cold debrief required, or a presentation of the findings to those who took part in the exercise?

PURPOSE

6. Why is the exercise being run?
7. Are there any regulatory, statutory, contractual or audit requirements for conducting the exercise?

OBJECTIVES

8. Are there any particular objectives you want to achieve from the exercise? Are you looking to improve knowledge, practise teamwork and leadership, validate plans, strategies and systems, build confidence, support continual improvement, or a combination of all of these?

SCOPE

9. Who will be exercised?
10. What plans and procedures will be exercised?
11. Are any external parties to be invited to take part in the exercise?
12. Who will be involved in the design and delivery of the exercise?

SCENARIO

13. Is there a preference for the scenario used in the exercise?

14 Once the scenario is decided, is there a design team or subject matter experts who can help develop the details of the scenario and injects?

TYPE OF EXERCISE

15 Will specialist exercise software be used to develop and deliver the exercise?

16 What type of exercise should be conducted?

17 Is pre-training required?

18 What is the team's capability and level of exercise experience?

19 Are there any risks or environmental issues associated with the exercise?

20 Are there any particular evaluation requirements?

21 Are there any thoughts on how the exercise will be delivered?

REQUEST DOCUMENTATION

22 Request copies of previous post-exercise reports.

23 Are there any relevant plans and other documentation available, such as BIAs, disaster recovery plans or business continuity audits?

The points not yet agreed upon need to be discussed in the kick-off meeting until all the design questions are resolved before starting on the development phase.

Will specialist technology or software be used to deliver the exercise?

As part of the design phase, you need to decide whether to use specialist software to develop and deliver your exercise. This decision should be made early, as the way the exercise is planned will be shaped by how the software is built and its functionality.

There are two different types of software to consider if you're planning to use technology in the delivery of the exercise. The first is game-like software, in which an individual or team plays within a simulated environment, responding to scenarios and learning from whether they successfully manage the incident. You may be able to choose the type of scenario, but it is unlikely you can tailor it much to the needs of your organization. At present, there are very few games explicitly designed to replicate a full exercise for individuals or teams. Perhaps in the future, more will be developed that help teams not only learn but also explore the consequences of their decisions, where different actions lead to different outcomes.

Micro-simulations are designed to provide some of the gaming experience. These can vary from short, computer-led scenarios lasting from 3–5 minutes to 30–45-minute multiplayer exercises. Again, these usually consist of multiple scenarios but cannot be tailored to the organization. They are useful if you want to deliver a high volume of short exercises to allow teams to practise without the effort of building a more substantial exercise each time.

The second type is software used to deliver and manage the exercise itself. Some platforms come with built-in automation to help develop the scenario, injects or assessments. While these may save time, planning the exercise within the platform still requires the same rigour and thought as planning an exercise without software. You will likely still need to produce an exercise instruction and post-exercise report to ensure the exercise details are properly documented and available for future reference. Relying solely on the platform risks losing important information due to software updates, data overwrites or a later switch to a new system.

When: choosing the right date and time of day

As a consultant, the first thing we try to agree with the client is the **date** of the exercise. Once that's set, we project-manage the entire planning process backwards from that date. A general rule of thumb: the more senior the people being exercised, the harder it is to find a time when all essential participants are available. For executive-level teams, the exercise date is typically set 3–6 months in advance, sometimes even a year ahead. If deputy participants are allowed, it adds flexibility, enabling the session to proceed if primary role-holders are unavailable.

There's no ideal time of year for an exercise, but some periods are best avoided: August, Christmas, New Year, school half terms, religious holidays and bank holidays. Similarly, while there's no universal best day of the week, many organizations avoid booking exercises for Monday mornings or Friday afternoons.

Time of day also matters. Starting at 9.00 am lets participants begin their day with the exercise and avoid the risk of being caught up in other work. A 10.00 am start may seem more relaxed, but people can get distracted, arrive late or miss the briefing, which can affect their understanding of the exercise format. Late arrivals can disrupt the flow and require the facilitator to pause or repeat key information. If the exercise is multinational, a convenient time has to be found for people in different time zones.

As many exercise participants have other meetings scheduled after the exercise, a key skill for the exercise director is **time management**. Ensuring the session runs on time and doesn't overrun is vital. I almost always schedule an additional hour after the exercise for a debrief with the umpires and delivery team to agree on the key findings for the post-exercise report. It's important to inform all facilitators and book the room for this extra hour in advance.

Ending the exercise at **lunchtime** can work well. It allows for an informal lunchtime discussion and gives the directing team the chance to gather immediate feedback. Alternatively, finishing close to 5.00 pm offers flexibility if the session overruns, though you may lose a few participants due to family commitments.

In conclusion, there's no single 'best' time of day to run an exercise; it often depends on organizational constraints. However, if you do have a choice, take time to consider the most appropriate date and time to maximize participation and impact.

How long should you run an exercise for?

The length of an exercise is determined by several factors. The shortest exercise I have run lasted 30 minutes, while the longest extended over three days. Oil company response exercises are often conducted over two to three days. National anti-terrorist or transport incident response exercises may also run for several days, and market-wide financial exercises can continue for up to a month. However, in such long-running exercises, the actual play is usually limited to one to two hours per day. It is very unlikely that the exercise play will run continuously, 24 hours a day.

Several factors affect the duration of exercise. These include the goals and desired outcomes, the availability and willingness of senior managers to dedicate time, the complexity of the scenario, the chosen type of exercise, the length of previous exercises, regulatory requirements, the scope of the exercise and the number of teams involved. Additionally, time should be allocated for the debrief.

The more complex the objectives, the more time the exercise will require. If the focus is on leadership and teamwork, the exercise needs sufficient time for the group to form, practise roles and develop team dynamics. In this case, at least a three-hour exercise is recommended. If the purpose is simply to test an organization's initial response to a scenario, the exercise could run for 30 to 45 minutes. This allows time to introduce the scenario, discuss the response and hold a short debrief.

Senior managers' willingness to allocate time is often the deciding factor. Most executives will commit between two and three hours, usually once a year. Occasionally, an additional hour may be agreed for training before the exercise, but it is rare for senior managers to dedicate more than three hours. One innovative approach is to run a three-day exercise in which executives participate for one hour per day. This allows time for reflection between sessions and for the scenario to be adjusted based on their decisions. In practice, three hours in total is the most common commitment executives are willing to make.

The type of exercise also influences length. A plan walkthrough typically lasts no more than an hour. A tabletop exercise usually takes between one and three hours, while a SIMEX should last at least two hours to allow team dynamics to develop properly.

If the annual exercise always lasts three hours, participants may be reluctant to accept a duration that is either longer or shorter. Regulatory requirements can also dictate length. A regulator may not consider 30 minutes sufficient to demonstrate that an organization has met its obligations.

Exercises involving multiple teams require more time. One team must consider an issue, brief a higher or lower team, receive feedback and then re-brief. A multi-team exercise, therefore, takes a minimum of two hours and may last between three and five hours to allow proper interaction between teams.

Planners are often tempted to cut the debrief time to maximize play. This should be avoided. A hot debrief should always be conducted at the end of the exercise. The minimum time should be 15 minutes, but ideally, 20 to 30 minutes should be allocated.

Fatigue also plays an important part in exercise duration. A full SIMEX can be stressful, with participants constantly processing new information, attending meetings, making decisions and contributing to discussions. Time is compressed in exercises, so events happen more quickly than in real life. I have often observed teams becoming tired as further injects are introduced, with enthusiasm declining as concentration wanes. Tabletop exercises are less intense, but participants must still concentrate and consider the implications of each question for their organization. This reinforces the view that, for high-intensity exercises, three hours is the maximum duration before participants' concentration begins to fade.

Where: location of the exercise

When considering where the exercise will take place, it is important to think carefully about the environment you are creating. The choice of venue should reflect the type of incident being tested and support the learning outcomes. For many exercises, the ideal location is the same room that the team would use in a real event. Setting up this space in advance with flip charts, whiteboards, place cards and the organization's 'battle box' (a pre-packed kit containing essential equipment, documents and tools needed to manage an incident from an alternate location) ensures that, when participants arrive, they are immediately immersed in a realistic setting and ready to begin.

If the scenario involves denial of access or the loss of a building, it is worth booking an off-site room. This reinforces the realism of the situation and avoids the artificiality of conducting an exercise in the very space that has supposedly been rendered unavailable. Alongside the main incident room, it is often helpful to provide an additional space for role-players, ideally situated close by so that interactions can flow easily during the exercise.

Room availability should be addressed early on, ideally as one of the client's first tasks following the kick-off meeting. Depending on the exercise design, there may be a need for multiple response rooms, one for each team, so this should be factored into the planning. If the exercises involve participants joining via video conference, the response rooms should be equipped to support this. It is wise to confirm whether IT support will be available on the day to deal with any technical issues that may arise.

For exercises that use on-site role-players, consider the communications they will need. Will they have access to desk phones? Can they use personal mobiles? Or does the exercise organizer need to provide temporary communications equipment? Clarifying these points avoids confusion and ensures role-players can deliver their part effectively.

Logistics such as parking and welfare facilities may appear mundane but are nonetheless crucial. Poor parking arrangements can cause delays, frustrate participants and undermine the professionalism of the event. Equally, ensuring access to toilets, refreshments, breakout areas and rest spaces is vital to keep participants engaged and able to perform at their best during what may be an intense day.

Finally, a decision needs to be made about how the room itself will be presented at the start of the exercise. Some clients prefer to have administrative staff set up the space in advance, so the team walks into a fully prepared environment as they would in reality. Others may wish the team themselves to arrange the room, which can also provide useful insight into how quickly and effectively they organize themselves under pressure.

Further considerations for the exercise location are discussed in Chapter 13.

Number of meetings to plan your exercise

Once you have the date for your exercise, you should start planning the exercise meetings. The number of meetings will depend on the complexity and length of the exercise, but generally, I recommend three to four sessions for a tabletop exercise and at least four sessions, plus an on-site rehearsal, for a SIMEX (see Chapter 3). Meetings should last between one-and-a-half and two hours to allow sufficient time to discuss all issues.

One of the criteria that affects the number of meetings is the exercise team's knowledge of the organization being exercised and its processes. If the exercise involves a complex scenario, then the exercise team needs to understand the processes in detail so they can craft a credible scenario. This may require a visit to where the activity is actually carried out, or meetings with different parts of the organization to understand how the scenario would impact each part. If the planning is not sufficient, then the credibility of the exercise can be lost, perhaps before it even starts. If you get into an argument with participants about the scenario, you have lost the exercise and your credibility.

When holding meetings and understanding the organization, you also need to understand the impact of the scenario and ensure it is sufficiently large for the team being exercised. This could involve speaking to several subject matter experts to check its credibility.

Naming your exercises

Not everyone who plans exercises chooses to name them, but I believe a good name adds value and makes the exercise more memorable. When I was in the Army, all exercises and operations had names, which gave them a certain formality and structure. A name also makes it easier to distinguish between exercises in a series, or to identify previously run exercises.

For example, a set of exercises I delivered for a local authority is called 'Loki'. The service-level exercises are named Loki A1, A2 and A3, while the strategic-level (Gold) exercise is called Loki B. These may not be the most imaginative names, but they make it simple to refer to each exercise in documentation and when reflecting on past activities.

WHY 'EXERCISE LOKI'?

Loki was chosen as the exercise name because he symbolizes chaos, disruption and deception, traits that align closely with the unpredictable and fast-moving nature of modern crises and cyber incidents. His role in Norse mythology as a trickster and shape-shifter makes him an ideal figure to represent complex scenarios involving insider threats, misinformation or cascading failures.

If you are running a series over several years, you might use a naming convention such as 'Exercise X 2025', followed by 'Exercise X 2026', or use sequential labels like 'Exercise X1', 'X2' and so on.

EXAMPLE

Exercise Sweet

Exercise Sweet was a series of 28 exercises delivered for a Scottish local authority. The aim of the exercises was to help each of their services develop a business continuity plan and then validate it through a tailored exercise. For most of the services, the chosen scenario was the discovery of an unexploded World War II bomb in the vicinity of their office.

The exercises were conducted pre-Covid-19 and the widespread adoption of homeworking. Therefore, a denial of access to their office for several days would have had a significant impact on service delivery. Using a World War II bomb scenario also allowed for the possibility that the bomb might detonate, making the office permanently unusable. Given that the area had been bombed during the war, the scenario was entirely plausible.

I wanted a 'clever' name for the exercise. Initially, I considered referencing the Blitz directly. During my research, I discovered that the glam rock band, Sweet, had played one of their early gigs within the local authority area in the 1970s. Reportedly, their song 'Ballroom Blitz' was inspired by that performance, which ended in chaos when bottles were thrown at them.

I named the series **Exercise Sweet**, and in each session, I challenged participants to see if they could figure out the connection. In one of the final exercises, someone finally made the link. The reference may have been obscure, but the name has stuck with me out of the hundreds of exercises I've delivered.

When naming an exercise, there are a few important principles to follow.

In the Army, I was taught that the exercise name should not reveal the scenario. In other words, participants should not be able to guess what will happen solely from the title. A name like Exercise Cyber Defender, for example, gives away too much and is best avoided.

You should also avoid choosing names that sound flippant or exaggerated. Titles such as Exercise Certain Death undermine the event's credibility.

In the past, I have used names based on historical events or significant local references, especially when conducting exercises in the UK. However, when delivering exercises internationally, this approach can be more challenging. What seems like a neutral or clever reference may carry very different and possibly offensive connotations in another cultural context. Always check your proposed exercise name with the design team to ensure it is appropriate for the audience.

These days, I often use names drawn from Greek or Roman mythology. I try to match the name to the nature of the exercise. For example, an exercise with a communications company might be called Exercise Mercury, after the messenger of the gods.

Consider risk

When planning an exercise, it is important to assess and consider any risks to participants and the organization. If the exercise involves carrying out real elements of a response, particularly in a live exercise, you need to ask whether the inherent risk is a key learning point or if the activity can be safely simulated without compromising the objectives.

For example, if you are planning a mass casualty incident, is physically placing a casualty on a stretcher and carrying them to an ambulance essential to the exercise? Or is the risk, such as the risk of someone injuring their back, too high for the benefit gained? Could the casualty walk to the ambulance, pretending they had been stretchered, without diminishing the learning outcome?

There is also the risk of an exercise unintentionally becoming a real event and impacting the organization. If the scenario involves a power outage, should you actually switch to the standby generator and test staff responses? Or, in a technical exercise involving IT, how much of the recovery and restoration should be carried out for real, and how much simulated? The organization's risk appetite must be considered, and the balance between risk and reward for each activity needs to be discussed. Any known risks should be documented, monitored and appropriate risk-mitigation measures put in place.

Environmental risks must also be considered, especially during live exercises. These could include waste generation, excessive noise, disruption to local wildlife or potential contamination. Where props are used, such as simulated oil spills, medical supplies for casualties, or equipment used in live exercises, there must be a plan to return the area to its original state and ensure that all materials are appropriately removed and disposed of.

'Who': understanding the organization being exercised

The more thoroughly you understand the organization you're designing the exercise for, the better it can be tailored to its context, risks and learning needs. Even if you work within the organization, you may not be fully familiar with the specific function or team being exercised.

Effective exercise design, therefore, requires gaining a clear understanding of what the organization does, how it is structured, where its staff and customers are located, how it delivers its core products or services and how it interacts with partners, suppliers and governing bodies. It is also important to understand its ownership or reporting lines, recent performance, past incidents and any cultural characteristics that may influence decision-making.

Without this organizational knowledge, an exercise may quickly lose credibility, as unrealistic assumptions about customer behaviour, market competition or organizational dependencies will become apparent to participants. For example, if customers are highly loyal or long-term contractual relationships limit switching, a scenario based on rapid customer loss may lack realism; conversely, where services are easily substitutable, incorporating competitive pressures may create a more authentic scenario.

Review current plans and other business continuity documentation

At a minimum, the plan for the part of the organization being tested should be requested and reviewed by the exercise design team. The following information is essential for developing the exercise:

1. The incident management hierarchy and where the plan fits into any other plans that the organization has developed.
2. What they call their incident team.
3. Any particular terminology they use in describing their response.
4. Whether their plans contain all the elements you would expect to see and if the plan needs substantial rewriting or is missing elements you would expect to find in good practice. This could be highlighted in the post-exercise report.
5. Which elements of the plan do we want included in the exercise and evaluated as PIs (see Chapter 17), such as SITREP forms, invocation criteria or response checklists?
6. Any specific elements of the plan which should be practised?

There may be other business continuity documents which might help you understand the team and how the organization responds. This could include relevant business impact analysis reports, risk reports, crisis communications plans or contingency plans outlining responses to specific incidents or scenarios.

You should also request post-exercise reports for the last two to three exercises the team has participated in. This helps review whether the same issues recur in the reports, indicating that learning has not occurred. There may be elements discussed in the post-exercise report that could be incorporated into the exercise you are planning.

Understanding the organization's use of media and social media

I always teach that an incident response is won or lost based on its communication, which is one of the most crucial parts of the organization's response. It is therefore very important for all exercises to understand the organization's use of media and how it is portrayed or considered in terms of reputation. For organizations with a poor reputation, an incident may have a greater impact than for organizations with an established good reputation. This is something the exercise planners should recognize so that the media, social media and customers' reactions to the incident can be depicted realistically.

The following are some considerations that can help to understand the organization and its use of media and social media:

1. Does the organization have a high or low profile in the international, national local or trade press?
2. Understand which social media channels the client uses, or if they use them at all. How frequently they post, and whether they use automated content or actively engage with customers.
3. Identify existing sentiment, including any negative posts or reviews that could influence an incident scenario.
4. Look at how many 'followers' or 'likes' each platform has.
5. Look at the 'news' section of their website to see the types of posts they upload.
6. Research any relevant stories, controversies or issues the organization may have been involved in. This could help when developing your scenario further / to increase pressure during the exercise.
7. If the client has been involved in any incidents in the past, look to see how they responded on social media or whether they were covered in the media.
8. Ask the organization being exercised for a copy of any crisis or crisis communications plans. Do they have any plans for internal communications with staff?
9. Which tools does the client use to monitor social media on a daily basis / during an incident?
10. Who posts on social media on a daily basis? Does this change during an incident or crisis scenario?
11. Do they have any public relations companies on retainer?

KEY LEARNINGS

- Early agreement on date, location, duration and participants is essential for effective exercise planning.
- A structured kick-off meeting helps clarify the exercise's logistics, scope, objectives and potential risks.
- Scheduling the exercise well in advance is crucial, especially when involving senior executives.
- Avoid scheduling exercises during peak holiday periods or times with low availability to maximize participation.
- The length of the exercise should align with its objectives, the complexity of the scenario and participants' availability.
- Venue selection should reflect the scenario's realism, including off-site locations when appropriate.
- Time must be allocated for a proper debrief; cutting this short undermines learning and feedback.
- Understanding the organization's structure, past incidents and communication habits ensures relevance and credibility.
- Naming exercises can improve recall and branding but should be culturally sensitive and scenario-neutral.
- Planning should include assessing risks to participants and the organization to prevent unintended real-world impacts.

10

Writing the purpose and exercise objectives

In this chapter, you will learn about:

1. Writing the exercise purpose
2. Writing exercise objectives
3. Developing a hierarchy of knowledge
4. Making objectives SMART

When I first started delivering exercises, I – as many practitioners do – followed the format used by others. These exercise instructions typically included an aim and a list of objectives. I followed this format for quite some time, even though I was never entirely clear on the difference between an aim and an objective.

I understood that the aim was meant to express the overall goal of the exercise, while the objectives were intended as smaller, specific outcomes supporting that goal. However, I often found it difficult to write them clearly or to explain the difference to others. At some point, I came across the idea of using a 'purpose and objectives' format instead. This approach made much more sense to me and helped clarify my thinking when designing exercises, which will be detailed in this chapter.

Writing the exercise purpose: why are we running this exercise?

Understanding the reason for running an exercise is the starting point for shaping its purpose. Often, the decision to hold an exercise is not just because someone thinks it's a good idea, but it's driven by organizational, legal or external requirements. Below are some common reasons to run exercises:

Annual policy requirement: Many organizations have internal policies requiring them to run at least one exercise each year.

Regulatory requirement: Exercises may be required under legislation or industry regulations. For example, regulated utilities, financial services and transport organizations are often required to demonstrate their ability to respond effectively to major incidents. Financial organizations subject to the operational resilience framework are required to test and exercise their arrangements to ensure they can remain within defined impact tolerances.

Licence condition (e.g. COMAH sites): For sites storing dangerous chemicals or other hazardous materials, running exercises may be a condition of the site's licence or operating permission.

Compliance with international standards: Organizations certified to standards such as ISO 22301 (Business Continuity) or ISO 27001 (Information Security) must regularly test their systems to maintain certification.

Client or contractual requirement: Some clients or third parties may require regular exercises as part of a service-level agreement or contract, especially in outsourced or critical service environments.

Multi-year exercise programme: Many organizations run a rolling exercise programme over several years, each with a different focus or level of complexity, as part of a longer-term capability-building strategy.

Sector-wide or national programme: Organizations may be required to participate in government-led or industry-wide exercises (e.g. electricity, water or telecoms sectors, as well as financial services), which may be part of national resilience frameworks.

Audit or assurance activities: Internal or external audit functions may request an exercise be carried out to test specific parts of the business continuity or crisis management arrangements.

Part of incident response maturity development: Exercises may be used to move an organization from a low maturity level (e.g. untested plans) to a higher one (e.g. well-rehearsed teams and integrated response).

Board or senior leadership request: Sometimes the request for an exercise comes from the top, a senior leader, chair or board asking for reassurance that the organization is ready for a crisis.

Response to recent incidents or near misses: A recent event, either internal or external, may prompt the need to rehearse a similar scenario to ensure preparedness.

Good practice or local initiative: Sometimes, running an exercise isn't driven by policy, regulation or a formal programme, it's simply recognized as good practice. A department, location or team might want to test their plan independently to build confidence, practise roles or explore how they'd respond to a scenario.

Raising staff awareness: Exercises, particularly workshops, discussion-based sessions or short simulations, can be an effective way to raise staff awareness of the organization's business continuity arrangements. These sessions help staff understand their roles in a response and increase overall organizational resilience.

Introducing a new partner or service: If you outsource part of your service or change suppliers, you may want to have a joint exercise with them to validate and coordinate the two organizations' response.

How the purpose of the exercise influences the exercise design

The purpose of running the exercise may influence its type, format and the individuals involved. This could also include whether external third parties need to be involved.

Format of the exercise. If the purpose is to meet licence conditions, such as those for a COMAH site, the format may need to be a tabletop exercise to involve multiple agencies and deliver the scenario in a particular way. These exercises often follow set guidelines and must meet specific testing objectives.

Who attends the exercise. The attendees can be directly influenced by the purpose. A customer-facing exercise may involve client representatives, while an internal exercise could just focus on internal incident management teams.

Level of reporting required. Where the report is shared externally, such as with regulators or parent organizations, it often needs to be more detailed and formal, including comprehensive observations and recommendations.

Scenario development. In multi-year programmes, the scenarios may be agreed upon in advance, allowing for continuity and progressive testing.

For regulatory or licence-based exercises, while the core premise might stay the same (e.g. a hazardous material leak with off-site consequences), the specifics of how the incident unfolds can change from year to year to keep the exercise fresh and challenging.

Taking part in industry-wide exercises. When taking part in these exercises, you may have little input into the exercise, but sometimes you can add your own local scenario elements to exercise particular internal issues.

The following are some examples of purposes:

- To fulfil our annual policy requirement for exercising business continuity and crisis response plans.
- To meet the COMAH licence condition by testing our off-site emergency procedures.
- To support ISO 22301 compliance through a scenario-based test of our continuity arrangements.
- To deliver Year 2 of our multi-year exercise programme, focusing on reputational risk.
- To raise staff awareness of continuity plans through a discussion-based exercise.

Writing the exercise objectives

Writing objectives for your exercise is a critical part of the planning process. Objectives form the foundation of the exercise, providing structure and clarifying what participants are expected to achieve. From these overarching objectives, more detailed performance objectives (see Chapter 15) can be developed during the exercise's development phase. Objectives describe how success will be measured and how you will determine whether the exercise has fulfilled its purpose.

It is important to focus on what you want the participants to achieve, not what you wish the exercise itself to accomplish. This distinction matters. When someone asks, 'Did the exercise meet its objectives?' they are really asking whether the participants achieved the outcomes that were set for them, not whether the planning and delivery of the exercise went well. Recognizing this nuance is key to developing meaningful and measurable objectives.

Exercise objectives typically fit into five areas.

1. **Know: Improving knowledge:** This focuses on enhancing the team's knowledge and is like setting learning objectives during training delivery. During an exercise, there will always be an element of learning, but we may want to specify what we want participants to learn. Learning can occur at various levels, from a basic understanding of issues associated with a scenario to the development of new strategies and tools in response to it.
2. **Do: Practising skills:** This element is about practising practical skills associated with incident management. Activities may range from individual tasks, such as logging phone calls, to more complex team tasks, such as decision-making. These skills are often taught prior to the exercise, with the exercise providing an opportunity to practise them in a realistic setting.
3. **Work: Teamwork and leadership:** This examines teamworking and leadership, both of which are essential during incident response. It also involves assessing how effectively individuals demonstrate their ability to carry out their incident roles and contribute to the team. If a participant has a specialist role that differs from their usual day-to-day job, the exercise offers a chance to practise and demonstrate their competence in that role.
4. **Check: Validating plans, strategies and systems:** This area focuses on technical recovery, strategies and solutions, evaluating whether they are fit for purpose and, if implemented, meet their intended requirements within the agreed timeframes. It can include 'tests' to determine whether a strategy can be executed within the required time, often resulting in a clear pass or fail outcome. A common objective in exercises is to validate a plan, ensuring it can be effectively used during an incident response.
5. **Feel: Building confidence and continual improvement:** This area assesses participants' confidence in fulfilling their roles, the team's overall effectiveness and the organization's ability to manage incidents. Measuring confidence before and after exercises can highlight trends or improvements. Continual improvement also involves reviewing previous post-exercise reports, checking whether lessons were learnt and ensuring the same mistakes are not repeated.

Having just suggested when writing objectives to break them down into five areas objectives don't always fall neatly into those five areas. For example, I was asked by a client to run an exercise based on an active shooter scenario for a project they were managing in the US. They were building a very large solar farm in the southern US, importing a large number of employees from different areas, and were concerned that tensions between groups of workers could escalate into violence, potentially even an active shooter incident.

As they didn't have a specific plan in place for such a scenario, one of the primary purposes of the exercise was to build participants' understanding of an active shooter event, how to respond, and the tasks and actions required. In this case, the objective fell into the 'know' category.

Had there been a contingency plan in place for managing such incidents, the focus might have shifted towards validating that plan, assessing whether it was fit for purpose, and ensuring it contained the necessary information for responding. If the team had already received training in active shooter response prior to the exercise, the exercise's goal could have been adapted to demonstrate their ability to apply that training effectively during the scenario.

What is important is spending some time developing the objectives and ensuring they reflect the wishes of the exercise sponsor and clearly define the intended output of the exercise, and if they don't fall neatly into my five areas, it doesn't matter. It should be noted that you don't need to have an element of all five areas in the exercise; you may just focus on one or two areas.

Developing a hierarchy of knowledge

Depending on the team's existing level of knowledge and experience, the required learning outcomes will vary. Bloom's Taxonomy provides a structured hierarchy of learning that can support the development of learning objectives and align with a maturity-based assessment approach.[1] It encourages a structured progression from foundational understanding through to more advanced, critical thinking. It is a valuable tool in exercise design because it promotes deeper learning beyond simple recall, ensures training is delivered in a logical sequence from basic understanding to advanced thinking, and helps align exercise objectives, participant activities and evaluation methods in a structured and consistent way. This structured progression has the following levels:

1. Know the facts.
2. Understand what they mean.
3. Apply them in a practical context.
4. Analyse patterns, decisions and outcomes.
5. Evaluate the quality of decisions or plans.
6. Create new strategies or tools based on insight.

In the most basic of exercises, such as the plan walkthrough, participants might focus on levels 1 and 2 from the above list, as they are still at the stage of understanding their roles, what is expected of them, and how, in an incident, the team works together to manage it. In more complex exercises like SIMEXs, then objectives may be developed for levels 3 to 6, where participants are expected to apply their knowledge.

Understanding various types of incidents and how to respond to them is a crucial part of the learning process and can be an important objective in itself. Managing a cyber incident involves many nuances that are quite different from handling a product recall. Gaining an understanding of the key issues involved in responding to different types of incidents can therefore be a valuable goal.

Know: Improving knowledge

Exercises are, at their core, an opportunity to build knowledge and deepen understanding. Before people can respond effectively in a real incident, they first need to know what is expected of them, how the organization intends to manage the situation, and which plans, processes and recovery strategies are available to support them. Knowledge is the foundation of capability: if individuals don't know their role, where to find information or how their actions connect to others, then the response will always be slower, less coordinated and more prone to error.

This is especially true when responding to specific scenarios, such as a cyber-attack, a mass-casualty event or a supply chain failure, where specialized knowledge is needed to understand the unique risks, tasks and decisions involved. A team may be confident in general incident management, but without scenario-specific knowledge, their response could miss critical actions or fail to recognize key issues as they develop. Writing 'know' objectives helps us focus on developing the essential understanding that underpins an effective, timely and confident response.

What we might want to write 'know' objectives on

The following are the different areas in which we might want to write objectives:

- Understand, follow and effectively implement relevant plans and procedures.
- Developing particular knowledge for dealing with specific incidents, e.g. cyber incident management or an event involving mass casualties.
- The tasks, issues, decisions and risks associated with a particular scenario or incident type.
- The incident management hierarchy within their own organizations, and the roles and responsibilities of each of the teams
- Interoperability with multi-agency or partner organizations.
- Their role within the plan and how it interfaces with other team members' roles.
- Any specialist tasks or responsibilities allocated to them outside their normal day-to-day activities which require additional skills or knowledge.
- How to implement particular recovery strategies.
- Familiarity with the recovery strategies and contingencies outlined within their relevant plans.
- Their incident team's ways of working.
- Internal and external communication procedures.
- Statutory notifications, regulations or contractual requirements which need to be taken into account in the response.
- The organization's post-incident recovery process

Objectives examples (with levels)

1. Promote awareness of the business continuity plan and its key components. (*Level 1: Remembering / Level 2: Understanding: Identify / Describe*)
2. Ensure that the teams are aware of the actions, impacts, tasks and risks associated with a data breach.
(*Level 2: Understanding: Describe / Explain / Summarize*)
3. Demonstrate an understanding of the team members' specialist roles. (*Level 2: Understanding: Describe / Explain / Summarize*)

TABLE 10.1 Words to write 'know' objectives

Level	Description	Descriptor words
1. Remembering	Recalling facts, terms, basic concepts or answers	Define, list, recall, identify, name, recognize
2. Understanding	Explaining ideas or concepts in your own words	Describe, explain, summarize, interpret, classify, paraphrase
3. Applying	Using information in new situations	Use, implement, carry out, execute, demonstrate, apply
4. Analysing	Breaking information into parts to explore understandings and relationships	Analyse, compare, contrast, categorize, differentiate, investigate
5. Evaluating	Justifying a decision or course of action	Critique, evaluate, judge, recommend, justify, argue
6. Creating	Putting elements together to form a coherent or functional whole; generating new ideas or products	Create, design, develop, compose, construct, formulate

4. Implement the organization's cyber incident contingency plan in response to a simulated attack.
   (*Level 3: Applying: Use / Implement / Apply*)
5. Evaluate the impact of the incident, and recommend and implement the appropriate strategy to address it.
   (*Level 5: Evaluating: Evaluate / Recommend / Justify*)

Do: Practising skills

There is a wide range of skills required to manage an incident. Some are individual skills, such as logging, while others, such as maintaining situational awareness and developing a shared understanding, can be carried out individually or collaboratively. It is generally most effective to teach these skills in dedicated training sessions before participants engage in an exercise, rather than learning them simply 'on the job'. This is because participants often do not practise them regularly, which can lead to forgetfulness. Additionally, some skills are complex, and there may not be enough time during exercises to learn them thoroughly. This approach allows individuals to develop and understand the skills in a structured environment, then apply and adapt them during the exercise in response to the specific scenario.

What we might want to write 'do' objectives on

The following areas are what we might want to write objectives on:

- Building situational awareness by gathering, interpreting and anticipating information during an incident.
- Managing information flow, including collecting, verifying and sharing updates to support informed decisions.
- Updating information boards to reflect the latest facts, actions and priorities for shared situational understanding.
- Logging decisions, actions and events accurately and in real time to support post-incident review and learning.
- Making structured decisions under pressure using available information, organizational priorities and risk assessment.
- Defining strategic intent to guide the team's response and ensure alignment with organizational objectives.
- Identifying impacts across people, operations and reputation, and developing a working recovery strategy.
- Applying the incident management cycle of situation – direction – action.
- Communicating strategic intent clearly to provide shared purpose to those responding.
- Completing key incident documentation such as logs, action plans and situation reports under exercise conditions.

Objectives examples (with levels)

1 Apply the situational awareness – decision – action model consistently to manage scenario progression and support effective team decision-making. (*Level 1: Executing: Apply*)

TABLE 10.2 Words to write 'do' objectives

Level	Description	Descriptor words
1. Executing	Carrying out learnt procedures or steps in familiar settings	Perform, use, execute, apply, respond
2. Practising	Repeating or rehearsing actions to build consistency and skill	Practise, operate, implement
3. Managing	Overseeing or coordinating actions and tasks during application.	Manage, direct, supervise, facilitate
4. Adapting	Modifying actions in response to feedback or changing conditions	Adjust, modify, tailor, recalibrate
5. Mastering	Applying skills fluently and confidently across varying contexts	Demonstrate, integrate, optimize, lead

2 Practise activating and operating designated emergency communications tools (e.g. Teams, WhatsApp, satellite phone) to support remote coordination.
(*Level 2: Practising: Practise / Operate*)

3 Manage the escalation process by identifying when the incident reaches the gold threshold, preparing briefing materials and communicating the handover effectively.
(*Level 3: Managing: Manage*)

4 Adapt the team's response actions to new information, shifting risks or inject-driven complications.
(*Level 4: Adapting: Adapt / Operate*)

5 Demonstrate the ability to log key decisions, actions and rationales accurately and in real time, using the designated incident logging process.
(*Level 5: Mastering: Demonstrate*)

Work: Teamwork and leadership

Incident management is all about the people who implement the response and how they work together to manage the incident. People perform differently under the stress of a live situation, and those who are very effective at managing routine activities may perform very differently and much less effectively under pressure.

By practising teamwork in a benign environment, participants can rehearse how they would respond in a crisis and identify individuals who may not have the temperament to be part of the incident team. For those who already work together day-to-day, it provides an opportunity to operate under different, more pressured circumstances. For those who don't usually work together, it allows them to get to know and understand the people they will be working alongside during an incident.

It is also a valuable opportunity for the team leader to practise leading the team and to demonstrate their ability to manage both the people and the response in a situation that may be very different from their usual way of working.

WHO SHOULD BE ON THE TEAM?

There's an ongoing debate about whether incident team members should be chosen based on their position in the organizational hierarchy; for example, the CEO automatically becoming the team leader and the chief people officer (CPO) taking on the people coordinator role, or whether roles should be allocated to the person best suited to perform them during a crisis.

For instance, a CEO may acknowledge that they're not at their best when leading under pressure and may instead designate their chief operating officer to lead the incident team. Similarly, a CPO may know, as many senior managers do, that they struggle to remain calm in high-pressure situations. In that case, someone from their team may be better placed to take on the people coordinator role.

If individuals are self-aware, they might recognize that they're not suited to incident roles and voluntarily step aside. In other cases, it might be necessary to remove someone from the team or not include them in the first place. That can be a difficult conversation, especially if the person deciding the team structure is junior to the one being left out.

My own personal view is that the role in the incident team should come with the job. So, the CPO should be the people coordinator, and if their performance in exercises is lacking, they should be supported through coaching and further practice. Incident management is part of their overall role, and they should be selected not just based on their ability to do their day-to-day job, but on their willingness to build the capability to manage during a crisis.

What we might want to write 'teamwork and leadership' objectives on

Some of the areas in which objectives could be written are:

- The ability to operate effectively as a team under pressure.
- The adaptability of individuals to unfamiliar or high-stress team dynamics.
- Do the team members possess the necessary skills, knowledge, competencies and authority?
- Do people know their roles and responsibilities?
- Practising handovers between teams or team members.
- Understanding of personal and team members' working styles under pressure.
- Team leader's ability to lead, make decisions and provide direction during a crisis.
- Effective delegation and collaborative decision-making within the team.
- Identification of individuals who may not be suited to crisis roles.
- Ability to build rapport and work with unfamiliar colleagues.
- Confidence of individuals in carrying out their assigned roles under stress.
- The capacity to recognize and manage team conflict constructively.
- Flexibility in team leadership and the ability to support or step into alternate roles.
- Is the team the right size? Does it work effectively? Are the correct people on the team? These can be useful objectives, especially if they have 25 people on their incident management team in their plan.
- Practising a number of deputies taking part in the exercise

Objectives examples (with levels)

- Demonstrate effective leadership under pressure in a dynamic incident scenario.
  (*Level 3: Applying: Demonstrate / Execute / Apply*)
- Collaborate with other team members to manage competing priorities and limited resources.
  (*Level 3: Applying: Collaborate / Contribute / Support*)

TABLE 10.3 Words to write 'work' objectives

Level	Description	Objective Words
1. Awareness	Recognizing the importance of collaboration and leadership in incident management	Identify, recognize, name, acknowledge
2. Understanding	Explaining roles, responsibilities and behaviours in teamwork or leadership	Describe, explain, summarize, clarify
3. Applying	Demonstrating effective behaviours in a realistic or simulated situation	Collaborate, contribute, support, participate, communicate, delegate, guide, use
4. Analysing	Assessing how team dynamics or leadership decisions affect outcomes	Analyse, compare, contrast, investigate, resolve, coordinate, negotiate
5. Evaluating	Judging the effectiveness of team performance or leadership style	Evaluate, critique, judge, influence, justify
6. Creating	Developing new ways of working together or leading a team	Lead, direct, facilitate, empower, adapt, model, design, develop

- Communicate clearly and consistently with internal and external stakeholders during the incident.
  (*Level 3: Applying: Communicate / Apply / Implement*)
- Evaluate the effectiveness of the team's response and leadership behaviours during the debrief.
  (*Level 5: Evaluating: Evaluate / Judge / Recommend*)
- Facilitate inclusive discussions to ensure all voices in the incident team are heard.
  (*Level 6: Creating: Facilitate / Compose / Construct*)

Check: Validating plans, strategies and systems

One of the main purposes of an exercise can be to validate a new or revised plan. The exercise is used to check the content, determine if the plan flows properly, ensure it contains all necessary information and assess whether it is fit for purpose.

Good practice says that a plan cannot be considered valid until it has been exercised and demonstrated to be effective. Exercises can also aim to verify specific recovery strategies, testing whether recovery activities can be completed within designated timeframes and with the allocated resources. This might include recovering an IT system within its recovery time objectives, relocating an activity to an alternate site or confirming staff's ability to work effectively from home if they don't normally do so.

TEST OR EXERCISE

In business continuity as a whole, we tend to shy away from describing any exercise as a 'test'. A key purpose of an exercise is to provide a learning opportunity in a non-confrontational environment, where participants are encouraged to make mistakes, because it's far better to make a mistake during an exercise than in a real event.

When the word 'test' is used to describe an exercise, it can immediately trigger a pass/fail mindset. This can lead to participants becoming defensive or hesitant to fully engage, for fear of being seen as having failed.

That said, pass or fail can be appropriate in certain technical scenarios, such as verifying whether a system or process can meet a specific recovery time objective (RTO). In such cases, the exercise is designed to determine whether a particular application can be recovered within the required timeframe. You either meet the RTO, or you don't, so a clear outcome, pass or fail, is valid.

I worked on a recovery plan for a supplier to the UK Government, where the contract explicitly stated that specific RTOs must be met for the recovery of key services. In the exercise clause of the contract, the term 'test' was used deliberately. The purpose wasn't just to practise the response; it was to prove the supplier could deliver on those RTOs. In this instance, calling it a 'test' was appropriate and more important than running a typical learning-focused exercise as outlined in this book.

What we might want to write 'validating plans, strategies and systems' objectives on

The following areas are those that we might want to write objectives for:

- Ensuring a plan is logical, usable and fit for purpose.
- Bringing two organizations' plans together, perhaps after a merger, and checking that they are fit for purpose.
- Whether contingency plans contain sufficient information for dealing with the situation.
- Whether application recovery plans can be used by individuals who are not familiar with the recovery of the application.
- Whether a severe but plausible scenario would breach a financial organization's impact tolerances.
- Invoking mutual aid and checking that the requested support is available and can be provided in time.
- Whether applications and services can be restored within defined recovery time objectives (RTOs).
- Whether critical operations can be relocated to an alternate site.
- If systems can be accessed from alternative locations or from home
- If members of the incident team can be contacted within an agreed timeframe.
- Whether incident rooms or virtual coordination spaces can be activated and used effectively.
- Whether the response and recovery capability of key third-party partners meets the timelines agreed in the contract.
- Can resources be mobilized or are they available?
- Compliance with relevant standards, regulatory or contractual obligations is maintained.
- Strategies and solutions can be recovered to agreed specifications.
- Challenging assumptions in the plans and making sure that they are valid.

Objectives examples (with levels)

- Check that crisis team members can be contacted out-of-hours.
  (*Level 1: Remembering: Check / Observe*)

- Confirm that the alternative call centre can be made operational, including staff relocation, within six hours.
(*Level 3: Applying: Confirm / Demonstrate / Test*)
- Test activation of the backup power supply for designated critical systems.
(*Level 3: Applying: Test / Execute / Demonstrate*)
- Validate that the current business continuity plan contains accurate, complete and up-to-date information.
(*Level 5: Evaluating: Validate / Verify / Measure*)
- Assess the ability of third-party vendors to respond within contracted timeframes during a simulated disruption.
(*Level 5: Evaluating: Evaluate / Audit / Judge*)

TABLE 10.4 Words to write 'check' objectives

Level	Description	Descriptor words
1:Remembering	Recalling facts, terms or basic information	Check, observe
2: Understanding	Explaining or interpreting information in one's own words	Review, ensure
3: Applying	Using information or procedures in a given situation	Demonstrate, confirm, test
4: Analysing	Breaking information into parts to explore patterns or relationships	Examine, monitor
5: Evaluating	Justifying a decision or assessing value based on criteria	Evaluate, validate, verify, audit, measure

Feel: Building confidence and continual improvement

This section assesses participants' confidence levels. It examines how confident individuals feel in fulfilling their roles, their confidence in the team as a whole and in the organization's ability to handle an incident. Confidence can be evaluated at various points to spot trends or whether confidence has increased after an exercise.

Continual improvement focuses on whether the team is improving its incident management skills or whether its capability has deteriorated over time. It can also include reviewing previous post-exercise reports, identifying past recommendations, ensuring those assessing the current incident are aware of them, and confirming that lessons have been learnt. This ensures the team is not repeating the same mistakes identified in earlier exercises.

What we might want to write 'building confidence and continual improvement' objectives on

The following list shows the different areas in which we might want to write objectives:

- Assessing confidence in the ability of organizations, teams or individuals to manage an incident effectively.
- Carrying out a quantitative assessment of the team's performance and checking if they have improved or got worse than in previous assessments.
- Checking that the observation and recommendations from the present exercise are not the same or very similar to those from previous exercises.
- Where technical exercises are conducted, the targets for recovery are met or improved upon.
- Ability to apply learning from previous exercises or training sessions.
- Awareness and recall of lessons learnt from past incidents or post-exercise reviews.
- Reduction in repeated mistakes noted in prior exercises or real events.
- Improvement in decision-making speed and confidence during high-pressure moments.
- Clarity and confidence in escalation protocols and when to activate plans.
- Consistency in applying recovery procedures across departments or incident management teams.

Objectives examples (with levels)

1. Check whether lessons from previous exercises are demonstrated in the team's response.
   (*Level 1: Awareness: Check / Observe*)
2. Compare team performance against previous exercises to track improvement or decline.
   (*Level 2: Reflection: Review / Summarize / Compare*)

TABLE 10.5 Words to write 'feel' objectives

Level	Description	Descriptor words
Level 1:Awareness	Recognizing confidence levels, past experiences or observed behaviours	Identify, check, observe
Level 2:Reflection	Interpreting trends, reviewing learning or summarizing past performance	Review, describe, summarize
Level 3:Evaluation	Judging the effectiveness of team capability or confidence improvements	Evaluate, assess, measure
Level 4:Development	Designing improvements based on lessons learnt or observed weaknesses	Plan, develop, improve

3. Reflect on personal performance during the exercise to identify strengths and areas for development.
   (*Level 2: Reflection: Review / Reflect / Summarize*)
4. Measure individual confidence levels pre- and post-exercise using a short survey.
   (*Level 3: Evaluation: Measure / Assess*)
5. Assess whether participants believe the organization would perform effectively in a real incident.
   (*Level 3: Evaluation: Assess / Evaluate*)

How the achievement of the objective will be measured

Some objectives lend themselves to having measurable objectives, especially in the 'check' area where the purpose could be to achieve recovery within a certain timeframe. In the 'know', 'do' or 'work' areas, it is more difficult to produce quantifiable or SMART (specific, measurable, achievable, realistic and time-bound) objectives. Examples of clearly defined SMART criteria can be seen below:

- Apply the crisis communication plan to issue a holding statement within 20 minutes of receiving the first media enquiry, in line with the procedures outlined in the organization's communications protocol.

- Identify all critical stakeholders impacted by a simulated cyber incident and notify them within the timelines specified in the business continuity plan.
- Conduct an initial incident team meeting within 15 minutes of team mobilization, ensuring all key roles are assigned and situational awareness is established, as per the incident management plan.
- Escalate a critical incident to the strategic team in accordance with the escalation criteria defined in the crisis response plan and document the decision in the incident log.
- Complete and submit a situation report using the approved template within the first 45 minutes of the exercise, ensuring it includes all required fields: impacts, actions taken, outstanding issues and next steps.

If you can write SMART objectives for your exercise, you should do so, but not every objective needs to be SMART. Your objectives might be a mix of both SMART and non-SMART formats. When assessing whether the objectives have been met, it is usually the umpires and the exercise director who decide. Additional ways to determine whether the objectives have been achieved include participants indicating this on a feedback form, through an online assessment at the end of the exercise, or during a discussion on the exercise objectives during the hot debrief. Whether objectives are met should be included in the post-exercise report, with an explanation of why the objective was considered achieved.

KEY LEARNINGS

- Shifting from 'aims and objectives' to 'purpose and objectives' can make exercise planning clearer and more focused.
- Exercises are often driven by policy, regulation, audit, contractual needs or strategic requirements, not just internal interest.
- The exercise's purpose directly influences its format, attendees, scenario complexity and reporting requirements.
- Objectives should focus on what participants will achieve, not what the exercise facilitator delivers.
- Effective objectives fall into five key areas: know, do, work, check and feel.
- Scenario-specific knowledge is critical, as different incident types (e.g. cyber vs casualty) require distinct responses.

- Using Bloom's Taxonomy helps structure objectives from basic knowledge to advanced critical thinking.
- Not all objectives need to fit neatly into one category; a single objective may touch on multiple areas.
- Objectives should reflect the needs of the exercise sponsor and the desired learning or validation outcomes.
- SMART success criteria help evaluate whether objectives were met, but not all objectives must be written in SMART format.

Note

1 Shabatura, J (2022) Using Bloom's Taxonomy to write effective learning objectives, University of Arkansas TIPS. https://tips.uark.edu/using-blooms-taxonomy/

11

Deciding on the scope of the exercise

In this chapter, you will learn about:

1 Deciding who will be exercised

2 Choosing who will lead the planning of the exercise

3 Any external parties that should be invited to take part in the exercise

4 Determining which plans and procedures will be exercised

The exercise scope defines the boundaries of the exercise and who is taking part, whether that is an incident management team, the incident management team including deputies, or a group of staff. The scope also covers which plans and procedures will be exercised, as well as which entities, parts of the organization or any other organizations will take part in the exercise.

Who will be exercised?

The first question to ask is who is taking part in the exercise. When conducting SIMEXs, you always want the members of the incident management team to be involved. This should include ensuring that every role is filled by the first call or their deputy. One of the main objectives of a SIMEX is usually to practise teamwork and leadership from the team leader, so having anything other than the team they would form in real life can skew the lessons and provide an unrealistic view of team dynamics. The challenge with this approach and having a full team is that often the same people attend repeatedly, meaning deputies or even the first call person may never take part in the exercise. On the day of an incident, if the usual participant is unavailable, it can result in a very inexperienced individual filling that role.

In a tabletop exercise, there is greater flexibility regarding who is involved. It may be an incident management team, but it could also be a group of staff. There is also the opportunity to include deputies alongside the first call for the exercise. When considering groups of staff, it could be all senior managers who are not part of the crisis team, or it could be all middle managers who have a role in responding within their own department's operational plan. The exercise could also serve as a learning experience for staff or department groups. A tabletop exercise can be conducted for different department groups, such as finance, HR and communications, and during the exercise, they are all presented with the same scenario, but the questions they are asked and the responses focus on how each department will respond.

Involving deputies

Exercising deputies can be difficult to do effectively. The ideal approach is to run the exercise a second time for the deputies, so they gain the same experience as the primary team. In practice, this rarely happens. Organizations often lack the resources or time to support a repeat exercise, even if the development work has already been completed. Exercise staff are still needed to deliver the session and report on the outcomes.

In some exercises, deputies attend as observers. They may sit to the side of the incident room or, in an online exercise, watch in the background. In both cases, they do not participate. Having multiple observers present can sometimes affect the exercise dynamic. Participants may feel as though they are being watched or assessed, which can make them more reluctant to engage fully in the exercise.

Inviting a wider team

This approach has been effective in several exercises, and I believe it is a good way to involve more people and raise team members' awareness of business continuity. The way to organize this is to invite all team members, their deputies and relevant subject matter experts to the exercise, and to ensure that everyone blocks out the time in their diaries. All attendees receive the scenario, and the incident team leader selects the appropriate individuals to form the team. The rest either sit out or continue as observers.

This process helps the team leader carefully consider who is needed on the team, especially which subject matter experts are essential. It also serves as a good reminder for all potential team members that they could be called upon to take an active role in a real incident.

Observers

Sometimes there may be observers of the exercise from within the organization. This could be an auditor looking to review the exercise or to understand how plans are organized. New or potential team members may be invited to observe. Graduate trainees or interns may also be invited to observe the team as part of their education and to understand how the organization responds to an incident.

Involving a 'red team'

Another way to involve more people in the exercise and to challenge the assumptions, responses, plans and decisions of those taking part is to involve a red team. The team could consist of three to four experienced members of the organization, who have the team's respect and can assist in reviewing the team's response. It may be beneficial to include them in the exercise design, but it is not essential. Their use is probably most effective in a tabletop exercise, where, once the teams have delivered their solutions, they can challenge or question their responses. It must be noted that extra time should be allotted to the feedback section of a tabletop exercise, as the red team's challenges may spark a lively debate.

In a cyber exercise, they can take on the role of a hacker and provide details of the actions a hacker would perform in response to the incident team's activities. They could also be tasked with representing stakeholders in a cyber or non-cyber exercise, then informing the teams how they perceive the team's response and whether actions, communications and responses would have the desired impact on the stakeholders.

Who will lead the planning of the exercise?

To ensure consistency in the planning of the exercise, the exercise director should be appointed at the start of the planning process and lead all planning meetings. This helps maintain consistency in the planning and development of the exercise. If the exercise will be a SIMEX, the role-player coordinator should also be involved from the beginning. This also provides a contingency if one person becomes unavailable at short notice or cannot attend a meeting. The exercise umpire may be involved throughout the planning, but this is not essential. I have often joined as an exercise umpire on the day of the exercise without being involved in detailed planning or attending every planning meeting.

Role of the business continuity team in the planning and delivery of the exercise

The role of the business continuity team or the individual responsible for business continuity must be decided before the exercise or at the exercise kick-off meeting. If they are planning, delivering or reporting on the exercise, they should not participate as part of the incident team. In some organizations, business continuity professionals do not have a role in the incident team, particularly at the strategic level, and this leaves them to plan the exercise. In other organizations, they may play a key role by advising the team leader, providing or managing the administrative support to the team and providing expert guidance on the organization's response.

In one organization, a senior manager from the BC team acted as the tactical incident team leader, managing departmental responses and leading the team. If the BC professional or team are not involved in designing or delivering the exercise, they should be encouraged to participate in their usual role during the scenario. This helps to guide the team during the response and provides a more realistic picture of how an incident would be managed in real life.

Are any external parties to be invited to take part in the exercise?

When there is a multi-agency or multi-organizational response to an incident, all organizations involved are often invited to attend the exercise. Without their participation, assumptions may be made about how they would respond, which could prove inaccurate and lead to false expectations of how an incident would be managed. Most exercises begin with only one organization attending, and they involve others only once confidence has been built in their internal response. Involving external parties can significantly improve an organization's response and should be encouraged.

The chosen scenario may influence the decision on which external organizations to invite. For example, if a train operating company selects a train crash scenario, then a key part of the response would rest with the emergency services. In such cases, it is worth considering whether to invite these agencies directly. Simulating their actions is possible, but it is difficult for exercise planners to accurately second-guess how, for instance, the police or ambulance service would react. As a result, their absence may reduce the quality of learning or lead to incorrect assumptions. In my experience, unless the scenario demands their involvement or the exercise is specifically about multi-organizational coordination, organizations typically prefer to exercise with their own incident team and simulate the actions of third parties.

Where an important element of the organization's response is outsourced, it is preferable to include that third party in the exercise, especially if they play a key operational role. In some organizations, the third-party representative is embedded in the incident team and works alongside internal staff. While this is uncommon, it can be effective. However, if the third party is responsible for the incident, there may be parts of the session when they are asked to leave, as internal teams may need to discuss sensitive matters.

Allowing third parties to observe the exercise is another option. Observers can gain valuable insight into the organization's response processes, but their presence may alter the dynamics of the session, particularly if staff are uncomfortable speaking candidly in their presence.

An alternative approach is to have the third party stand up their own incident management team, either co-located or online, and simulate the communication flow between the two teams. I once supported a government organization that outsourced a critical IT function. Their exercise tested not only operational response but also communication dynamics. Interestingly, the IT provider was a major household name, arguably more powerful in public image than its client. Practising joint messaging became a key learning objective of the exercise.

Involving third parties in the design of the exercise is another good practice. They can contribute to scenario planning and ensure that their role is accurately reflected and realistically played. Even if they do not actively participate in the exercise itself, input into the design helps ensure their expected actions, working methods and communications are reflected correctly. Understanding how key partners respond can be a core objective of the exercise, helping to surface meaningful lessons and improve cross-organizational coordination.

Which plans and procedures will be exercised?

It is good practice to identify which plan or plans are being exercised and to document this within the exercise instructions. Sometimes, there may be no plan in place, and the exercise is meant to develop actions and responses and to understand the potential impacts on the organization. I have done this ahead of Brexit for several organizations that wanted to explore how the change would affect them. I have also conducted exercises focused on a known future event, aiming to help an organization develop its plans and responses. Events like the Commonwealth Games in Glasgow, the Olympics in London and a planned protest that might turn violent are examples I have planned exercises for. The main challenge with planning for these types of events is identifying potential impacts and making assumptions about how the incident might unfold to shape the exercise scenario. If real-life development differs from these assumptions, it could result in a false sense of security or in incorrect lessons being drawn.

Usually, existing plans and procedures are being exercised. It is important to state these in the exercise instructions so that those taking part can read the plan and understand its contents rather than turning up on the day and making up the response. When you have an organization with multiple plans for different scenarios, such as cyber or product recalls, you give away a little by asking participants in advance to read the main incident management plan and the cyber plan. Although they will know the scenario type it should mean they have read the plan, hopefully, and are thinking about the scenario prior to taking part in the exercise. Personally, I don't think telling participants the exact scenario in advance is detrimental to the exercise. They will still gain from the experience. It is often the exercise sponsor who insists that the scenario is not known until it is revealed during the exercise.

KEY LEARNINGS

- SIMEX must reflect real-life team structures to accurately test leadership and teamwork.
- Tabletop exercises offer flexibility to engage wider staff groups and foster cross-functional learning.
- Deputies need active involvement to ensure they're ready to step into critical roles.

- Involving a broader team increases awareness, preparedness and succession planning.
- Observers must be carefully managed to maintain a psychologically safe learning environment.
- Red teams can provide valuable challenge and reveal weaknesses in assumptions and plans.
- The exercise director must be involved throughout the exercise planning to ensure coherent planning and delivery.
- Clearly define whether the BC team is participating or facilitating to avoid role conflict.
- Multi-tier exercises reveal how well strategic, tactical and operational levels coordinate.
- Include key external partners when their actions are critical to a realistic response.

12

Designing the scenario

In this chapter, you will learn about:

1. What the scenario should achieve
2. Using a design team to get the fine scenario details
3. Choosing the scenario
4. Overcoming issues when choosing a scenario

When the planning starts for a new exercise the discussion almost immediately turns to discussing the scenario. In my experience, this can very quickly become the primary focus. In some cases, the scenario is already determined before planning starts, perhaps as part of a multi-year exercise programme or due to a regulatory or contractual requirement. For some exercises the focus is on the scenario, such as responding to a ransomware attack. However, in other situations, the scenario is just a way to frame the exercise, and the real value lies in practising incident management rather than exploring the incident itself. While the scenario matters, it should not dominate; its importance depends on the exercise objectives.

For a simple tabletop, only a minimal scenario may be needed; for example, 'your headquarters has just burnt down'. That may be sufficient to practise plan invocation and response structure. More complex exercises require greater detail. Sometimes the sponsor arrives with a clear testing aim; in other cases, the scenario is agreed during the design phase.

In the design phase the broad scenario is selected, whether an earthquake, cyber-attack or IT outage, and later refined in the development phase.

Scenarios may also reflect emerging risks, such as protests, global events or supply chain disruptions. Where no established plan exists, the exercise can explore impacts, identify gaps and inform plan development.

What should the scenario achieve?

If there isn't a strong preference for a particular scenario, a good starting point is to focus on what you want the exercise to achieve. Being clear about the exercise objectives will help shape the scenario and guide its development. Even if you already have an outline idea in mind, it's still useful to step back and ask what the scenario needs to deliver in terms of learning and challenge. A list of key questions can help clarify this, whether the overall scenario has already been chosen (for example, a ransomware attack) or is still being decided.

The following are some of the considerations when making a decision on the scenario or developing a predetermined scenario:

Objectives: Do the objectives of the exercise suggest specific scenario requirements? In other words, do they naturally align with a particular type of incident? For example, if the aim is to develop HR-related skills, then a people-focused scenario would be appropriate, such as an accident involving injuries or fatalities, or a pandemic resulting in the medium-term loss of a significant number of staff.

Complexity: What is the level of complexity required for the scenario? Is a straightforward scenario needed without technical details, or does it require something more complex?

How the incident occurred: Do we need to know how the incident occurred? In many scenarios, especially those focused on the first few hours of response, it's often not necessary to explain how the incident happened. These details are unlikely to be known at the time and may only emerge later. This is particularly relevant for cyber exercises, where not specifying how attackers gained access can help avoid unnecessary complexity.

Timescales: Do you want the exercise played in real time, over a time frame (the first day of the incident), or over multiple time frames with a time jump in between?

Starting point: Do you want the exercise to start with the occurrence of the scenario, some way into the response hours or even days after the incident has occurred?

Who will be affected by the incident? Are there particular organizations you want to practise engaging with, such as regulators or partners? Do you want the exercise to involve just internal stakeholders or external ones as well?

Media and social media: Do you want these involved? Remember, the story needs to be of sufficient magnitude for the press and social commentators to be interested.

Align to invocation criteria: Review the invocation criteria outlined in the team's plan for the exercise. The scenario should meet these criteria: neither so broad as to be unrealistic, nor so detailed as to fall outside the team's usual responsibilities and be handled as a routine incident.

Temporary vs permanent issues: Do you want your scenario to involve a temporary denial of access to a particular building, or do you want full destruction of the building and all its contents? Is the data centre just down, or is it entirely destroyed?

Including hidden agendas: Are there any hidden agendas that the exercise planners or the sponsor wants to explore through the exercise? For example, a sponsor might say, 'I don't know what the specific scenario should be, but I want the crisis management team to realize that disaster recovery is underinvested in', or 'The team are not as good as they think they are'. Are there also known risks that the exercise could subtly highlight to the participants? These can be woven into the scenario to help expose gaps or challenge assumptions.

Noise or 'red herrings': Does the scenario have to be purely around the incident, or should additional noise and unrelated items be included? Are there items that could be included in the exercise as a distraction, and do the exercise team recognize them as such, or do they devote time and energy to dealing with the situation?

Procedures, skills demonstration, reporting, forms: Are there elements with the plan which you want the team to demonstrate they can do, e.g. fill in the situation report (sit rep) form, or skills taught that you want them to demonstrate, such as logging? Ensure these are included in the exercise, or brief them at the beginning that you expect them to do the reports for real during the exercise.

Realism: Is the exercise realistic? Has it occurred somewhere else? Could it possibly happen?

Resolvable actions: Are there actions which could quickly shut down or solve the incident, leaving you with no exercise?

Something for everyone: Does the scenario need to include impacts or challenges that engage all members of the team? Review the team composition to ensure each function is meaningfully involved. Typical roles to consider include operations, technology, facilities, HR and communications.

Risks: What are the risks associated with the incident and the response? Are there any knock-on consequences that should be included in the exercise to test how the team handles them; for example, reputational damage, financial implications or legal exposure?

Team experience: What other scenarios or elements of a response has the team exercised before? Their level of exercise experience may also determine how complex the scenario is.

There may need to be several discussions on what the scenario aims to achieve before it is finalized, and several scenarios may be presented to the sponsor before a decision is made.

Using a design team to get the fine scenario details

Depending on the complexity of the scenario, additional members may need to join the exercise-planning design team as subject-matter experts. Unless the scenario is straightforward, it is always beneficial to have a design team, or at least a subject-matter expert, involved in developing the exercise scenario and the detailed injects. Using people from the organization being exercised will always help build a better and more credible scenario during any exercise, as they are familiar with the workings of the organization and perhaps previous incidents. They can also help develop the questions for a tabletop exercise. As my colleague Gavin always says when talking about using an internal design team, 'they know where the bodies are buried' and then they introduce appropriate details into the exercise.

Those on the design team often learn just as much from planning and delivering the exercise as the participants do. Therefore, if you have business community professionals in the organization, you should ensure they are included on the planning team.

Designing a SIMEX usually requires a dedicated design team. When putting together a design team it is important to bring in people with a good knowledge of the business and the way it operates. The team should also include subject-matter experts from facilities, IT, security, HR, finance and cyber, as well as representatives from the departments most likely to be affected by the scenario being exercised. It is also essential to involve those responsible for communications and external relations, as their role in shaping the organization's message and handling the media is often critical during an incident. By including these people, the design team is better equipped to develop a realistic scenario and ensure the exercise addresses the organization's key areas.

Choosing the scenario

There is no golden rule for selecting the scenario for an exercise, but several considerations can help make the most suitable decision. The following points should be taken into account when choosing the scenario:

- **Organization's documented risks:** One of the first ports of call for the scenario should be to look at the organization's risks outlined in the business impact analysis or in their organizational risk register. It is a very important place to start, as these are the identified risks and should be the ones with the highest likelihood and impact. Once these are exhausted, then other risks should be considered.
- **Industry risks:** All industries have their own risks, and these should be considered as potential scenarios. For **manufacturing**, they could consider events such as plant fires or explosions, hazardous material leaks or disruptions to just-in-time supply chains. **Retail** scenarios might involve supply chain disruption, product contamination/recall or a major IT failure during peak trading periods like Christmas or Black Friday. **Healthcare** scenarios might involve a mass casualty incident, disease outbreak, failure of critical medical equipment or a ransomware attack that locks patient records.
- **Location risks:** When considering scenarios, it is also worth looking at the risks associated with the organization's location. An organization situated close to a flood plain may be vulnerable to seasonal flooding, while those in areas susceptible to tornadoes, hurricanes, tsunamis or even volcanic activity need to be mindful of the impact these natural disasters could have on their operations. The location of the organization may also expose it to risks, such as being near a major transport hub, an industrial facility or other critical infrastructure, which could be affected by an incident and have knock-on consequences.
- **Looking at causes:** When designing scenarios, it is often helpful to think not just about the impact of the incident, but also the cause. The cause

can make the exercise more engaging and believable, and in some cases can add an additional dimension of uncertainty to the scenario. However, sometimes providing the cause of the incident can cause an argument with participants, who say, 'that wouldn't happen because...' To avoid this happening, you need to engage a technical expert to explain how the cause could bypass the defences, or simply avoid providing details on how it occurred, as this is still under investigation.

EXAMPLE

World War II bomb scenario

One of my favourite examples is the discovery of an unexploded World War II bomb in the vicinity of a building. This scenario works well because it combines both denial of access, sometimes for several days while the bomb is dug out and defused, with the possibility, however unlikely, of it going off and destroying the building entirely. This gives participants two different challenges to think about: a temporary loss of access and a total loss of the site. World War II bombs are still found in Europe quite regularly, so the scenario is a realistic one.

- **Look at the news:** Monitoring the news often provides inspiration for realistic incident causes. Many exercises I have run use scenarios drawn from recent events, sometimes with only minor changes, because they are fresh in people's minds and resonate strongly. A realistic cause helps participants visualize the incident unfolding and engage fully with the exercise, while reminding them that the 'unthinkable' does happen.
- **Loss of key asset:** Another way to develop scenarios is to consider the loss of a key asset, such as an office, warehouse or data centre, due to fire, flooding or structural failure. Building collapse or subsidence can be realistic, particularly in areas prone to sinkholes or disused mine workings. Risks may also stem from construction defects, such as structural degradation. Smaller but disruptive incidents include cutting power or communications cables, or external equipment damaging the building and making it unsafe.
- **Loss of people:** Staff loss can affect any organization and take many forms. It may involve a single critical individual or a larger group unavailable due to sickness, strike action, travel disruption or a major incident. A pandemic

is an obvious example of prolonged absence, as demonstrated by Covid-19. Other scenarios include outbreaks such as legionella or food poisoning at corporate events. The impact concerns not just numbers but capability, authority and access to essential knowledge. These exercises often reveal weaknesses in succession planning and over-reliance on key individuals. Teams may assume someone will step in, but without exercising this, smooth handover under pressure cannot be guaranteed.

EXAMPLE

Airbus Atlantic's Christmas dinner outbreak

In December 2023, Airbus Atlantic held a Christmas dinner for around 2,600 employees at its Montoir-de-Bretagne facility in France. The event was catered internally. Within 24 to 48 hours, hundreds of employees reported symptoms of vomiting and diarrhoea, with media estimates suggesting up to 700 staff were affected. French health authorities launched an investigation, and the company cooperated fully. No hospitalizations were reported.

There was no published evidence of disruption to manufacturing or customer deliveries. However, the incident exposed the vulnerability of workforce availability following large staff events and generated national and international media coverage, creating a reputational impact for the company.

- **Supplier failure:** Supplier failure can be a critical risk, particularly where the organization relies on a single source for materials, logistics or specialist services that are key to delivering products and services. The loss of utilities such as electricity, gas or water can quickly halt operations, while loss of connectivity, such as internet access or internal networks, can cripple communications and business processes.
- **Reputational issue:** Reputational issues can serve as excellent exercise scenarios, but they pose specific challenges. Senior management is often aware of a problem before it becomes public, so they rarely arise suddenly. Exercise design should consider this lead time, during which the organization may already suspect trouble, and then focus on how the issue develops once it becomes public. Determining the person who caused the issue can also be tricky. Using a real staff member is inappropriate, but involving a fictitious senior manager may seem unrealistic. Other reputational examples include a product recall in which faults were internally flagged for months before media attention, or a data breach in which

suspicious activity was noticed but not addressed until customer data appeared online. Supply chain issues might involve allegations of unethical practices, such as awarding contracts to family members or affiliated organizations. In most cases, the organization had some prior knowledge or suspicion, and incorporating this into the scenario helps assess how leaders manage issues that smoulder before erupting publicly.

- **IT infrastructure outages:** Loss of IT systems is one of the most common and disruptive scenarios, and it can take several forms. At its most severe, it could be the loss of a data centre due to fire, flooding or technical failure, impacting multiple systems. More often, it may be the loss of a single critical application such as finance, call handling or booking systems. Increasingly, organizations rely on cloud services or Software-as-a-Service applications, which introduce additional risk.
  Services may be unavailable due to provider outages, cyber-attacks or contractual disputes. Where systems are hosted or supported by a third party, the response may depend on how quickly and effectively the supplier resolves the issue. Even losing email or video conferencing for a few hours can cause disruption, highlighting dependence on IT. These scenarios help explore resilience, test workarounds and assess reliance on external providers.

- **Cyber-attacks and data breaches:** Cyber-attacks and data breaches are a serious threat to most organizations. In the Appendix, there are details of 10 possible exercise scenarios focusing on these threats.
- **Physical security threats:** For many organizations, particularly in the US, workplace violence or an active shooter is considered a high risk and should be practised in an exercise. Terrorist attacks are often suggested as a UK scenario, but unless you are a high-profile target, it is unlikely the attack would be specifically aimed at your organization. Such incidents could cause casualties and denial of access to a building, but access denial is often limited to hours or days. If the focus is on casualties, a more realistic scenario might be a car or bus crash involving key staff.

  Bomb threats can test operational staff response, but they are unlikely to require strategic input. Protests in the local area or wider civil unrest can also make good exercise scenarios, particularly if there is an upcoming event which could trigger unrest. These scenarios also force organizations to carefully consider the information they provide to staff, reducing the risk of people being unnecessarily caught up in disturbances.

Overcoming issues when choosing a scenario

There are numerous potential issues you might face when choosing the scenario. The following section details these, and the ways to address them:

Incident not severe enough: One of the worst things an exercise director can do is make the incident not severe enough, particularly if senior managers are involved. This happened to me: I assumed the scenario would involve the senior team, but when presented with it, they responded, 'The HR manager would deal with this; it wouldn't come to us.' At that point, you are stuck. You either adjust the scenario on the fly to increase its severity, or you pretend it warrants their involvement. By then, the exercise may have lost credibility, and most likely you have too.

Scenario not plausible: For an exercise to work, participants must believe the scenario is plausible and could realistically happen to their organization. The likelihood may be low, but if it feels possible, people will buy into the exercise and engage properly. I always say: 'do not fight the scenario. Reality, fate or bad luck can create far more convincing situations than we can design'.

Exercise not linked to the objectives: Review the scenario against the exercise objectives and purpose to ensure alignment, and confirm that the injects provide sufficient scope to meet those objectives and deliver meaningful content for all participants.

Beware the 'law' of unforeseen consequences: You may decide to use denial of access to a building and choose asbestos discovery during refurbishment as the cause. It may be a realistic scenario, especially in an older building. However, participants may focus on the health implications of asbestos rather than the denial of access itself, shifting attention away from the intended learning outcomes.

When to decide when the exercise should start: In a large multinational, senior managers are unlikely to be informed of an incident immediately. It may take hours for them to become aware, or the issue may have to escalate before it becomes a crisis. Not all exercises need to begin at the moment the incident occurs; the scenario may start several hours or days into the event, when the crisis team's involvement is required.

Ensuring the exercise must be solvable: During business continuity analysis, you define the maximum incident level the plan can manage. The chosen scenario must remain within that boundary. Avoid adding elements that make it almost impossible to resolve, such as layering multiple extreme events together. An unsolvable scenario should only be used deliberately to highlight a major risk requiring mitigation.

Avoiding unnecessary complexity: Do not overcomplicate a scenario for its own sake. The situation must be manageable for the team being exercised. Combining multiple major events can overwhelm participants and limit learning. Often a simple scenario, such as a building fire, is sufficient. Excess detail can distract from the response and allow participants to bypass the intended focus.

Use the same scenario for multiple exercises: Consider reusing a well-developed scenario across several exercises. The first may focus on immediate response, while a later session explores longer-term consequences. This approach maximizes the value of the design work and allows different teams or deputies to practise within the same evolving context.

The scenario is key to the exercise, but it's only one part. All the work on the exercise shouldn't be focused on making the scenario fiendishly difficult to respond to or trying to catch participants out with how clever you've been in coming up with it. Yes, the scenario is important, but how you structure the rest of the exercise can be just as crucial.

KEY LEARNINGS

- Start with clear objectives, then design a scenario that helps you achieve them, not the other way around.
- The scenario should be realistic, engaging and plausible enough for participants to buy into it.
- Simple scenarios are often best: avoid unnecessary complexity that can confuse or derail the exercise.
- Match the scenario's severity to the level of team being exercised; its being too mild or too extreme will lose credibility.
- Use the organization's real risks, industry threats or local hazards as a foundation for the scenario.
- Include impacts that engage every participant role; everyone should have a reason to contribute.
- If the scenario has a 'lead-in' phase (e.g. reputational risk), build in that slow burn to make it believable.

- Think about the timing of the scenario: will the exercise begin at incident onset or mid-response?
- Use subject-matter experts and internal knowledge to co-develop scenarios that reflect the organization's realities.
- Consider reusing or evolving scenarios across multiple exercises to deepen learning and test long-term resilience.

13

Determining the type and structure of the exercise

In this chapter, you will learn about:

1. Factors which determine the types of exercise
2. 'Mixing and matching' the exercise play
3. Dividing the exercise into distinct phases
4. The importance of training prior to the exercise
5. Exercising elements within the plan
6. Developing tabletop phases
7. Structuring a SIMEX
8. Structuring multiple team exercises
9. Hybrid and online only exercises
10. No-notice exercises

In this chapter, we look at choosing the type of exercise to be conducted, whether it is a SIMEX, tabletop or live exercise. Once the overall style of the exercise has been decided, we then need to determine how the individual phases will be delivered. These phases might be structured around time jumps, specific events or different elements of the response.

Factors which determine the type of exercise

Prior to Phase 1 design, the sponsor or organization may already have a clear idea of the type of exercise they want to conduct. This could be influenced by budget constraints, as tabletop exercises are easier and less costly to design and develop than a SIMEX.

Regulatory requirements may also influence the type of exercise. The Control of Major Accident Hazards regulations (COMAH) require an internal tabletop exercise once per year and a multi-agency tabletop exercise every three years. NHS England's Emergency Preparedness, Resilience and Response (EPRR) framework applies to all NHS-funded organizations. It sets out an annual training and exercising requirement: a communication exercise every six months, a tabletop exercise every year, and a live exercise every three years.

Contractual obligations may dictate the required format. An organization might require a supplier to demonstrate the recovery of an IT application, activity or process within a set time. In such cases, the exercise should be conducted as a test to validate recovery performance.

If the organization follows a three-or five-year exercise programme, the exercise type may be planned as part of a progression in complexity. This might start with a plan walkthrough in year 1, a tabletop exercise in year 2 and then a SIMEX in year 3. The sophistication and capability of participants must guide the chosen format. There is little value in placing inexperienced participants into a complex SIMEX, as they may not know how to respond effectively. This could damage their confidence and reduce their willingness to participate in future exercises or real incidents.

Therefore, exercise design should aim to build skills, knowledge and confidence gradually. The skills, knowledge and experience of the team being exercised need to be taken into account to ensure that the exercise is 'pitched' at the right level. Each exercise should develop the participants' capability step by step. The objectives of the exercise will largely determine the most suitable format. SIMEX is valuable for practising leadership, teamwork and applied incident management skills. Understanding responses and testing plans are often better explored during tabletop discussions, where participants can consider the scenario and plans without the pressures of real-time response.

Ultimately, many factors determine the appropriate exercise type. Planners must ensure the format supports the intended outcomes. If necessary, they should challenge the sponsor if the chosen type is not suitable. Some participants may prefer the excitement of a SIMEX, viewing it as a challenge similar to a TV adventure game. However, a tabletop exercise may provide the same benefits and be more appropriate for meeting the organization's actual needs.

Dividing the exercise into distinct phases

I find it helpful to divide exercises into several phases, each serving a specific purpose. This excludes the first part of the exercise, which typically includes introductions and an explanation of how the exercise will be conducted, and the final part, which is usually the hot debrief. In a standard three-hour exercise, there is usually time for three or four phases. These do not need to be lengthy; for example, a discussion on incident invocation criteria may take only 15 minutes.

However, it is important that each phase allows enough time for participants to explore the issues in depth, so that the exercise feels paced and not rushed. Not giving participants sufficient time to review and digest each part of the scenario or inject can lead to cognitive overload, where individuals are given more information than they can process effectively. Striking the right balance between simulating the pressures of a real incident and avoiding participant overload is a fine line. If this balance isn't managed carefully, the exercise can turn into a negative experience where little is gained.

I planned an exercise for a client who previously engaged another organization to plan and deliver their cyber exercise. Although the original brief was for a full-day session, it was cut to a half-day at the last minute. It is unclear whether the planners had time to revise the exercise or simply ran the original version with a compressed schedule. There is always a temptation to proceed without adjusting the content, particularly when significant effort has been put into developing a detailed scenario and injects. However, participants, all senior managers, reported that the exercise felt rushed and lacked meaningful engagement. This outcome reflects poorly on those who planned and delivered the session and underscores the importance of adjusting exercise structure to fit the time available.

The importance of training prior to the exercise

As discussed in Chapter 5, pre-exercise training significantly enhances both learning and participant engagement. Where possible, all participants should undertake some form of training before an exercise. This helps reduce distractions and unnecessary questions, allowing participants to focus on applying their knowledge rather than figuring out their role during the exercise.

Training sessions should be held about one to two weeks before the exercise. This gives participants the chance to learn and practise skills and knowledge, while also allowing sufficient time for learning to be retained to apply during the scenario. The type and extent of training should be based on the team's experience and capability. New team members may require individual training to ensure they are operating at the same level as more experienced colleagues.

Self-paced or one-to-one training can be an effective alternative to formal training before the exercise. When working as a business continuity manager, I often conducted individual briefings with senior managers prior to exercises. This gave them an opportunity to ask questions and build confidence; many requested this support to avoid appearing unprepared in front of their peers. The advantages and disadvantages to training delivery methods are outlined in Table 13.1.

Where resources permit, training can be professionally produced. However, the priority should be on ensuring content is current, reflecting updates to plans, procedures and recent lessons learnt, rather than perfect production values.

If training is done immediately before the exercise play takes place, this is not the time to teach new skills; rather, the focus should be on refreshing

TABLE 13.1 Advantages and disadvantages to training delivery methods

No.	Delivery method	Advantages	Disadvantages
1.	One-to-one face-to-face sessions	• Tailored to the individual • They can ask questions	• Time consuming • Difficulties in diarizing the meeting with busy senior managers
2.	Slide decks with voice-overs	• Quick and easy to do • Can update easily	• Could be seen as unprofessional if the voice-over is not well done
3.	e-learning modules	• Can check if people have done it • Can have a quiz to check for understanding	• E-learning fatigue and people not wanting to engage with another e-learning topic. • Cost and time to develop the module
4.	AI avatars delivering dynamic, tailored content	• Quick and easy to do • Can update easily • Relatively cheap	• Some people don't like listening to an avatar delivering training

existing knowledge and reinforcing prior learning. Training immediately before the exercise can be helpful when diary time is limited, as senior managers are more likely to attend if the training is embedded in the session. Although there is often enthusiasm for separate pre-exercise training, attendance may drop over time, leaving only the most confident individuals.

Topics for immediate pre-exercise training may include:

1. **Plan familiarization:** Covering team roles, inter-team collaboration, individual responsibilities, existing strategies and communication protocols.
2. **Crisis management landscape:** An overview of key crisis management principles, supported by contemporary case studies. This approach ensures concepts covered in training are often reflected back during the exercise.
3. **Lessons learnt:** Reviewing prior exercises or real incidents, highlighting both areas for improvement and examples of good performance. This reinforces organizational memory and helps avoid repeated mistakes.
4. **Scenario-specific briefing:** If the scenario is known, providing contextual information helps participants better engage and apply their knowledge effectively.

Participants are often keen to dive straight into the scenario and may not see the value of training immediately beforehand. However, as exercises are intended as learning experiences, training should be considered an essential part of the exercise life cycle and a key step in building team capability.

Call-out

If appropriate to the exercise, I like to include a call-out element as part of the exercise. This can be especially valuable if the organization uses a mass communication platform. It adds a sense of realism when participants receive a message early in the morning, say around 7.30 am, notifying them of a major incident. The message might include a few scenario details and ask them to report to the incident room at 9.00 am.

Using the organization's mass notification system reminds participants that it exists and prompts them to respond, thereby confirming their availability. It also means they start thinking about the scenario and potential responses before they even arrive at the exercise, which can significantly improve engagement and focus from the outset

Exercising elements within the plan

Running phases that focus on individual elements of the plan and response can help participants better understand specific aspects, without having to focus on a full incident response. These exercises allow teams to practise key activities in isolation and gain confidence in specific roles. Several elements naturally lend themselves to being played out as stand-alone phases within a broader exercise. They are more suited to a tabletop exercise, but they could be included in tasks within a SIMEX triggered by an inject.

1. **Escalation:** Explore the various escalation pathways to senior managers or those authorized to invoke the plan. Testing escalation procedures out-of-hours can be particularly useful, as it may reveal weaknesses or gaps in coverage.
2. **Plan invocation:** Present a series of short, realistic scenarios (one to two lines each) and ask participants to debate whether the plan should be invoked. This helps reinforce invocation criteria and promotes discussion around thresholds.
3. **Setting up the incident room:** Discuss the practicalities of establishing an incident room, including the equipment required, layout and who is responsible for set-up. This is especially relevant if the incident will be managed on-site.
4. **Stakeholder identification:** Review your communications plan to ensure it includes a list of stakeholders, when they should be contacted, their information needs, how they should be contacted and who is responsible for communication.
5. **Stakeholder influence matrix:** Ask participants to identify relevant stakeholders for the scenario being exercised. Then, plot these stakeholders on an influence matrix (using interest and power as axes) to determine which ones require the most attention. This exercise helps prioritize communication during an incident.
6. **Developing a working strategy:** Get participants to discuss an initial working strategy for responding to the incident. Then, build on this to consider the longer-term recovery strategy and how this might evolve.
7. **Battle box:** Practise using its contents and check if anything is missing.

Some of these activities can be completed in as little as 15 minutes. However, avoid running too many in one session. Alternate them with longer exercises to ensure the session feels structured rather than rushed.

Tabletop phases

Each phase of a tabletop exercise consists of a number of standard elements that can be repeated over several time jumps or distinct stages. Each phase should be self-contained, though it may influence, or be influenced by, previous or subsequent phases.

The standard elements within each phase are:

1. **Introduction to the scenario:** This sets the scene for the participants. It could be a brief two- to three-line summary, leaving details to the participants' imagination, or a more comprehensive description that includes the nature of the incident, actions by other stakeholders and media or social media commentary. As the scenario develops during the exercise, you may need to retain some of the details because you must consider decisions and actions taken in earlier phases.
2. **Discussion:** Participants are given one or more scenario-related questions to consider and respond to. If the exercise involves multiple phases, you may choose to divide participants into smaller groups, each focusing on a different aspect of the response; for example, communications, people, operations and service continuity, and partner/supplier coordination. Each group can be tasked with specific questions and then share their conclusions with the wider group.
3. **Feedback and reflections:** Participants or groups are asked to present their responses, either to the exercise director or to one another. It's useful to prepare a model answer (ideally presented on a slide), which the exercise director or umpire can use to highlight key points and identify any areas the participants may have overlooked.

If you are running a multi-phase tabletop, it's good practice to vary the structure across the phases. For example, Phase 1 could involve whole-team discussion; Phase 2 might split participants into groups; Phase 3 could test understanding of specific plan elements; and Phase 4 might focus the entire team on managing the longer-term implications of the incident.

Incident team meetings

This is one of my favourite exercise phases. The team is given a scenario and then role-plays their first incident team meeting. Each person is assigned a role (or fulfils their actual role as defined in the plan). They then evaluate the situation, share information, decide how to handle the incident and assign actions under the team leader's direction. Once the meeting ends, actions are agreed upon and then each team member, as they would in a real event, moves from the team meeting to communicate with their stakeholders and carry out their assigned actions. It is a simple but powerful exercise, as people are encouraged to make decisions and agree on actions to address the situation. There are several ways to run this type of exercise:

The team works to an agenda: The team is given an overall scenario but limited detail on how it affects each participant, requiring them to think through the impact in their own area. In incident meetings, an agenda is essential to guide discussion and ensure nothing is missed. The exercise director can refer participants to the agenda in their plan, if one exists, or allow them to structure the meeting themselves. If they struggle or plan to hold a second meeting, a standard agenda can be provided. The meeting should begin with updates from each participant covering what they know, key risks and issues, and likely actions within their responsibility. This can be followed by discussion on strategy, communications, objectives and action allocation. The team leader or administrator should then confirm the agreed actions.

Give each participant individual injects: In the agenda-based approach, participants receive a short scenario and must imagine its impact. This does not always work, as some struggle to apply it to their specific role. An alternative is to give each participant an individual script outlining what their character would realistically know. This mirrors real life, where information is fragmented, and encourages the team to build situational awareness from multiple inputs. Media updates can be provided to the communications coordinator, who then briefs the wider team.

Include administrative support: For a more SIMEX-style exercise, ensure administrative support or a note-taker is present to practise producing minutes. Preparing the incident room in advance, with seating cards and information boards, adds authenticity. Even in a tabletop, using an administrator as scribe helps the team become accustomed to working with them. Once actions and the date of the next meeting are agreed upon, this phase can be debriefed.

FIGURE 13.1 Three-stage team meeting / incident management cycle for a SIMEX

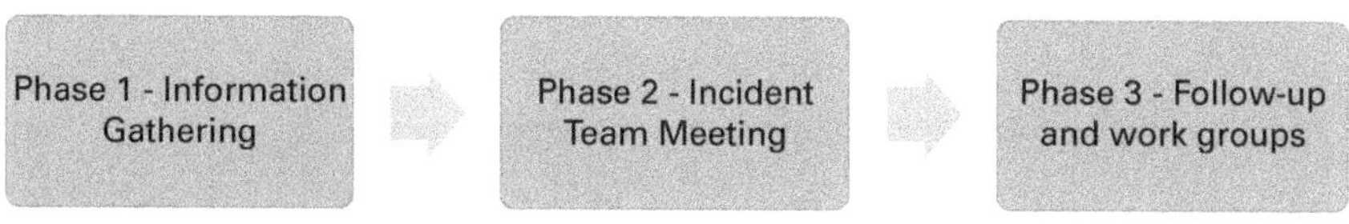

Structuring a SIMEX

A typical three-hour SEIMEX consists of initial incident notifications, followed by an unfolding scenario over the next two-and-a-half hours. The incident team sits in their room and receives a series of injects via telephone, email, in person or a social and media simulator. They are expected to respond appropriately to each inject, share updates with the team and move the scenario forward. The exercise runs as one long continuous phase.

This format works reasonably well but has a few issues. There is often little time for the team to have a focused meeting, as injects keep arriving relentlessly. Even if they call a 'time out' to focus on their position, they have little time before the next inject comes in which they feel they must address. This means there is also a limited opportunity for people to carry out their actions, as they are constantly responding.

A more effective approach for a three-hour SIMEX is to run it in **three distinct phases**, which allows for better learning and gives the team more realistic opportunities to manage the situation, as seen in Figure 13.1.

Phase 1: Information gathering. Once the team has been briefed on the initial scenario and the exercise director has briefed the team on the existing scenario, a series of injects can be delivered to update them and highlight key issues requiring attention. This phase typically runs for 20 to 30 minutes. Injects should be given to all participants, though selectively not giving injects to certain people can test whether team members proactively support colleagues under greater pressure if they have no update or task themselves.

Phase 2: The incident team meeting. The team should then hold an incident meeting, either as required by their plan, prompted in advance or requested by senior leadership seeking an update. During this meeting, injects should be limited so the team can concentrate on building situational awareness, agreeing priorities and shaping their strategy. The focus should be on structured discussion, decision-making and allocation of actions. This phase should last approximately 30 to 45 minutes.

Phase 3: Follow-up and work groups. After actions have been agreed and assigned, participants move into implementation. This may involve drafting communications, identifying stakeholders, developing operational plans or preparing documents outlining strategic intent. This stage also provides an opportunity to involve wider colleagues, particularly to support operational or communications activity. Further injects can be introduced at this point, either continuing the scenario timeline or responding to the team's agreed actions.

Depending on the length of the exercise, there could then be a second cycle of Phase 4: Information Gathering, Phase 5: Incident Team Meeting and then conclude with a Phase 6, which could involve follow-up and work groups or a presentation to senior managers on the incident so far and the actions they have taken.

Exercise time jumps

For many crisis teams, the initial response may not be enough to create a 'crisis'. It is often only after the response goes wrong that the crisis team's involvement is required. Sometimes, the first phase of an incident is the easiest part, simply firefighting the immediate issues with the resources available. Only once the incident has been ongoing for a few days do the major reputational issues emerge, potentially escalating the situation into a full-scale crisis requiring senior management involvement.

Poor maintenance, failure to take health and safety seriously, cost-cutting and inappropriate communications are all reputational issues, but they usually take time to become public and enter the incident narrative. It should also be noted that the larger the organization, the more severe an incident must be before it requires a crisis-level response.

Time jumps in a tabletop exercise can allow participants to look at the initial response, then fast-forward a few days to address reputational issues, and finally jump a week into the incident when the team can begin planning for long-term recovery.

In a SIMEX, time jumps are not normally used, as it is difficult to account for what people would have done in the intervening period. Participants might respond to an inject by saying, 'I would have done that already, so why are you asking me this question?' If you want to introduce a time jump in a SIMEX, it may be more effective to run the final phase in a tabletop style, with structured questions rather than injects. This approach can offer a better way to explore some later-stage issues.

Incorporating live elements or 'stands'

You may want to incorporate an element of live play into your exercise, particularly at the beginning, and then spend the remainder of the time dealing with the consequences of the event. I once ran an exercise for a shipping company that had a ship in dry dock. They wanted to practise a rescue scenario involving the dry dock owner's staff, who were working on the ship. The exercise was carefully planned, with plenty of health and safety risk assessments and checks. We placed a dummy in a compartment on the ship and activated the fire alarm.

The dry dock breathing apparatus (BA) team had to respond by donning their BA sets, searching the ship and evacuating the dummy. I never quite knew how long they'd been waiting around the corner with their kits on, but the exercise was a success; they proved they could carry out a fire rescue on board a ship in dry dock. Once the evacuation was complete, notifications were sent to the shipping company, marking the beginning of the exercise for their tactical and strategic teams. Their role was to manage the consequences of the fire, the impact on the ship in dry dock, and support the casualty.

In a similar way, you could run a live hazardous materials response on-site, followed by a transition to the notification process and the mobilization of internal teams. This allows participants to fully respond to the scenario. A live-play event can be a strong opening phase to a broader exercise that focuses on the organizational impact of the incident. Where there is a statutory or regulatory requirement to run an exercise, incorporating a live element followed by a command-level or tabletop session adds value without too much extra effort. These two parts do not need to be run back-to-back; they could be run a day or two apart.

When I was in the Army, one of the training methods commonly used was the 'round robin'. This involved a rotation through a series of 'stands', each one focused on a practical skill or drill. For example, one stand could be focused on dealing with a casualty. A soldier would be made up to simulate injuries, and participants would be given a brief scenario explaining the situation and their task. They would then approach the casualty while assessing for hazards, determine what was wrong and provide the appropriate first aid. At the end of each stand, participants received a debrief covering what they did well, what could be improved and lessons learnt, before moving on to the next scenario.

Example stands could include:

1. **Kim's game:** Participants view 20 objects for a few minutes. The items are then covered, and they must recall as many as possible.

2. **Pacing practice:** Learning how many steps it takes to pace out 100 metres so participants can use this for navigation and hitting distance markers.
3. **Distance judgement:** A set of features is identified on the ground, and participants estimate how far away each one is.

Using a series of stands is a great way to deliver a half-day or full day of resilience training, allowing participants to refresh and practise core skills in a focused, engaging format.

EXAMPLE

Example live element 'outside now'

This is an exercise I like to use with tactical and operational teams, and it works particularly well for those who spend part of their time office-based. This works for organizations such as schools, manufacturing sites or warehouses. The concept involves delivering the exercise briefing, then informing participants that the fire alarm has sounded and they must evacuate the building. The exercise takes place outside at the fire evacuation point, focusing on a range of issues beyond routine staff accounting. These may include identifying who will manage the scene and make key decisions, such as whether to send staff home, who will liaise with the emergency services, how to deal with any casualties and how to handle any press present at the scene.

A functions phase or working groups

Sometimes, in an exercise, it's useful to split the group and practise individual skills, allowing for more in-depth development of procedures, working strategies or particular elements of the response, such as strategic intent or communication collateral. This helps people better understand their role, and it can also include 'support staff', who may not be part of the incident management team but would be brought in to support their team member during a real incident.

Groups could look at the following areas:

- **Human aspects of the incident:** Develop an approach to responding to casualties or dealing with trauma associated with the incident.

- **Operations:** Explore manual workarounds or alternative service delivery methods to meet customer needs. This could also include securing sites, salvage operations or prioritizing customers and deliveries.
- **Communications:** Work on developing press statements, questions and answers, internal communications, preparing spokespeople for media interviews, developing a media strategy or deciding how to respond to negative press or social media coverage.
- **Strategic intent:** Focus on developing strategic objectives or other high-level elements of the response.

Three-phase exercise conducted over three days

Some exercises benefit from being run over multiple days, especially when testing how actions and decisions evolve over time. A useful format is the three-day exercise model, where a one-hour session takes place each day, typically at the same time, to maintain continuity and minimize disruption to participants' schedules. This approach allows the scenario to develop organically based on participants' decisions, with time in between sessions for scenario recalibration.

On day one, the initial scenario is introduced, and the team meets to discuss and agree on their response actions. Following this, the exercise director updates the scenario overnight, taking into account the decisions made. This works exceedingly well for a strong media story, allowing the media to be updated in between meetings as if they are reacting to the team's decisions. These updates, along with tailored feedback or prompts, are shared with participants in preparation for the next day. This might include individualized responses that participants can use to feed into the following session, helping to drive a more immersive and responsive narrative.

This cycle continues over three mornings, allowing the team to see the consequences of their decisions unfold in near real time. The format also provides an opportunity to explore escalation, emerging risks or second-order impacts based on how well the team has responded. In some cases, a final session is added for a structured debrief, capturing learning points and identifying areas for improvement.

An additional element can be added by having the main team member hand over to their deputy between meetings, ensuring handovers and continuity of response.

Providing a finale to the exercise

There is a danger in SIMEX and tabletop exercises that they can simply fizzle out as participants become tired. They may have responded to the injects thrown at them and feel they have had enough. To avoid the exercise ending on a downbeat note, I like to give the team a final task that requires focus and accuracy. I also believe it is good practice to have the team summarize their response and be clear about their actions and decisions to date.

To this, I often make the final task to brief upwards to their seniors on the progress of the response or to prepare for an interview with the media. Both tasks require the team to think carefully about their actions, and a key part of the value comes from involving them in the preparation and decision-making about what they will say.

When briefing upwards, I try to identify a senior person in the organization who is senior to the team being exercised, making it important for them that the briefing is well-delivered. For bronze/operational teams, this might be their director; for silver/tactical teams, the CEO; and for crisis or strategic teams, it could be the chair of the board, the company owner, someone senior from the parent company or, in the case of a government organization, a senior figure within government. Ideally, this should be the actual person who would receive such a briefing in real life. You may only need them for 15 minutes, and you can provide them with appropriate questions to ask. Having the real person attend makes the team take the briefing seriously, simulates what it would be like in reality and reminds senior managers that the organization is actively exercising its plans. If the real person is unavailable, someone from the exercise team can play the role. While the team will quickly realize it's not the real individual, playing it straight and treating it as real still delivers valuable training benefits.

Another way to achieve a similar outcome is to make the final task a mock media interview or a meeting with another body, such as a regulator. Again, the preparation is the key benefit, with the incident team (or a subset of it) brainstorming the questions they might be asked. This has the added advantage of getting the team to think through their 'lines to take' on various aspects of the incident. In some cases, I haven't actually conducted the interview if time ran short but even scheduling it into the exercise is enough to get the team thinking about their response.

Multiple team exercises

When running an exercise with multiple teams, it is crucial to plan in advance how those teams will collaborate and interact during play. Getting teams to work together has the clear benefit that each team learns how the others operate and observes first-hand the processes, approaches and decision-making at different levels and in various departments. It also helps to ensure that issues are addressed at the appropriate level within the response structure, rather than being left unresolved due to confusion over responsibilities. One of the main benefits of bringing multiple teams together in an exercise is that it challenges assumptions and reveals underlying beliefs. In many organizations, there is often a tendency for one team to assume that 'the tactical team would handle that' or 'the crisis team would make that decision'. In reality, without exercising the teams together, there is no certainty that the tactical team is actually doing what the crisis team expects, or that the tactical team even perceives the task as part of their role. Multi-team exercises help clarify these misunderstandings and establish who does what, when and how.

From my experience, particularly when dealing with senior managers, I strongly believe they should not be left sitting around waiting for another team to produce an answer before they can take part. Senior managers' time is valuable, and if you are going to involve them in an exercise, the design must ensure that their involvement is purposeful and active. If you plan to have multiple teams working on the same exercise, you need to give careful thought to how to keep all teams engaged and involved throughout.

EXAMPLE

Exercise Gold Dawn

When I was working as business continuity manager for a large utility firm, one of my responsibilities was supporting a division that handled customer service and billing. The biggest risk for that division was the loss of its headquarters building in Glasgow, which at the time housed around 2,200 staff. I wanted to run an exercise to test the complete end-to-end response, starting with the immediate reaction to a major incident such as a fire in the building, and ending with a significant number of staff relocated and working from our workplace recovery (WAR) site in Edinburgh. The exercise would involve the division's 10 operational teams, its tactical (silver) team, and I was also keen to involve the company's crisis (gold) team. As well as providing a real test of our processes, this was a good opportunity to showcase the division's business continuity work at a corporate level.

When planning, I decided to break the exercise into four linked but separate events instead of running one large, continuous one. Each part would run two to three days apart, which meant that if something went wrong in one phase, we would have time to adjust plans, re-brief people or make changes before the next. This also meant that one stage of the exercise wouldn't inadvertently derail the next. The four parts were imaginatively labelled A, B, C and D.

Exercise A: Live-play evacuation

The first part of the exercise was a live-play event. We set off the fire alarm for the entire office, which meant that all 2,200 staff went to their normal muster points as part of a standard fire drill. Once everyone was assembled outside, instead of sending them straight back into the building, we delayed the return by about 10 minutes. During this time, staff were asked to discuss in their teams what they would do if the evacuation were for a real incident and the building were out of use. Senior managers discussed how they would organize people at the evacuation points and manage the situation in those first critical minutes.

The next step involved selecting staff from each of the 10 operational teams, about 120 people in total, and busing them to a local conference centre. There, they were given 90 minutes to discuss their response in more detail and complete a situation report (SITREP) form. This SITREP was then sent to the division's tactical team, outlining exactly how they would manage their part of the overall response.

Exercise B: Tactical incident team meeting

The second part of the exercise involved the tactical team, led by the division's managing director. Their task was to hold a formal incident team meeting, review the SITREPs provided by the operational teams and confirm whether they were satisfied with the proposed responses. The finale for this stage was a real briefing to the company's CEO. I'll admit I was slightly nervous at this point: there was always a chance they would simply read from the meeting notes, which might not be polished enough for a senior audience. To avoid this risk, I was asked to prepare a draft briefing script well in advance of the exercise so they would not look unprepared in front of the boss.

Exercise C: Technical set-up at the workplace recovery site

This stage involved the IT department. Their job was to travel to the WAR site in Edinburgh and prepare it for staff use the next day. They set up PCs and printers and configured the call centre telephony so it could take live customer calls. In the afternoon, we brought in a number of testers to make live calls and check that everything worked as planned. This allowed us to iron out any problems before the main group of people arrived for Exercise D.

Exercise D: Large-scale live relocation

For the final stage, 300 people from across the division, roughly a third of the number we would move in a real incident, were selected to take part. I felt this was enough to prove the concept while also giving those responsible for managing incoming staff the chance to practise at a realistic but manageable scale. On the morning of the exercise, everyone gathered in the car park at Hampden football ground. They were loaded onto buses for the hour-long journey to the WAR site.

When they arrived, they were met, given a health and safety briefing and shown around the building. They then went to their designated workspaces, logged in and began taking live customer calls. After two to three hours of live operation, we conducted a short debrief, and they were bused back to their cars.

The entire series of exercises successfully validated the end-to-end process for relocating staff to the WAR site and confirmed that the strategy was both workable and practical. As with any major exercise, lessons were learnt at every stage, but the fundamental concept was proven beyond a doubt.

Different ways to structure multiple team exercises

There are multiple ways that multiple team exercises can be structured.

Sequentially: This approach is used when two or more teams take part in the same exercise. You may have several operational teams that feed their responses up to the tactical team, which then consolidates and coordinates the response, ensuring sufficient resources are available to implement requested actions. Once the operational teams have delivered their response, they are stood down. The tactical team can then brief the strategic team, who consider their response and address any guidance sought or decisions required by lower-level teams. This is how I ran

Exercise Gold Dawn earlier in this chapter. The timing between briefings can be immediate or spaced by hours or even days. Handover may take the form of a written SITREP or handover document, or a direct briefing from the lower team leader to the higher team. Feedback or clarification can later be provided to complete the loop, ensuring lower teams understand how their input shaped the overall response.

In parallel: In this model, two or more incident management teams work on the same scenario simultaneously, communicating and exchanging information as they would in reality. This requires umpires with each team to monitor activity. Parallel play works particularly well in SIMEX-style exercises, as information can flow quickly between teams. It is less suited to tabletop exercises, where passing information between groups can slow the exercise. Running in parallel is an effective way to test whether tasking, information sharing and the passing of strategic intent are clearly understood at all levels.

Staggered start: This format is particularly useful when working with senior managers, who are unlikely to sit waiting for updates from a subordinate team. In a staggered start, the first team begins the exercise and develops the scenario. Once they reach a natural briefing point, the second team is brought in to receive that update, make decisions and issue direction.

A good example is Exercise Zeus, which involved both an incident management team and a crisis management team. The incident management team responded for an hour before briefing the crisis management team. Two incident management team members attended the crisis management team meeting, delivered the briefing and remained while decisions were discussed. They then returned to the incident management team and updated them on the crisis management team's deliberations. Meanwhile, the remaining incident management team members continued working and receiving injects. This structure ensured both teams remained fully engaged without unnecessary downtime.

Simulating a team: If you wish to practise team interactions but cannot assemble all participants, you can simulate a single team. This may be done by the absent team's leader, another team member or an exercise staff member. In SIMEX exercises, for example, the tactical team leader might brief the crisis team and later return to receive further tasking. In tabletop exercises, a participant may represent another team, providing feedback and challenge. Whoever plays the role must have sufficient authority and knowledge to do so credibly.

Running multiple teams in a single exercise requires more planning and increases complexity. However, the value is considerable, as it tests assumptions, improves coordination and confirms that what one team expects from another is what actually happens in practice.

Choosing where and how the exercise is delivered

When I first started delivering exercises, they were very simple and always conducted face-to-face. Part of the exercise process involved notifying team members, who would then jump in their cars and head straight to the incident room. Only occasionally would some participants join the meeting via a conference or 'star' phone, as they were known at the time.

Today, with people working from home, virtual teams and senior staff potentially spread across continents, incident meetings may be run virtually, in a hybrid format with some participants face-to-face and others joining remotely, or if the organization is small and everyone lives and works close by, entirely in person.

When deciding on the format of the exercise, it is important to determine whether it will be conducted face-to-face, virtually or in a hybrid format. This decision may depend on how the real-life response is expected to take place. Alternatively, those being exercised may choose to run the exercise face-to-face to enhance the training benefits, even if they would usually respond via video conference.

The following are a few considerations when running virtual or hybrid exercises.

Hybrid exercises are exercises where some people are in the room and others are joining by video conference. This format can be tricky, and if not managed well can reduce the value of the exercise. One of the big problems is that those online can easily get forgotten, especially when the scenario gets busy, or the pace picks up. In real incidents or exercises, there are side conversations, quick chats and breakout discussions, which are almost impossible for remote participants to follow.

The result is that online people can end up out of the loop. It's also harder for them to get into the conversation because those in the room often speak more and dominate, so the person online either has to interrupt or sit quietly. Remote participants miss out on body language, facial expressions and the 'feel' of the room, which can tell you a lot about the urgency or stress levels of a situation. They also don't see things like whiteboards, flipcharts or incident room boards, which in a SIMEX helps everyone share the same picture of what's going on. Without these, online attendees can feel disconnected, less confident and less likely to speak up.

What you often end up with is the people in the room naturally taking the lead, making most of the decisions and getting more out of the exercise. If you're going to run a hybrid exercise, you need to actively manage it so that everyone is included, otherwise the learning and engagement will be heavily weighted towards those in the room.

Running online-only exercises. For some organizations, especially at the senior management level, they may already have a virtual crisis team and, as part of their procedures, expect to respond virtually. If this is their documented way of working, then it should be practised during an exercise. To make the exercise a success, you need to check what is in place in terms of the platform and ways of working before you conduct it.

If the team has regularly used their platform for managing incidents, then go ahead and plan the exercise. But if this is the first time, even if the team regularly uses video conferencing for day-to-day meetings there's a need to check how they intend to run their meetings and, in turn, how you will run the exercise. The main issue is that while video conferencing is fine for running incident team meetings (something they will have done before), the question is what happens when the meeting is over – how will the rest of the exercise take place? It's also important to think about how you will get injects to participants if the exercise is a SIMEX.

If teams are going to use video conferencing for running incident team meetings, their platform should be set up with a main area for team meetings and then a number of breakout rooms where members can move to work in smaller groups on specific subjects. For example, you could have a communications room, an operations room, a stakeholder room, an IT room and a number of spare rooms, all set up in advance. If you just let people finish a meeting and then call each other one-to-one, the exercise staff won't be able to hear what is going on, and much of the benefit of the exercise may be lost. A way around this could be to make it part of the exercise rules that, if breakout conversations are happening, an exercise umpire is invited into the group.

Getting injects into the exercise can be more difficult if the exercise is a SIMEX. If a participant is on a Teams call, it can be awkward to get them off that call to receive another. Injects could be given directly to their mobile phones, but you would have to make sure they answered and knew to accept calls from a certain number. As stated earlier in this book, we tend not to have participants use email for exercise communications, as they can easily get drawn into day-to-day work, and there's also the danger of an email being sent outside the exercise and being mistaken for a real event. If the video conference allows one-to-one chat, that can be a way of giving individual injects, or, if the exercise is conducted inside an exercise platform, it usually has the ability to conduct one-to-one communications built in.

Personally, I think that online exercises, if you have the choice, are better suited to tabletop exercises than to SIMEXs.

Should you run a no-notice exercise?

Running a no-notice exercise is often considered the gold standard for testing an organization's incident management readiness. It provides a true-to-life scenario, allowing crisis teams to be assessed from a standing start, just as they would be in a real-world event. The benefits are compelling: no-notice exercises reveal genuine gaps in capability, test the organization's response under pressure and avoid the polish that comes with pre-exercise preparation. Participants must rely on their actual knowledge, confidence and teamwork, offering an honest gauge of their level of preparation. The realism, urgency and unpredictability of such exercises often enhance engagement, pushing participants to think on their feet and demonstrate their true ability to lead and act in a crisis. When I conducted a cyber exercise involving five teams, many participants commented that the unannounced nature made it feel more like a real incident, highlighting who knew their plans well and who didn't.

No-notice exercises can carry significant risks and are not suitable for every organization. Poorly executed, they can damage morale, disrupt live business operations or descend into confusion if participants are unsure whether the event is real or an exercise. Key personnel may be absent, business-critical meetings may clash, and if leadership doesn't visibly support the exercise, engagement can wane. Additionally, organizations miss out on the pre-exercise preparation phase, where teams often review and update plans and brief new staff. For these reasons, best practice is to start with announced or partial-notice exercises, using no-notice formats only once teams are mature, well-drilled and organizational buy-in is strong.

In summary, while no-notice exercises can be immensely valuable, they must be used strategically, with careful planning and senior support to maximize learning and minimize disruption.

KEY LEARNINGS

- The type and structure of an exercise should be guided by its purpose, objectives and practical constraints, such as time, budget and team experience. There's no need to stick rigidly to a single format; blending styles and methods across phases can often deliver better outcomes.
- Exercises should be 'pitched' at the right level. Overly complex formats like SIMEX can overwhelm inexperienced teams, while overly simple formats may not challenge more experienced participants. The chosen structure should build capability in a way that's engaging, progressive and aligned with learning goals.
- The format may also be dictated by external requirements, regulatory, contractual or organizational policies. These need to be understood early on to avoid last-minute surprises or misalignment.
- Training is vital and should be provided before the exercise to provide a shared foundation for everyone.
- Training can be delivered in various ways from one-to-one briefing to AI avatars, but the focus should always be on making participants feel confident, not catching them out.
- Exercises are most effective when broken into manageable phases. Each phase should be well-paced to avoid overload and should allow time for discussion and reflection.
- Technology can support exercises but shouldn't drive them. Whether using platforms for injects or game-based micro-simulations, planning and thought still matter most. Always consider how learning will be captured and preserved beyond the platform.
- Structuring exercises to include live elements, individual tasks or role-play scenarios can make them more immersive. Variety keeps people engaged and allows different learning styles and skills to be exercised.
- Multi-day and multi-team exercises add realism and complexity but require more careful planning to keep everyone engaged and aligned. These formats are great for testing escalation, handovers and longer-term strategic thinking.
- As a final point, don't be afraid to challenge the exercise format if it doesn't fit the objectives. It's better to ask hard questions early than deliver an ineffective session later. The structure must always serve the objectives, not the other way around.

14

Developing the storyboard

In this chapter, you will learn about:

1. Developing the storyboard framework
2. Developing storyboard content
3. Ensuring there are issues for all
4. Including 'difficult issues' in your exercise

How the scenario, storyboard and injects or questions fit together

During the design phase, you should agree on the overall scenario to be used, whether the exercise will include time jumps or be played in real time and how the exercise will be structured. Each phase should have clear activities for the team and an agreed duration. Developing the storyboard is when detailed planning takes place, and for each phase, the exercise content is built.

Storyboards can be used in both tabletop exercises and SIMEX. In a tabletop exercise, the storyboard outlines the events that occur during each phase and frames the context for the questions participants must answer. In a SIMEX, the storyboard provides the framework for creating and delivering individual injects into the exercise.

The storyboard describes how the incident unfolds over time and how stakeholders, including staff, customers, the media, regulators and the public, are affected. Writing a storyboard can be compared to writing a film script: a series of linked events is created that together drive the exercise and shape participant responses. Storyboards may be structured either by time blocks, for example,

15–30 minutes, or by incident phases. The storyboards may also contain the 'back story': the context of what has occurred before the exercise begins.

The level of detail in a storyboard will vary depending on the exercise's complexity, type, number of phases and its length. In simpler exercises, the storyboard may summarize the main events in each phase, with the details added later during inject development. More complex exercises may require greater detail, but it is important not to make the storyboard so complicated that the overall flow of events is lost. The exercise director should be able to see how all elements of the exercise connect and ensure that the story does not drift out of sequence.

Understanding the impact of the scenario on the organization

When planning an exercise, designers must undertake a structured assessment of the likely impact of the scenario on the organization as part of the development of the storyboard. Those planning the exercise need to understand how that incident would realistically affect the organization's ability to deliver its key services. This requires identifying which functions would be disrupted, which clients or service users would be affected, which contractual or regulatory obligations might be breached, and which activities could continue with modification. Planners should also consider whether a similar event has occurred previously, either internally or within the wider sector, and what lessons were identified at the time.

Exercise planners should consider the impact of the scenario across the whole organization. This includes the effect on people (availability, safety, welfare, industrial relations), physical assets (buildings, access, utilities), technology and data systems, suppliers and outsourced partners, and financial stability. Reputational consequences must also be mapped in advance: how might regulators, customers, shareholders, media and other stakeholders perceive the incident and the organization's response? Exercise planners should also conduct research and consider the organization's past incidents. If an incident has happened before or multiple times, the impact on reputation may be greater than if it is the first occurrence. A scenario that disrupts operations but ignores stakeholder reactions, for example, may fail to test communications, governance and strategic decision-making under pressure. By systematically analysing operational, financial, reputational and stakeholder impacts during the design phase, planners ensure the exercise reflects the complexity of real-world disruption and meaningfully tests the organization's continuity and crisis arrangements.

Developing the storyboard framework

When developing a storyboard, it is typically laid out in a table or spreadsheet. The column headings represent the exercise timeline, either divided into time blocks (e.g. every 15–30 minutes for a half-day session, or hourly for longer ones) or aligned with the scenario's phases. See Table 14.1.

> TIP
>
> It should be noted that the time spent on the initial briefing of participants and the final debrief is not included within the storyboard timings.

When developing the phases or timescales across the top of your table, it's helpful to include a brief description of the team's expected activities during each phase. For example, if a phase involves an incident management team meeting, injects should be limited to avoid disrupting the discussion. Alternatively, the phase before a meeting might include multiple injects to provide the information needed for that discussion.

Once the table or spreadsheet headings have been agreed, the next step is to identify the stakeholders, both internal and external, who would be affected by the incident, as well as those you wish to feature in the exercise. If there are any requirements from specific stakeholders for inclusion in the exercise detailed in the objectives, these should be taken into account.

TABLE 14.1 Storyboard framework

Scenario The overall story that frames the exercise			
Storyboard: Back story	Storyboard: Phase 1	Storyboard: Phase 2	Storyboard: Phase 3
SIMIX: given as part of the exercise briefing	Inject 1 Inject 2 Inject 3 Inject 4	Inject 5 Inject 6 Inject 7 Inject 8 Inject 9	Inject 10 Inject 11 Inject 12
Tabletop exercise: given as part of Phase 1	Question 1 Question 2	Question 3 Question 4 Question 5	Question 6

Stakeholders may include internal staff, which can be further broken down into categories such as general staff, staff directly affected by the incident and customer-facing staff. External stakeholders might include customers, regulators, the media, social media and members of the public. Any organization or stakeholder group that will play a role in the exercise should be included in the table on the left-hand side. Useful sources for identifying stakeholders include the organization's crisis management plan, crisis communications plan, the plan for the part of the organization being exercised, and the supplier lists developed during the business impact analysis (BIA). Asking AI for a list of stakeholders may identify stakeholders not already detailed in plans or incident documents.

A typical storyboard layout, therefore, has time phases or incident phases across the top, and key stakeholder groups listed down the side.

Developing the story over time

Once the table is built, the first task is to develop the story and determine how events will unfold across different phases or timescales. The scenario will define the overall incident type, but it will be up to the design team, using their experience, knowledge of how a particular scenario would impact the organization and understanding of the various impacts, to drive the development of the storyboard over time.

In the following example, the exercise is designed for the crisis management team. The scenario involves a fire in the organization's largest building, which houses much of its IT infrastructure and the greatest number of staff. The crisis management team itself is based in a separate location and would not be directly affected by the fire. The exercise begins with the team being informed of an incident and required to attend a briefing in the boardroom. This initiates them responding to the incident.

The exercise is designed as a SIMEX and has several phases that align with the evolving scenario. This storyboard would be just as suitable for a tabletop exercise.

Typical storyboard: Fire scenario

1 **Prior to the exercise (back story)**: There have been several minor fires in the Rankin Building over the past three years, but no significant action has been taken in response. In the last 24 hours, staff reported a burning smell in the basement. Facilities management investigated the smell but found nothing.

2 **Phase 1, 0–30 minutes:** At 12.00 pm an explosion occurs in the basement, and fire quickly spreads throughout the building. Staff evacuated the building, but due to the speed of the fire and many staff having left the building prior to the fire to get lunch, it has not been possible to account for all staff.
3 **Phase 2, 30–60 minutes:** Several staff members are taken to the hospital, with some in a critical condition.
4 **Phase 3, 60–90 minutes:** It is confirmed that there are 10 casualties: four walking wounded, five serious and one critical. All staff have now been accounted for. Staff at the warehouse, located 20 miles away, report that their IT and warehouse management systems are down, preventing orders from being fulfilled. They have lost access to the company network, and all systems are unavailable except Microsoft 365.
5 **Phase 4, 90–120 minutes:** Customers, having seen news coverage of the fire, begin calling to ask about the status of their orders and the wider impact. One casualty has died. Media outlets report claims from a whistle-blower that the company had experienced multiple previous fires in the building but failed to act.

Once the overall story is developed, the impact on each stakeholder group can be explored. When creating the storyboard for each stakeholder, there are several ways they can influence the story, help achieve the exercise objectives and educate respondents about the importance and needs of different stakeholders.

Developing storyboard content

Developing content for the storyboard requires research, imagination and experience, and it must align with the exercise's objectives. The purpose of the storyboard isn't just to present an engaging, compelling story to participants; it's to prompt discussion, emphasize key learning points and explore issues that arise from a specific scenario. It also offers participants a chance to practise incident management skills, apply knowledge and leadership, and build teamwork skills. The balance of these elements, and which should be most emphasized, should have been agreed upon during the exercise's design phase and reflected in the exercise objectives.

When developing the storyboard content, it's important to ensure there's something for everyone. If participants come from a range of departments or hold different roles within the incident team, the scenario should include elements that are relevant to all of them. Otherwise, some may disengage or feel the exercise isn't a good use of their time.

There are a number of ways in which content can be developed and where inspiration for the content can be found.

Research the event: If your scenario involves a building fire, research similar incidents through news reports, academic papers, publicly available incident reports or reputable online sources. Consider what generally causes fires, how emergency services respond, and the likely number of casualties. Keep the scenario realistic rather than extreme, so participants learn the correct lessons. You may slightly increase the impact to create pressure, but exaggerating the incident's likely impact risks teaching the wrong lessons or making it so unlikely that the exercise loses credibility. The same applies to cyber incidents involving ransomware as a scenario: research how such attacks usually occur in other organizations and use this information to guide your own exercise planning.

Give the 'what', not the 'how': During an exercise played in real time, there will not be enough time for a formal investigation, so the exact cause of the incident may not be known until later when the exercise play has finished. Avoid focusing on how the incident occurred, as this can lead participants to dismiss the scenario as unrealistic. This is particularly important in cyber exercises. If you avoid specifying how the attacker gained access, IT staff are less likely to become defensive and more likely to focus on the consequences and their response.

People, facilities, technology, operations, communications: When developing injects, utilize these headings as a framework. Consider how the incident impacts:

1. **People:** staff directly involved, the wider workforce or the public, including physical injuries, mental health, boycotts or protests.
2. **Facilities:** loss of access to buildings, safety concerns or evacuation.
3. **Technology:** IT systems, applications or communications networks.
4. **Operations:** the organization's ability to deliver products or services.
5. **Communications:** how information is shared internally and externally.

Validating the plan: One objective of an exercise may be to validate the organization's plan. Storyboard injects can be used to test whether the team applies documented escalation thresholds, forms the correct team and develops required reports, such as a situation report (SITREP). Injects can also request that recovery strategies from the plan are explained or implemented, ensuring the team works through their response in practice.

Leadership and teamwork: Introducing multiple injects at the same time can pressure the team, allowing for the practice of teamwork and leadership skills. Effective leaders should help the group prioritize, stay calm and address issues in a structured manner. Providing decision points with no perfect answer, and applying time pressure, helps develop resilience and demonstrates how the team behaves under stress.

Incident management skills: Incident management skills can be incorporated into the storyboard by organizing phases where the team runs meetings, allocates actions, documents decisions and develops a working strategy in response to the evolving scenario. New events may prompt them to record key information in logs, reassess priorities and share crucial details among all participants or teams, if multiple groups are involved.

Managing overload: Deliberately increase the volume of communications in the room to assess the team's ability to prioritize and manage information. This highlights the importance of filtering inputs and maintaining control during a high-pressure incident.

Situational awareness: This can be woven into the storyboard by including information that must be gathered, interpreted and prioritized as the scenario develops. Injects may provide separate pieces of detail that only make sense when combined, requiring the team to connect the dots. Conflicting accounts of the situation can originate from different stakeholders; for example, varying casualty figures, which demands that the team clarify discrepancies and verify facts before acting. Storyboards can also incorporate operational information that is accurate but irrelevant at the crisis team level, prompting managers to recognize what should be delegated or deprioritized. Last, providing incomplete updates encourages the team to identify what they do not yet know and actively seek out missing information.

Including interactions with the media: Including media elements in the storyboard can help assess the team's readiness for communications under pressure. Injects might include various press enquiries for interviews on the incident, asking the team to prioritize which interviews to accept or whether to accept any at all, then prepare suitable spokespeople. A request could be made for a media statement with a tight deadline, or a journalist might share the outline of a draft article to be fact-checked and corrected by the incident team. Simulated interviews, whether live radio, videoconference or phone calls, challenge participants to deliver clear, accurate messaging. Additional complexity can be introduced by a request from technical/industry media, requiring subject-matter expertise on the incident, or by responding to off-the-record comments from staff. Storyboards can include a leak of internal information on social media that could cause reputational damage if it goes viral or is picked up by the media and assessing whether the team recognizes its significance and plans accordingly. Preparing senior leaders for media engagement also tests briefing skills, especially if the exercise references previous adverse incidents or sensitive, unrelated topics that could be raised in interviews.

Adding a media story: In most exercises, including a media story adds depth and realism, even if the team being exercised isn't directly responsible for managing the media. It serves as a reminder that media outlets may pick up on the incident, potentially driving the response timeline and revealing details before the organization is ready to release them.

TIP

Media bandwidth is limited. National outlets usually focus only on major stories, while local media teams are often stretched thin and may cover only the most critical local incidents. As a result, some of the media coverage used in exercises might come across as slightly unrealistic, unless the organization is particularly high-profile or the incident is large enough to capture national attention.

To ensure realism, it's worth researching how similar incidents have been covered in the past. Most media outlets check their facts, and while misinformation can happen, it's unlikely they'd publish something blatantly untrue. You should also remember that there are protocols for releasing sensitive information, such as casualty names or incident causes, so any simulated media content should respect those boundaries.

If media management is a key part of your exercise, consider involving a media specialist, external PR consultant or someone from your internal communications team as part of the design team.

Media stories could include:

- Media coverage from the scene of the incident, providing the basic facts, could include images or video.
- Reporters who begin referencing unnamed sources to suggest prior safety concerns state 'this was an accident waiting to happen'.
- The media get their facts wrong, and the organization needs to contact them.

- A statement has not yet been released from the organization, and so news reports comment on this.
- Media outlets run background pieces on the organization's history and previous incidents.
- Analysts and commentators speculate on the financial and reputational impact of the incident.
- Media stories compare the response to similar past incidents in other organizations.
- Editorials and opinion pieces call for accountability and transparency.
- News outlets begin approaching stakeholders (e.g. unions, regulators, industry experts) for reactions and comments.

Social media responses and stories: In exercise terms, there are no rules governing how people behave on social media, making it a useful tool for introducing disinformation and falsehoods as well as breaking incidents, so focusing the team's attention on the external environment. While mainstream media stories are often researched and generally accurate, anything goes on social media. Media and social channels can be key themes in the exercise, enabling communication professionals to practise their responses. They can also be used to inform stakeholders about the scenario, allowing them to contact the organization with any specific concerns.

TIP

The following could be included within social media posts:

- Use of a hashtag.
- Complaints about products or services unrelated to the incident.
- People are angry or upset about the incident itself.
- People are requesting information or prompting for an update or statement on the incident.
- People repeating disinformation.
- A fictional organization posing as the client is posting humorous or untrue information.
- Some posts defending the company.

- Concerned relatives of employees are inquiring about well-being, seeking information about the incident or trying to locate someone.
- Trolling and use of memes, people mocking the incident or the response.
- Personal attacks on organization's staff or senior managers.
- Sympathy posts for people affected by the incident.
- Images of the incident or areas surrounding the incident. For example, a picture of a smoky building or a traffic jam due to a car crash.
- Posts bringing up past incidents or controversies the company has been involved in.
- Members of staff or ex-staff members saying it was an incident/accident waiting to happen.
- Members of staff slating their own company.
- Influencers, celebrities or influential politicians commenting on the issue, especially those with large numbers of followers.
- Use of doctored pictures and videos or pictures out of context/taken at a different time or incident.

Senior manager, board, government or regulator briefing: As discussed before, I like to use this as a finale to the exercise, as it allows the team to consolidate their thinking and prepare for a formal briefing. Although this can be effective at the end, the briefing could occur at any point during the exercise and, if appropriate, there could be multiple briefings, especially if the organization is heavily regulated. A request for an update often arrives from the party, usually with some notice, giving the team time to prepare. The briefing can be delivered by phone, video conference or in person. The party can ask probing or politically sensitive questions to test the exercise participant's confidence and strategic clarity.

Timely actions and communications: Exercises should also assess whether actions and communications are being properly followed through. This can be incorporated into the storyboard by including several calls or requests that require a prompt response, then verifying that the answers are returned and acted upon. Injects can follow up on previously agreed actions to confirm progress or to highlight any omissions. It is also helpful to include decisions or tasks that have time limits, encouraging the team to prioritize effectively and ensuring they maintain momentum throughout the exercise.

As you develop your storyboard, especially regarding the impact on stakeholders, decide on new ideas or story elements, and then adjust the overall story so that the latest information aligns. Developing the stakeholder elements of the storyboard is an excellent opportunity for the design team to demonstrate their knowledge of incidents and their impact on the organization. It's one of the most interesting parts of exercise development, where planners can really showcase their skills and imagination.

Examples of stakeholder timelines for the fire scenario

The following are example timelines of individual stakeholders.

STAFF / CUSTOMER IMPACT TIMELINE

1. **Phase 1, 0–30 minutes:** No customer activity is reported.
2. **Phase 2, 30–60 minutes:** Several customers call the contact centre expressing shock about the fire. One customer asks about their account manager, Seonaid Ferry, based in the Rankin Building, and whether he is safe.
3. **Phase 3, 60–90 minutes:** A call comes from the warehouse: two customers have arrived in person to pick up their orders. Staff explain that orders cannot currently be fulfilled because the company's systems are down. The customers say they will wait, but staff are unsure how to respond.
4. **Phase 4, 90–120 minutes:** An increasing number of customers contact the call centre to ask whether their orders will be fulfilled the next day. They have seen media reports of the fire and emphasize that their deliveries are critical. They press for reassurance that services will not be disrupted.

MEDIA AND SOCIAL MEDIA ESCALATION TIMELINE

1. **Phase 1, 0–30 minutes:** There is no media coverage. The incident is only known to those directly involved.
2. **Phase 2, 30–60 minutes:** The media reports the basic facts about the fire. Social media activity increases as colleagues and family members inquire about possible casualties, as some people are not answering their phones. There is also some disinformation that isn't gaining much traction; it is based on claims from an ex-employee who states the building was poorly maintained and that she was asked to cover up a fire she extinguished in the basement.

3. **Phase 3, 60–90 minutes:** Further details emerge in the media. Reports state there are 20 casualties, 7 of them critical. Social media posts claim that staff had smelt burning earlier in the day, suggesting the incident could have been preventable.
4. **Phase 4, 90–120 minutes:** The company is criticized for failing to release a media statement. Social media claims about the smell of burning are now repeated in the mainstream press. There is speculation about the identity of one of the deceased, and outrage builds online as reports of previous fires linked to the organization resurface.

USE OF THE RISING TIDE MEDIA STORY IN EXERCISES

For scenarios where the incident is not immediately obvious externally, such as an IT failure or a cyber incident, using a 'rising tide' media and social media story can be highly effective. This approach prevents the incident management team from choosing when to make the incident public and instead forces them to consider their external communications strategy under pressure.

In a cyber incident exercise, I often begin with social media speculation that a major organization has been impacted. At first, there may be general rumours without organizational names attached. As the incident develops, posts start to identify the specific organization under attack. This leaves the team with a dilemma: whether to break the story themselves or ignore the speculation.

The scenario can be escalated further when a customer or partner calls to ask whether the social media reports are true. At this point, the organization must decide whether to deny the incident and risk credibility or acknowledge it openly. As the exercise progresses, the story may spread into the technical industry press and then into mainstream media. At this stage, the organization could face a deluge of stakeholder queries and criticism for not issuing a statement sooner.

This technique adds realism to exercises by testing how the team manages speculation, responds to stakeholders and times its media statements. It highlights the importance of proactive communication and the risks of delay or denial during a cyber incident.

Checking there are issues for all

Once you have decided on your storyboard, it is important to ensure that all members of the incident management team being exercised have a role relevant to their department or responsibility within the team. I have seen exercises where a participant sits silently with their arms folded for the entire session, believing that nothing in the scenario applies to them.

To avoid this, I sometimes create a matrix that lists all team members against the exercise phases. This allows me to check that each person has content relevant to them at some stage. If a phase appears to offer little for a participant, I develop additional material to ensure they are engaged.

In other cases, I deliberately avoid assigning specific tasks to some participants. This allows me to see whether they take the initiative to support colleagues who may be overloaded, or whether they contribute to strategic tasks such as drafting strategic intent. These activities often require focused thought, separate from the operational response.

It is worth making the point, during the exercise or in the debrief, that incidents affect team members differently. Not everyone will always have a full workload. Team members should actively seek tasks or offer support to others, as there are always activities that need to be carried out.

Including 'difficult issues' in your exercise

Occasionally, it may be necessary to include what I call 'difficult issues' in an exercise. These might be elements that are emotionally charged or potentially distressing. For example, your scenario might involve a terrorist attack, serious injury, a transportation disaster or reputational incidents involving allegations of sexual misconduct, assault or rape.

If these elements are essential to the scenario and the exercise objectives, it is important to ensure that no members of the design team or the participants are likely to be adversely affected. Sensitive content should never be included without forethought and discussion.

In exercises where I've included such issues, I have sometimes opened with a short statement to inform participants in advance. This might include a warning that the scenario contains potentially distressing material and an offer to anyone who feels uncomfortable to discreetly withdraw from the exercise. In practice, I've never had anyone leave, but I felt that the warning was appropriate and appreciated.

This approach supports psychological safety and ensures that the exercise remains a learning experience for everyone involved. It also allows you, as the exercise facilitator, to manage any emotional impact with professionalism and care.

EXAMPLE

Black Basta

In autumn 2024, I planned and delivered a cyber exercise for an organization, having been invited to do so by another consultancy. The scenario centred around a ransomware attack accompanied by a ransom demand. The attacker group we used was Black Basta, who were particularly prolific at the time.

We agreed to include them in the scenario because they were active, widely reported on in the media and the team could access threat intelligence about their tactics and techniques. I also knew that the group's name had uncomfortable associations, particularly due to its phonetic similarity to racist terms, and I believed this discomfort could be used purposefully. The external consultant and the rest of the design team all agreed on the exercise content, including the use of the name of the attackers.

However, during the post-exercise debrief, the consultant's colleague expressed, in front of the entire group, that he was very unhappy with the use of the name. I felt he was trying to score points or undermine the success of an exercise that had otherwise gone extremely well.

I replied that I had used the name with intent: part of running a good exercise is invoking emotion. If a name or event causes discomfort, it often leaves a stronger impression and helps embed learning more effectively. I believe the exercise achieved that aim.

The situation, however, served as an important reminder: all significant details of an exercise, especially anything potentially sensitive or controversial, should be documented in the exercise instruction. That way, if anyone on the delivery or planning team has concerns, they can raise them before the exercise. It's far better to address difficult issues in advance than to express discomfort afterwards, once the scenario has played out in front of participants.

When developing the storyboard, you always need to consider whether the incident will truly challenge the team being exercised. Is it pitched at the appropriate level, severe enough to warrant their involvement and management, but not so extreme that it would be escalated beyond them? Does it meet the exercise objectives? Is it believable, realistic and does it contain enough depth and complexity to challenge all the teams and participants involved?

In conclusion, a storyboard can be as detailed as the exercise demands, which depends on its type and duration. A tabletop exercise might require a simple storyboard with few events, while a SIMEX lasting several hours will need a more detailed and complex story. The design team should always review the exercise objectives and ensure that the story remains aligned with its intended goals.

KEY LEARNINGS

- A storyboard translates the scenario into a structured, time-based sequence that drives the flow of the exercise.
- Each phase of the storyboard should align with clear activities and be calibrated to match the team's level and exercise objectives.
- The scenario, storyboard and injects must connect logically to create a coherent and realistic unfolding story.
- Stakeholder impacts should be developed across time to ensure realism and relevance for each participant group.
- The storyboard table typically maps time phases across the top and key stakeholders down the side to track injects and impacts.
- Content should be developed using real-world research and structured using categories such as people, facilities, operations, technology and communications.
- Injects can test a wide range of capabilities, including incident management skills, leadership under pressure and decision-making.
- Situational awareness can be challenged through incomplete, conflicting or misleading information that teams must interpret in real time.
- Including media and senior leadership briefings adds realism and tests both communications and strategic clarity under pressure.
- A well-designed storyboard ensures all participants are meaningfully involved, supports the exercise's learning objectives and maintains psychological safety.

15

Verisimilitude: making your exercise come to life

In this chapter, you will learn about:

1. Use of pictures
2. Reporting from the scene of the incident
3. Radio clips
4. Simulated media and social media
5. Internal communications
6. Call with regulators, government bodies or parent organizations
7. Casualties
8. Use of props

Verisimilitude, when used in exercises, is about the appearance of being real, which adds to the realism of the exercise and immerses the participants in the experience.

POLICE AND FIREFIGHTERS' HATS

One of the first big exercises I ran required the evacuation of a utilities head office in Glasgow. The exercise was in four parts, and the first part involved a full office evacuation during a fire drill, with 2,200 people participating. Those not involved in the rest of the exercise returned to work once the fire drill was completed, while the heads of department remained outside to take part in the second phase. The scenario was a World War II bomb discovered by workmen while digging a trench for a new water main.

To brief the exercise participants on the scenario, I used the local policeman. He agreed, as the company was a large employer in the area and he had a good relationship with us. I felt the exercise would feel a lot more real and get off to a better start if he briefed those responding, rather than me as the exercise director. This worked well, added realism and practised company police liaison. The problem is that for many people running exercises, unless you have a friendly policeman, if you want police involvement, you might have to pay for their time, or a police person who agreed to do the briefing may be called away to other duties at the last moment.

I ran an exercise a few years later with a different client, which also involved senior managers from their campus site being briefed first by a policeman and then, about 10 minutes later, by a firefighter. The client wasn't going to pay for a real police or firefighter. In this instance, I sent one of the consultants delivering the exercise to a fancy dress shop and they purchased fire and police hats.

The same person first gave the briefing while wearing the police hat, and ten minutes later provided an update while wearing the firefighter's hat. In both instances, there were no silly jokes or gimmicks; they played it straight and delivered the briefings in character. For those participating in the exercise, it did not matter that a man in a suit was wearing a fancy dress police hat; they perceived him as a police officer, listened carefully and acted on the briefing. This demonstrates a great example of verisimilitude: the appearance of being real. Although it isn't, if participants believe it is real, it enhances the immersive nature of the exercise.

Ways to deploy verisimilitude in your exercise

We've seen in Chapter 5 that people learn better when they are immersed in the scenario. The more they believe in the scenario, the more effective the learning. There are many ways to deploy verisimilitude in your exercise, and advances in technology are making it easier and cheaper to produce.

A picture paints a thousand words

If the exercise participants are directly affected by the incident they are responding to, you need to inform them of the details of what has occurred.

Often, with a senior team, they are responding to an incident at another site to where they are located. In the exercise briefing, you, as the exercise director, could brief them on the scenario: 'At 4 am this morning, a fire broke out in our manufacturing plant in Hull. Despite the fire service's efforts, it burnt to the ground. Your manufacturing site has been destroyed, as well as all the stock in the warehouse.'

For some exercises, this is sufficient; it gives the team enough information to start thinking through the response. If you want to add some more verisimilitude, you could mock up some pictures from the site, which can have an emotional as well as an intellectual impact. The pictures could have been sent from the site by a member of staff, shared by a senior person on social media or via the media.

There are several ways to develop and use these images in your exercise. You can find a picture of a similar site online that matches the type of disaster you are simulating. For example, showing an image of another manufacturing facility on fire and telling participants that it represents their building is often enough to draw them into the scenario. It does not need to be perfect. It just needs to feel real enough to help them visualize what is happening.

In the past, I've gone to the incident site, taken a picture and added smoke as a layer so participants can see their recognizable site, with smoke coming out of it. I used to hire a freelancer via an online specialist work marketplace, but lately I've found it just as easy to do it myself. With AI, it's even easier to generate the pictures you want from the scene of an incident.

I've also taken video and then had a freelancer add in flames, starting small and building to thick black smoke. I've shown this during exercises, and on two or three occasions, participants have looked out of the window to check that the adjacent building really wasn't on fire. With AI tools, this type of video is now very easy to generate, and they can be hyper-realistic.

You can use the picture to brief participants at the beginning of the exercise, but to make it more realistic, you could send the image to participants' mobile phones ahead of the start, just as it might happen in real life. Then, the incident team could meet in response to this alert.

Sending the picture in the same format and methodology it might be received in reality adds to the verisimilitude. It could be sent via a WhatsApp group, through the organization's mass alert system or as part of a message calling out the crisis management team. It could also be sent via email with a short message or as part of a simulated social media post. The picture doesn't always have to be used at the start. It can be part of injects throughout the exercise.

When using props or pictures, it's easy to get carried away trying to find the perfect image or generating exactly the right AI version. This can become a distraction and take time away from developing the overall exercise. Remember, pictures should enhance realism, not become the main focus or an opportunity to show off your AI picture or video generation skills.

Reporting from the scene

A news report from the scene of the incident can be another way to introduce the scenario and explain what has happened on-site. People are used to learning about incidents from the news, on TV or radio, so a news reporter speaking either from on-site or from a studio can introduce the scenario more effectively than the exercise director reading it out.

When I first did this, several years ago, I used to hire an ex-news reporter who would go near the site and film a piece to camera as if she were reporting live. This worked really well and got the participants engaged straight away. The challenge was the cost and logistics. The reporter had to travel to the site, record the segment, which, before mobile phones, involved hiring someone to film it, then it needed to be edited and burnt onto a CD to be played at the start of the exercise.

All this was expensive, and the clip could only really be used at the beginning because later in the scenario, news coverage would depend on how the incident management team handled the situation.

Another simple tool is a voicemail recording. This could be made to sound like it was left on a participant's phone, informing them of the incident, giving details and inviting them to a crisis meeting or it could be information from the scene of the incident from someone caught up in the incident. You could send this by email as an audio file, or include it in the introductory slides.

Use of avatars and AI presenters to break news

The use of avatars, AI-generated news presenters you can feed a script to, has changed the dynamic of using a news site to provide injects and the initial description of the incident. The avatar could be in a virtual media studio, like a newsreader, or appear on-site with a video or still image of the scene behind them. They can then introduce the scenario.

Since these clips only take minutes to produce and render, they can even be created during the exercise. So, depending on the actions of the incident team, the avatar can respond with fresh news commentary, forcing the team to react to what's being said publicly.

This makes the exercise much more realistic and introduces a live communications challenge for the team. Some avatar-generating platforms will not allow you to create news clips on controversial subjects, such as disasters or terrorist attacks, for fear of spreading disinformation. Other platforms are more flexible and allow you to create your own content.

Producing media during the exercise is a really effective way to drive the scenario and ensure the communications team and senior managers stay fully engaged. Although mainstream media organizations are usually pretty good at getting their reports factually right in an exercise, you can have them put out false information that the organization then has to correct. This could be around the number of casualties, the extent of the incident or the type of hazard involved.

Radio clips

Radio broadcasts can also be used, either at the start or during the exercise. I've used a mobile phone recording app to record a 'radio' segment. You could add a jingle at the beginning of the clip to make it clear it's radio, and whether it's national or local.

As people tend to listen to radio less these days, this might not have the same impact as it did a decade ago. However, it's still a useful tool, especially if you're looking for variety in delivery styles.

Media articles

Media and social media can play a significant role in both exercises and real-life incidents. I'm a big believer that even the simplest exercise should include some kind of media or social media component. At the most basic level, this could be a mocked-up news article presented in an envelope, or displayed on a slide, styled to resemble the BBC News website or a local newspaper.

Before AI, these articles had to be laboriously written, often taking an hour or two per piece. With AI, news articles can be generated in minutes. You can specify the tone and outlet: for example, 'Write this article in the style of *The Times*'. However, there is now a temptation to write too much or produce too many articles. Unless your exercise lasts several hours, much of this won't be read, and time spent developing content could be wasted.

You can also deliberately insert inaccuracies into articles that the team will need to spot and correct. This adds pressure and tests whether they are properly monitoring information. You can reinforce the effect by asking other role-players to refer to the article, either repeating what they have read or questioning whether it is true. This encourages the team to challenge misinformation rather than accept it at face value.

Another way of getting media to play into your exercise is to give participants, especially those responsible for communications, a media briefing pack. This could be a two- or three-sided document that provides an overview of the media coverage of the incident, including the main talking points, social media sentiment, whether the coverage is improving or worsening and headlines from various newspapers or news websites. This method is easier to understand and consider than a collection of individual articles. It is also practical because many organizations have media monitoring services that track articles about them daily. If the organization already uses such a service, you can utilize their existing format and simply include your articles.

Simulating social media

For some organizations that provide goods or services to the public, social media can be an important part of their response, and they maintain a managed presence online. Other organizations may have no social media presence or a somewhat half-hearted one, which they update only occasionally. Similar to media articles, social media posts can be distributed on paper. In the past, I've even handwritten them on Post-its and stuck them on a whiteboard in the incident room. This at least encourages the communications team to get up from the table and read them.

For me, using numerous social media channels isn't necessary. We typically simulate social media as coming from 'X' and treat it as a generic platform. We've never had anyone in an exercise say, 'We're not on X, we're on Facebook, so this isn't realistic.'

When using social media in exercises, you don't need multiple channels. All we do is simulate the organization's social media page and post everything there. In our simulated tweets, we include the poster's number of followers, reposts and likes. This allows the organization to assess, based on the numbers, whether to ignore the post or engage with the person. A hashtag may also be used in the posts to see whether the organization picks it up and uses it themselves.

Providing a handful of social media posts is enough to convey to the communications team that there's an active online response; you don't need to create dozens. Just a few relevant ones will do the job.

Using a media and social media simulator

For PlanB Consulting's exercises, we've developed a portal called MITS (media incident training simulator) for managing media and social media injects. Participants can log into the portal during the exercise, and this is where the media and social media elements play out. The portal is discrete to the exercise, ensuring that nothing shared within it is accidentally made public.

MITS allows us to break news and social media stories throughout the scenario. Relevant media sources are researched and then simulated within the portal. During the exercise, media and social media posts are released periodically, and participants must monitor the portal, inform the incident team and decide how to respond.

One advantage of MITS is that it allows participants to post responses as if to their own organization's website or social channels. Before we had MITS, communications teams were often asked to draft a holding statement, but since they had nowhere to publish it, they would simply pretend to write one. With MITS, teams can genuinely post their statements on the platform, providing a realistic environment for practice.

MITS is operated by an individual during the exercise, who monitors the organization's responses and can quickly generate reactive media content, such as a journalist commenting on the holding statement, or people on social media responding to the organization's posts.

There are several providers of similar software which serve a similar role, as well as exercise software providers that include media and social media features within their platforms.

Internal communications

Getting the organization to exercise its internal communication is an integral part of its response. In a similar way to press statements, it is easy to say they will be written but more difficult actually to write them. Simulating this activity in an exercise can be tricky, as different organizations have different ways of communicating with staff. They may use the 'chain of command', where the message is conveyed through layers of management; there may be an informal intranet where staff communications are posted; or messages may be sent via email or a mass notification system.

There are several ways to simulate internal communications. If the 'chain of command' is used, then the communication can be written, and it can be agreed with the exercise director that this has been sent to managers to brief their staff. If the organization has an intranet, you can again ask participants to write the text as if it were posted there. To add realism, the post can be sent to role-players or directing staff, who can then factor the content into their injects during the exercise.

If the message would be sent by email or mass notification system, the text can still be written, and it can be assumed by exercise staff that the communication has gone out.

PlanB Consulting has also used our social media simulator, MITS, to mimic the organization's intranet or internal platform. It has a space where participants can post internal communications, and we only accept that staff have been briefed once the message has been posted there.

Call with regulators, government bodies or parent organizations

If the organization being exercised is regulated, then preparing for a call or issuing a statement to the regulator can be an important part of the simulated response.

EXAMPLE

Regulators taking part

When I was working in the water industry as an emergency planning manager, we were expected by the regulator to run company-wide response exercises at least once a year. Whenever there was a company-wide exercise, our contact in the government department that regulated the water industry was always keen that reporting the incident to the regulator be part of exercise activities. During the exercises, they would play themselves and expect a phone call to inform them of the incident.

They would also phone the organization's crisis team and say, 'The Minister is going into Parliament in 30 minutes, please can you give me a brief so I can update them?' This put the chief executive under pressure to produce a comprehensive brief and really added realism to the exercise.

You may want to approach the regulator, other government bodies or a parent organization to play themselves during the exercise. This has a number of benefits: it adds realism, gives the real individual a sense of what kind of briefing they would receive, and after the exercise, you can discuss whether the briefing met their expectations. It also demonstrates that the organization is taking its responsibilities seriously. Real individuals can ask probing questions, as they understand the subject and know what information they need. Some organizations may not feel comfortable involving real regulators in their exercise and prefer to simulate their involvement.

In larger regulated organizations, there's often a department whose role is to liaise with the regulator. A member of this team can play an excellent role as the regulator in the exercise. They understand the kinds of questions the regulator might ask and can challenge the team with more difficult queries. The role – players as part of an inject, can phone into the incident room to arrange a time for an interview with the 'regulator'. This gives participants the chance to prepare and think through their responses.

Often, as the finale of an exercise, I've arranged a briefing to the chair, regulator, parent company or another senior individual. This helps the organization gather its thoughts and prepare a structured summary. If you are the person being briefed with a few tough questions, it ensures those doing the briefing are properly prepared.

Getting the real person, even if they're only available for 15 minutes, can enhance the realism of the exercise. If the real individual isn't available, a member of the exercise team can make the call and play the role. Make sure they are aware of the situation and have thought through some difficult questions to ensure the call challenges the members of the incident team.

Media interviews

In the days before the widespread use of video conferencing, if you wanted to practise a senior manager being interviewed as part of an exercise, you had to hire an interviewer, a camera operator and perhaps a sound technician. They would need to travel to the location of your exercise and conduct the interview on-site.

The alternative was to take the spokesperson to a hired studio to record the interview. All these options were expensive, and unless there was a large budget for the exercise or the senior manager specifically wanted to practise their interview skills, this often wasn't done. As a result, media response was frequently overlooked or under-practised.

These days, many media interviews are conducted via video conferencing, with the interviewer in the media studio and the interviewee located anywhere. Video interviews can now be included in most exercises if required. As part of the scenario, a media outlet can request an interview. It's usually best to agree in advance whether the organization wants the interview to proceed, otherwise members of the incident team may refuse the request.

A time can be scheduled, and the media team can then develop key messages and help the spokesperson prepare. To add realism, a real journalist could conduct the interview, budget allowing, or a member of the exercise team could take on the role. It's important that the interviewer is well prepared, able to ask difficult questions and to apply pressure. While confrontational interviews are less common in modern broadcasting, applying some pressure during the exercise can give the interviewee valuable muscle memory and highlight the need to be well prepared.

By conducting a video interview, the exercise director can also provide feedback on the setting, the individual's mannerisms, body language and overall impression, which can be very useful in real events.

Casualties

In your exercise, you may wish to simulate casualties, either members of staff or the public, especially during live exercises or practical drills. Including casualties in your scenario can be valuable for practising:

- Casualty triage procedures
- Communication with emergency services
- Reporting from the scene of the incident to an organization incident management team
- First aid skills
- The psychological response to attending a mass casualty event
- Scene management and coordination under pressure

In large national or government-led exercises in the UK, volunteers are often recruited to play the role of casualties. For example, in a scenario involving an underground train crash, volunteers would be briefed on their injuries and made up to look realistically wounded. They would act out their roles, and responders would treat the scenario as a real event. In some cases, amputees are included to enhance realism, allowing a participant to call out, 'It's my leg!' while responders are confronted with the scenario of a limbless person with a severed leg.

This level of realism might not be appropriate for all exercises, and sourcing volunteers can be time-consuming and, unless publicly beneficial, expensive.

A more practical approach is to ask staff members to play the role of casualties. Make-up and fake blood are not always necessary; if participants remain in character and describe their injuries in role, this can be effective. In drills I've run, I've also included 'witnesses' or individuals in shock.

Participants are then required to:

- Approach and assess if the person is injured
- Gather witness statements
- Record names and details
- Manage the psychological state of those at the scene

For simulating an unconscious or deceased person, you can use a stuffed boiler suit, perhaps dressed in a company uniform, to represent a body. Attach a tag to indicate their condition, e.g. 'unconscious' or 'deceased'. This provides a useful prompt for participants to rehearse scene safety, initial assessment and subsequent control of the incident area.

Dealing with groups of people

Dealing with a large number of staff or members of the public may be part of the issues your organization faces when responding to an incident. The pressure of an incident, even if it is relatively minor, can have different effects on people and requires good people management skills. This should be practised during an exercise.

EXAMPLE

'The unruly mob'

I ran a live exercise for a client who wanted to simulate the evacuation of part of their campus office site. The location had only one road in and out, and they were concerned that an incident blocking this route would trap staff on-site, with no easy way to leave except by walking across several farmers' fields, which were either usually ploughed or had crops in them. The exercise aimed to practise managing a group of staff stuck on-site and unable to leave.

The scenario introduced the challenges staff might realistically face, including being trapped on-site, being escorted to the site incident management team, needing to pick up children from school, caring for elderly relatives, requiring medication or becoming emotionally distressed or angry. We asked for 20 volunteers to play the role of these stranded employees and designated a team of responders to manage them during the exercise.

We gave the group a name, 'the unruly mob', and assigned each volunteer a character trait (angry, quiet, hysterical, bullying) and a personal issue (e.g. missing medication, diabetes, single parent needing childcare). This added fantastic realism. Each volunteer played their part convincingly, and the post-exercise debrief revealed that those tasked with managing the group gained a much deeper insight into the complexity of managing staff in a real incident.

This is a relatively simple, cost-effective way to add realism to a live exercise or drill. Giving each person a back story and character profile in advance ensures consistency and keeps the exercise realistic. Local staff often excel in these roles as they know the company culture and site layout, and can anticipate which actions will most challenge responders.

A short briefing is essential to prevent volunteers from playing their role too intensely or traumatizing participants. In reality, managing people during incidents can be unpredictable and difficult. Simulating these dynamics helps build resilience and 'muscle memory' for those who may one day need to deal with affected staff or the public in a crisis.

Use of props

Models, props, maps and plans can all be used to add to the realism of the exercise and help those taking part to visualize the incident and to formulate their response.

The use of props and the set-up of mini-exercises can be an effective way to train staff to respond. This is especially valuable for on-site managers or staff who would be required to respond to an incident at their workplace and are likely to be the first people on-site or involved in post-incident response. Where specific responses are required, such as in a hazardous materials spill, this is a good way to practise responder skills. I used coloured water poured on the floor and a container of hazardous liquid on its side as props, then had the local response team respond. A few visual clues to the type of incident they are dealing with are all that is required. Having the stands set up in locations where the incident might realistically occur helps add to the realism and enhances the training value.

USE OF PROPS IN DIFFERENT 'STANDS'

I was asked to develop a training course for a train track maintenance organization. They had engineering maintenance crews working at different times of the night. They had a designated duty engineer who, if there were an accident on-site involving their people out working, would have to manage the scene in conjunction with the company's crisis team and the emergency services. I wrote a two-day duty manager course that covered all aspects of their role, from initial actions at the scene to reporting to the crisis team, working with emergency services and preserving evidence on-site. Half of the training was classroom-based, and the other half was focused on practising the skills in a realistic setting.

On the final afternoon of the course, I arranged a series of three stands or mini-exercises to practise the skills they had been taught. A 'stand' is a word used in the military to describe a mini-exercise where soldiers practise a certain skill they have just learnt. There are usually a number of them, each focusing on an aspect of training, and participants then rotate through to complete all the stands.

In small teams of three to four people, the duty engineers were introduced to the exercise, given a scene to respond to, and then had to act as they had been taught during training. The teams had 10 minutes to complete the exercise before receiving a debrief on their performance. As the training took place at their training school, there was a rail track, signals, and buildings, all of which we used as props to make each mini-exercise realistic. We didn't have additional staff to play casualties or role-players, so as each group approached their stand, one or two people were taken aside, briefed on their role as casualties or members of the public and inserted into the scene.

Setting up the different stands with props was simple. A ladder lying on the ground with a groaning casualty was all that was needed to simulate a fall from height, the need to deal with the casualty, ascertain what happened, report the incident and preserve forensics at the scene. Another stand was a 'casualty' trapped under a rail maintenance vehicle, who was presumed dead, requiring participants to manage the scene. The 'casualty' was played by a dummy in a company boiler suit. The props were simple and only suggested an incident; elaborate scene setting was not required. The mini-exercises helped bring the classroom sessions to life and gave participants the confidence to manage an incident scene if required.

EXAMPLE

Use of a model

As part of my role as a water company emergency planning manager, I had to make sure our plans were coordinated with multiple agencies. I was asked to run an exercise on the collapse of a sewer, which would lead to flooding over a wide area. A sewer was identified which would cause flooding over a wide area. I wanted to design a multi-agency exercise with a multi-agency team on-site, feeding back to their respective higher commands. To add realism, I decided to have the on-site team co-located at the incident scene, near where the collapse would occur. I hired a church hall for the exercise to take place in, and at the start we walked to the potential collapse site.

Rather than providing a standard map to show the spread of flooding, I had a physical model built of the local area, complete with contours, houses and roads. We used Perspex overlays to track the real-time progress of the flooding and show which houses were affected. We also had model vehicles so emergency services and local authorities could decide where to set up cordons and position command vehicles. This all added to the realism of the exercise and forced those attending to make real-time decisions, such as where to place the cordon, and they could then report this to their control rooms. I could have used a map, but having the model made the response much more tangible. I reused the model several times after the exercise to train internal teams on the same incident.

EXAMPLE

Use of site plans and paper lorries to verify a recovery strategy

For a logistics client, we aimed to validate a contingency plan that, in the event their central UK sorter was lost, would allow four local depots to temporarily assume its role. There had been much internal debate over whether the four yards would become too congested with the volume of vehicles arriving, parking and leaving. To validate the contingency plan, we used printed plans of each depot and cut out to-scale lorry icons. During the exercise, each site had two to three participants, including the site manager. Attending the exercise was the linehaul logistics manager, who oversees vehicle movements throughout the country and in and out of sites. We simulated 12–13 hours of typical nightly vehicle movements across the four depots. We progressed through the exercise hour-by-hour, with the linehaul logistics manager calling out which vehicles were arriving and leaving each of the sites. The depot teams would then place their paper lorries on the plans, checking for adequate space for vehicles to park and to come in and out of each depot without their being a traffic jam. By the end of the exercise, we had proven that the contingency plan was viable, no site had an unacceptable traffic jam and the plan was validated through the simulation.

The use of models, plans or maps helped participants visualize the scene of an incident and forced them to make practical decisions. For example, instead of just saying 'we would deploy four vehicles to the scene', they had to place them physically, revealing whether there was actually room for four, or if only two would fit. In incident management, it's often these small details that make the difference between a successful or unsuccessful response. The use of models, maps and plans ensures participants think through the specifics of their response plans in a realistic and practical way.

Verisimilitude doesn't need to be expensive or overly complicated. It's about creating a setting where, from the moment participants engage, they pick up on the visual cues and feel instinctively that what they're dealing with is real. Whether it's a mocked-up picture, a convincing role-player, a simple prop or a realistic message delivered in the right format, these elements immerse people into the scenario straight away. The aim is to make them respond as they would in a real incident without questioning or overthinking. Believability is the goal, not perfection. If it looks and feels real, it drives realistic behaviours and creates memorable learning that sticks long after the exercise is over.

KEY LEARNINGS

- Verisimilitude enhances immersion; if it feels real to participants, it is real for exercise purposes.
- Low-cost props like police or firefighter hats can effectively simulate external agencies and set the tone.
- Images and AI-generated visuals add emotional depth and realism, helping teams visualize the scenario.
- Pre-recorded or AI-generated news reports can deliver injects with more credibility than direct briefings from staff.
- Sending scenario content through realistic channels, like WhatsApp or internal alerts, boosts authenticity.
- Simulated media and social media elements help test communication teams under pressure and misinformation.
- Casualty role play, even with minimal props, helps teams practise triage, scene management and staff care.
- Simulating group dynamics (e.g. 'unruly mob') helps participants understand the complexity of people management.
- Models, site plans and paper-based simulations drive practical decision-making and validate response strategies.
- Believability, not perfection, is the key; small, well-placed details can trigger genuine responses and lasting learning.

16

Developing tabletop questions or injects

In this chapter, you will learn about:

1. Developing tabletop exercise questions
2. Developing scripts and briefing documents
3. Developing a set of injects for a SIMEX
4. Guidance on writing injects

Once your storyboard has been agreed upon, you will need to convert it into a series of chronological injects to drive the exercise forward. For a tabletop exercise, using one inject per phase is a practical approach. This inject outlines how the scenario has progressed, and the exercise director then poses a set of questions for participants to explore based on the updated situation. In a SIMEX, there will typically be several injects per phase.

Developing tabletop exercise questions

When developing tabletop questions, start with the exercise objectives and the intended outcome for each phase. There are several ways to structure your questions, depending on the outcomes you're aiming for. The storyboard also needs to be considered. When delivering the questions during the exercise, participants should first be provided with the scenario or an updated scenario, followed by an initial question. The questions can take several forms. See Table 16.1.

TABLE 16.1 Tabletop possible questions

No.	Type of question	Description	Examples
1.	Open question	Ask an open question.	• 'How would you deal with the situation?' • 'What are you going to do?' • 'What is the impact of this incident?' Open questions avoid directing participants and allows insight into how they naturally approach the situation and what plans and procedures they use to guide their response.
2.	Functional question	This targets specific team functions.	• For people: 'What information, advice and support will you give to staff affected by the cyber-attack?' • For technology: 'How long will it take to rebuild the systems affected by ransomware?' • For communications: 'Will you issue a holding statement?' or 'What will your overall communication strategy be?' • For operations: 'How will you continue to deliver services to customers, and which activities have workarounds?' Questions could be directed to the participants as a whole or they could be split into functional groups and answer a question tailored to their group.
3.	Developing a response	Ask about the organization's response to the scenario.	• 'What is your working strategy for dealing with this incident?' • 'How will you continue to serve customers, and at what level?' • 'How will you recover operations, and how long will it take?' • 'How will you develop a communications strategy for this incident?' • 'What activities will you prioritize in the recovery and why? Produce an outline timeline for recovery.' Follow-up questions may focus on required communications, staff instructions and procurement actions to support recovery.

(continued)

TABLE 16.1 (Continued)

No.	Type of question	Description	Examples
4.	**Responding to new information**	New information which changes the situation.	• 'The casualty has died.' • 'The incident is now trending on social media.' • 'Your backups are corrupted.' • 'The entire warehouse is destroyed.' Provide new information via an inject, which changes the situation. The aim is not to overwhelm, but to highlight realistic developments and encourage consideration of worst-case scenarios and how to manage them if they occur. The team must decide if it alters their response.
5.	**Decision point**	Pose a decision requiring judgement where there may be no clear right answer. The team must evaluate available information to make the call.	• 'Shall we disconnect our systems from the internet?' • 'Shall we put out a holding statement or wait for further information?' • 'Should we activate the backup site even though systems might recover soon?' • 'Do we go public with the data breach now or wait until we know the full impact?' Provide new information via an inject, which changes the situation. The aim is not to overwhelm, but to highlight realistic developments and encourage consideration of worst-case scenarios and how to manage them if they occur. The team must decide if it alters their response.

(continued)

TABLE 16.1 (Continued)

No.	Type of question	Description	Examples
6.	**Task-based questions**	These ask the team to evaluate or gather information, to demonstrate incident management skills or display their knowledge.	• 'Develop the strategic intent for this incident.' • With the information available to you, conduct the first incident team meeting.' • 'What are your priorities in this incident?' • 'What are your information gaps, and where can this information be found?' • 'Which processes must be recovered first, and why?' • 'What actions will you take in the first hour?' • 'What direction will you give the operations (bronze) teams?' • 'Develop a media statement.' Make the team demonstrate they can actually carry out this task.
7.	**Plan or procedures prompt**	The question is about an aspect of the plan.	• 'Using the invocation criteria in the plan, should the plan be activated?' • 'What strategy should be used to respond to the incident?' • 'What specific plans and procedures apply to this situation?' • 'Do the procedures provide clear guidance for this situation, or would they need to be adapted? If adaptation is necessary, what changes would be required?' • 'Looking at the list of stakeholders identified within the plan, are there any stakeholders for this incident that should be added to the plan?' Make sure that they have access to copies of the plan.

(continued)

TABLE 16.1 (Continued)

No.	Type of question	Description	Examples
8.	Sub-questions	After an initial question is answered, you may use follow-up questions to explore specific elements further. The number and nature of these will depend on the time available and the quality of the original response.	• 'What assumptions are you making about how this incident will evolve?' • 'If your assumptions prove false, what's your backup plan?' • 'What are you assuming about the availability of external support or contractors?' • 'If your planned approach fails, what's your Plan B?' • 'How would your response change if this incident continues for another 7 days?' • 'What would you do if another, unrelated crisis occurred at the same time?' It is always worth having a couple of spare questions for the phase, just in case the team gets through their questions faster than the time allocated.

When writing these questions, consider developing your own model answers. Prepare a slide with expected responses to help guide the debrief. If participants come up with better answers, acknowledge this; it's part of the learning process.

Developing scripts and a briefing document

As described in Chapter 3, in a SIMEX, instead of using individual injects as information to drive the scenario, inputs for participants are delivered to the team through scripts or briefing documents.

The scripts can be detailed, containing half a page or more of information, or short, comprising just three or four lines. The concept is to give each person a piece of the jigsaw of information, which they then bring into a team meeting to share what they know. Each participant may receive different information, or some may receive contradictory details. A key part of the exercise is for the team to identify where the scripts conflict and resolve those discrepancies.

Another method to conduct this type of exercise is to give team members a briefing document that includes information on the incident, along with briefing papers as if they have been prepared by a specialist within the organization. For example, the briefing for a cyber incident might consist of an incident situation report, a ransom note, a technical assessment, media coverage and a legal briefing. Each stage of the exercise can then introduce a new update and a corresponding set of documents. These could be used as well as individual injects or reduce the need for the numbers of injects.

Developing a set of injects for SIMEX

The starting point for developing injects is the storyboard. This provides a list of actions or activities for each phase or time period of the exercise. From here, each element needs to be developed into an inject by noting the approximate time it will be delivered, who will deliver it, who will receive it and the method of delivery. Once the delivery channel has been chosen, the inject should be scripted and formatted appropriately. Finally, the expected response should be documented.

Developing injects shouldn't require a great deal of extra thinking, as most of the groundwork will have already been done during storyboard development. At that stage, each stakeholder should have been identified, the storyline confirmed and the reasoning behind each element considered. So, by the time you're writing the injects, the purpose and intent of each one should already be clear.

A structured list of injects should now be created. This is typically done using a table or spreadsheet, with standard headings across the top and each item entered as a separate row. Each inject should include the following information:

Reference number: Assign a unique number so all facilitators know which injects have been delivered.

Approximate timing: Indicate when you expect the inject to be issued. The exercise director may adjust this based on exercise flow.

From whom: Specify who is delivering the inject: a person or organization.

To whom: Indicate whether the inject is directed to the entire team or a specific individual.

Delivery method: This could be via phone call, email, media simulator or in person. (Refer to Chapter 15 on verisimilitude.)

Script: Provide the exact text to be delivered. If the inject is an email, format it with sender, subject line and body text.

Expected response: For each inject, planners should clearly document the expected response it aims to elicit. This could include an answer to a specific question, a decision the team must make, a shift in how the incident is perceived or the addition of information that enhances situational awareness. In some cases, the inject might intentionally act as a 'red herring' that the team is expected to recognize as irrelevant and dismiss appropriately. Clearly articulating the expected response in advance clarifies the purpose of the inject and ensures it directly supports the exercise objectives and intended learning outcomes.

Actual response: Document the team's real response during the exercise. This could be scored (e.g. 3 = full response, 2 = partial, 1 = none, if looking for quantitative scoring) and used in the post-exercise report.

Notes: Include delivery tone (e.g. panicked, under pressure), any contingency actions or additional context for the inject.

Guidance for writing injects

The following guidance can help ensure that your injects are realistic, inclusive and effective in supporting the objectives of your exercise, and that you have enough of them.

How many injects? For a three-hour exercise, approximately between 50 and 70 injects is a reasonable estimate, if the exercise is being run continuously. If there are multiple phases that don't require injects, such as a team meeting or a senior manager briefing, less will be required. The exact number will depend on the content and intent of each inject. It is generally better to have too many than too few, as this gives the exercise director flexibility in pacing and content delivery.

Avoid real names for casualties: Including casualties is a great way to involve the human resources department and introduce people-focused elements into your exercises. However, I'm slightly superstitious and always feel that if I use someone's name in the organization as a casualty and they have an accident soon after, it might be blamed on the exercise! To avoid this, I suggest using placeholders such as Mr/Ms X, Y or Z.

Use discretion with customer names: If you refer to customers in your injects, consider whether it is appropriate to use their real names or agree with the design team to use made-up names. Take care to protect privacy, brand sensitivity and reputational concerns.

Use a realistic tone and delivery: People under pressure at the scene of an incident are unlikely to speak in calm, structured statements. They may struggle to find the right words, be emotional or have poor phone reception. Injects delivered verbally should reflect this. Encourage role-players to use their acting skills and deliver messages as if the incident were real.

Stick to the script: Injects often contain information essential to building situational awareness. Ensure that role-players do not go off-script or improvise in ways that omit or dilute this information.

Write injects dynamically when needed: Injects can be written during the exercise if the scenario takes an unexpected turn. This can help bring the team back on track or allow the exercise director to explore a new issue that has emerged. Flexibility in inject creation can enrich the realism and relevance of the exercise.

Include diversity and inclusion where appropriate: When scenarios involve the public or groups of people, consider whether the people represented in your injects reflect real-world diversity. Do they include elderly people, children, people of different genders, ethnicities, cultures or faith groups? Cultural insensitivity in an organization's response can damage its reputation. Including this dimension in your injects is a powerful way to raise awareness during an exercise.

EXAMPLE

Example Inject 1: An inject phoned into the incident team

Reference Number: 003

Timing: 12.30

From: Bill Smith, Divisional Director, at the incident scene

To: Crisis Management Team

How: Telephone (suggest using speakerphone)

Script: 'Hi, this is Bill Smith at the Rankin Building. I've taken command. At 1200 there was an explosion in the basement. The fire spread through the lift shafts. Although the alarm was triggered, the west wing escape was blocked by smoke. We believe we evacuated everyone, but staff are scattered, some on-site, some in cafes, some unaccounted for. Emergency services are on-site. The building appears completely destroyed. I'll call back in 30 minutes. Please handle external calls, I can't keep answering the phone.'

Expected Response: The team should convene an incident meeting, develop a checklist of on-site actions, assign a casualty coordinator and prepare a holding statement.

Actual Response: (*To be completed during exercise*)

Notes: Deliver in a panicked tone with possible poor line quality.

EXAMPLE

Example Inject 2: An email inject

Reference Number: 015

Timing: 13.30

From: BBC News Desk

To: Communications Coordinator

How: Email

Script:

> **To**: Hilary Jones
>
> **From**: BBC News Desk
>
> **Subject**: Explosion at the Rankin Building
>
> Dear Hilary,
>
> We have a reporter on the scene and would like to interview a senior manager at 18.20 for the Six O'Clock News. This can be done from our Glasgow studio or via Zoom. Please confirm within the hour.
>
> Regards,
> Jane Dean
>
> Deputy Editor, Six O'Clock News

Expected Response: Decide who will give the interview and begin preparation and briefing.

Actual Response: (*To be completed during exercise*)

Notes: The chair has requested the organization engage with media, so this request should not be refused.

EXAMPLE

Example Inject 3: A face-to-face inject

Reference Number: 021

Timing: 14.00

From: Graham Wright: Facilities Manager

To: Crisis Team

How: Face-to-face briefing: he has just driven from the site of the incident

Script: I have just come from the site of the incident, and things do not seem too severe. I spoke to some staff and the evacuation appears to have been conducted in an orderly fashion, and only a few minor injuries occurred from people slipping on the stairs. The building is damaged, but I think it will only take a couple of days to repair, though I haven't been able to get close enough because of the cordon.

Expected Response: This contradicts all previous information, so see if the team quizzes them further or revisits the information they have from the site.

Actual Response: (*To be completed during exercise*)

Notes: If questioned closely by the team, Graham can admit they arrived on-site an hour after the incident and were not really able to see how badly the building was damaged, and he only spoke to one member of staff.

Creating media and social media injects: The first thing you need to decide is how you'll deliver the media and social media scripts during the exercise. Will they be issued on paper as injects? Revealed to participants via a social media simulator? Or presented as part of a media briefing pack? Once you've chosen the format, you can begin writing the injects. If the media or social media scripts are short, you can include them directly in the inject spreadsheet or table. However, if they're longer, especially media articles, I usually keep the full text in a separate appendix, attached to the exercise instructions.

EXAMPLE

Example Inject 4: Social media post

Reference Number: 025

Timing: 13.10

From: A number of X social media posts

To: Crisis Team

How: Delivered by social media simulator

Script:

@LucyF_B
Can someone please tell me what's happening at the Rankin building? My husband "Big B" (Brian) works there and I haven't heard from him since this morning. He left his phone at his desk. I'm terrified. If anyone knows anything, please DM me.

#RankinFire🔥

362 comments 1,049 retweets
3,872 likes 412.5K impression

@Samia_FM

I used to be a facilities assistant in that building. We reported fire risks SO many times. I even put out a small fire myself once!!! Management brushed it off, told me not to make a fuss and keep quiet. This incident was preventable.

#RankinFire #Negligence

56 comments 327 retweets
964 likes 226.9K impressions

@InTheKnow2025
A friend who knows someone inside says there are at least 10 more people unaccounted for... and they think the worst. Why aren't they telling us the truth?

#RankinFire #CoverUp?

3 comments 23 retweets
5 likes 100 impressions

Expected Response: Use the hashtag #RankinFire on social media posts. Get in touch with LucyF_B and tell her husband is safe. Find out more about Samia_FM to see if her story is true. Ignore InTheKnow2025 as his comments are not getting traction.

Actual Response: (*To be completed during exercise*)

Updating the storyboard after injects have been written

During the development of an inject, it's common to stray slightly from the original storyboard. As you work through the details of each inject, you may discover better ways to present the story or improve the learning experience.

If you're particularly diligent, you may choose to revise the storyboard to align it with the injects. However, in practice, this is not always necessary. The storyboard primarily serves as an initial framework to guide development. By the time you reach the inject stage, it has usually fulfilled its purpose.

Final task

Once all the injects are agreed upon, the final task is to produce printed copies of the incidents. These can be used on the day of the exercise, either to give to the role-player entering the inject or to the appropriate exercise participant. I usually copy and paste them into a single continuous document, with one page per insert, and then print them on A4 paper, single-sided.

KEY LEARNINGS

- Injects are used to bring the scenario to life and keep the exercise moving forward.
- Tabletop questions should always link directly to the exercise's learning objectives and the storyboard.
- A range of tabletop question types – open, functional, strategic, decision-based and task-focused – helps test different aspects of the team's thinking.
- Sub-questions are useful to explore initial responses further and add depth to the discussion.
- Each SIMEX inject should be carefully planned, including timing, delivery method and who it's from and to.
- It's important to record actual team responses during the exercise to support learning and evaluation.
- As injects are written, the storyboard may evolve; this is natural and can improve the final product.

- It's better to write too many injects than too few to allow flexibility during the exercise.
- Injects should be realistic, avoid using real names and reflect diversity and human experience.
- Every inject should have a clear purpose, with an expected response that supports the learning outcomes.

17

Evaluating the incident team's performance and assessing the exercise

In this chapter, you will learn about:

1. Different ways to evaluate an exercise team
2. How to conduct a quantified assessment of the exercise team
3. The role of the umpire
4. How to assess the overall success of the exercise and feedback forms

All exercises should be evaluated to identify learning points and improve team performance. At its simplest, evaluation can be carried out by the exercise director, who draws on their experience and incident management knowledge to highlight key observations, which are then captured in the post-exercise report and shared with participants. At its most sophisticated, evaluation may involve multiple umpires observing the incident team's performance and reporting against a range of frameworks or predefined evaluation criteria.

The evaluation of an exercise is a crucial part of its design and should be considered throughout the development process, not as an afterthought. How participants and teams will be assessed or evaluated is an important discussion to have with the sponsor, as different organizations prefer their exercises to be reported and evaluated in different ways. Umpires and others responsible for reporting on team performance must be provided with clear guidance on what to observe and how to evaluate the team.

Evaluation considerations

The UK Resilience Academy defines evaluation as 'a systematic assessment of exercise objectives, design and delivery'.[1] They state that 'The process should measure against recognized, predetermined criteria that enable the team to determine any discrepancies between intended and actual outcomes.' If incident teams are to continue improving, lessons learnt during exercises must be identified and documented in the post-exercise report.

During an exercise, if a different team undertook the same scenario with the same injects or questions, they would likely produce different outcomes. Even if the same team repeated the exercise, some of their responses would vary. What's important in evaluating the exercise is not to assess every action blow-by-blow, but to focus on areas where meaningful changes can be made and where the response can be improved in future exercises or incidents.

If the team was too large, key roles were missing, or it operated at too low a level, these issues can be observed, documented and used to inform improvements. Adjustments can be made, the plan revised and the team observed in a subsequent exercise to assess whether performance has improved.

Observations such as the team not using the plan at all or struggling with decision-making highlight training needs. These areas can then be addressed so they no longer present challenges in the next exercise.

Commenting on the minutiae of every team decision or action, for me, adds limited value. If circumstances had been slightly different or if a different team had been involved, the same information might have led to an entirely different decision. Often, it's only in hindsight that we can judge whether a decision contributed to the success of the response or might have attracted criticism. Decisions that initially appear wrong may, in fact, turn out to be the right call.

Of course, there are some absolute instances where a decision is clearly incorrect. For example, if a team decided to pay a cyber ransom to a proscribed terrorist group, that would be illegal under UK law, and it would be entirely appropriate to label this decision as wrong. Similarly, in specific scenarios such as responding to a chemical hazard, there may be established best practices or documented procedures. If the team deviates from these, it should be noted and commented on in both the debrief and the post-exercise report. For this reason, I believe that including a detailed, moment-by-moment commentary on the team's actions in a post-exercise report generally doesn't add value, unless a response was clearly inappropriate, against established procedures or unlawful.

During an exercise, umpires should focus their evaluation on three key areas: structure, process and behaviours. Structure refers to how the team is set up, including who is in it, whether the hierarchy functions effectively, and whether roles, responsibilities and levels of authority are clearly defined and operate as intended in practice. Process involves observing whether individuals and the team follow the procedures outlined in the response plans and whether they demonstrate the incident management skills appropriate to the tasks they are performing. While behaviours can also be evaluated, it is most effective when predefined behavioural criteria are in place, so that all participants are aware of what is expected of them and assessments are consistent and objective.

As part of the evaluation process, the last two post-exercise reports should be reviewed to identify previous observations and recommendations. These reports should either be examined before the exercise, so that key points can be included within the evaluation criteria, or reviewed before writing the new post-exercise report. If the same observations or recommendations appear repeatedly, this should be highlighted and commented upon in the final evaluation.

Evaluation against a recognized framework

There is currently no single, universally recognized exercise evaluation standard within business continuity and crisis management practice. Documents such as ISO 22301 (Security and resilience – Business continuity management systems – Requirements), ISO 22313 (Business continuity management systems – Guidance on the use of ISO 22301), ISO 22398 (Guidelines for exercises and testing), the Business Continuity Institute's Good Practice Guidelines, and NIST SP 800–84 (Guide to Test, Training, and Exercise Programmes for IT Plans and Capabilities) provide guidance on exercising and testing, but they do not define a common approach to assessing team incident response performance. While these sources offer useful inputs, practitioners must establish their own structured evaluation framework tailored to organizational context and learning objectives.

A simple evaluation criteria framework

At its simplest level, evaluating exercise participants can be done using common sense and prior experience to comment on team performance without using a criteria framework at all. Although this can provide insight, it is more effective to use a structured framework. This ensures that umpires examine all aspects of the response rather than focusing only on the most visible or obvious elements.

A helpful mnemonic for this is PICTS. It can be used for all exercises, especially for plan walkthroughs and tabletop exercises. It can be used during SIMEX or live exercises, but for these, you may want to develop a more detailed framework that I call expanded PICTS. PICTS stands for the following:

- **P: Plans:** Did the team use the available plans? Did the plans include the required information? Were the procedures within the plans followed?
- **I: Incident management:** Was the incident managed effectively? Did the team gather information to understand the situation, make informed decisions, share information appropriately and work to an agenda while coordinating with other responding teams?
- **C: Communications:** Was a list of stakeholders identified? Were their information needs recognized? Was communication timely and logged accurately, both incoming and outgoing?
- **T: Teamwork and leadership:** Did the team collaborate effectively to manage the incident? Were the right people involved, and was the team of an appropriate size?
- **S: Scenario response and recovery:** Was the response to the scenario appropriate? Did the team demonstrate the ability to resolve the incident?

These criteria can create a framework for the umpire or umpires to assess all aspects of the team's response and to use it to give feedback to participants during the debrief and afterwards in the post-exercise discussion report.

Tabletop evaluation criteria: 'What does good look like?'

However, instead of using PICTS or another framework for the evaluation of a tabletop exercise, you should develop a set of 'what does good look like?' answers for each of the questions. The following example is taken from a tabletop exercise in which the scenario was a severe fire in a manufacturing plant that resulted in numerous casualties.

The first question for the team, after they had received the scenario, was: 'What actions regarding people need to be taken, including immediate action on casualties and those missing, and what information do you give to staff at the fire evacuation point?'

Once the team had considered the issues and shared their responses, I displayed a slide with the following points: staff casualties; foreign casualties, including correctly identifying them; staff trauma; NOK of staff: identification and support; confidentiality; and social media.

I then discussed their answers in relation to this list and highlighted areas they hadn't considered. One issue that arose was that the site frequently hosted visitors, often from overseas, and the team had not taken into account foreign nationals, whether they knew their names, which company they represented or how to contact those companies if the visitors were injured, missing or deceased. Having a list of best-practice responses helps reinforce the areas that were overlooked or not fully thought through by the team.

Complex evaluation criteria frameworks (expanded PICTS)

For SIMEX, you may want to use a more comprehensive framework to evaluate the incident team, breaking PICTS down into greater detail. Below is an example of an expanded PICTS framework, offering more specific criteria under each of the five areas. This is the version I use in my evaluations, but you should adapt it to suit your organization's needs and the specific demands of your industry.

1 **Plans and procedures**
   - Was there information within the plans, or a specific checklist, or contingency plan for the situation being managed?
   - Were the guidance, predetermined strategies and information within the plans and business impact analysis (BIA) used during the exercise to inform the response, working strategy, actions and recovery?
   - Were the procedures within the plans, such as checklists, flow charts, agendas and forms, used throughout the response?

2 **Incident management**
   - Was information actively sought from all appropriate sources? Was this evaluated and considered when formulating the organization's response?

- Were the risks associated with the incident identified, monitored and were appropriate actions taken to mitigate them? Was there a shared understanding of the situation and its impacts? Was information proactively distributed, made accessible to all incident team members and communicated up or down the incident management hierarchy as needed?
- Were actions delegated to appropriate persons? Did they understand their requirements? Were they logged, and was their progress monitored?
- Was an accurate record or log of key events, actions, options, decisions and communications maintained?

3 Communications

- Was a list of interested parties for this incident documented? Were their information requirements identified? Were they contacted through appropriate channels and were the responsibilities for communicating with each interested party designated?
- Was an overall communications strategy developed; were lines to take agreed and used consistently across all internal and external communications? Were communications delivered in line with the organization's brand, tone of voice, purpose and values?
- Were communications carried out proactively and in a timely manner?
- Were the communication and messaging adapted to new developments, the changing situation and feedback from interested parties?
- Were the communications emotionally intelligent, containing an appropriate level of information and advice, and meeting the needs of interested parties? Were the victims of the incident identified, and their communication requirements fulfilled? Did the team consider the diverse needs of interested parties, including language differences, cultural backgrounds, preferences for receiving messages, ages and needs of the vulnerable? Were actions taken that complemented the communications?

4 Teamworking and leadership

- Were objectives/strategic intent written and communicated to all those responding to the incident to ensure that all were working to a common aim? Were these appropriate to the issues associated with the incident and the recovery strategy?

- Were the roles and responsibilities assigned to team members appropriate? Did they possess the skills, knowledge and understanding needed to perform their roles? Was the team size suitable, and did the team collaborate effectively to manage the incident?
- Was incident team members' welfare considered during the response, including monitoring for stress, establishing psychological safety, avoiding excessive working hours, providing refreshments, rotating staff within roles and monitoring morale? If the incident was expected to be prolonged, were team members rotated?
- Was the team directed and coordinated with a calm, decisive, effective and systematic manner by the team leader? Did they show the personal characteristics of willingness to take a leadership role: emotional stability, stress resistance, decisiveness, controlled risk-taking, self-confidence, emotional intelligence, self-awareness and empathy?
- Were decisions made at an appropriate level, with designated authorities and in line with incident guidance?

5 Scenario / response

- Were the impacts of the incident identified, was a working strategy developed for how the organization would respond to the incident, were assumptions challenged, priorities agreed and was the strategy updated to reflect changing circumstances?
- Did the team understand the requirements of the scenario and have a basic understanding of the issues associated with it, and understand the actions required to respond to the situation?
- Did the response consider the regulatory, statutory and legal requirements associated with the scenario as well as safety norms?
- Did the response consider the medium - and long-term issues as well as the immediate ones? Medium-term issues could include the recovery of operations, while long-term issues might involve rebuilding the organization's reputation.
- Was the response coordinated appropriately and did it make use of the resources, skills, capabilities and knowledge of other parties both externally and internally?

These criteria can be put in a table and then the umpires use them to guide their own thoughts. They can tick if the team have met the criteria either during or after the exercise and use this as a prompt to ensure they haven't missed any element of the response.

Development of performance indicators (PIs) tied to objectives

You may want to focus on specific aspects of the team's performance and link these to the organization's exercise objectives. This allows you to focus on particular aspects of the team's response. For each exercise objective, several capability assessments (PIs) can be developed. These indicators can be derived from the plan, good practice, former post-exercise reports and/or understanding of the scenario and how it is likely to impact the organization.

These PIs may relate to tasks for the entire team, individual team members or specialist roles. It should be discussed with the sponsor whether they want PIs developed alongside the objectives, and which areas they should be written on. The sponsor should also decide whether the PI results should be included in the post-exercise report, presented as a separate document or used solely for internal assessment purposes.

The following are examples of exercise objectives and their corresponding PIs written to align with each objective.

EXAMPLE

Objective

To make the team aware of some of the issues they will face when dealing with an active shooter incident.

PI

What was discussed or considered during the exercise?

- Was there a plan in place for dealing with an active shooter, including reporting to the company and emergency services, as well as evacuation procedures?
- Were there any indicators that this was going to happen, and did people respond to them?
- Were proper background checks carried out on all employees?
- What actions were in place to support those involved, including managerial support such as the provision of trauma counselling and wider staff support through access to an employee assistance helpline?
- The trauma impacting those involved: what help is going to be provided?
- Legal issues of responsibility.
- What about other sites? What actions are being taken to ensure the same incident doesn't occur at their site?

EXAMPLE

Objective

Increase the crisis team's understanding of their plan's content and how it applies to their roles during an incident.

PI

Were the following elements of their plan referenced or used during the exercise?

- Incident escalation and initial assessment of the exercise.
- Use of the severity category.
- Incident team meetings.
- Arrangements for recording information: logging of calls and decisions.
- Situational awareness and making sense of the situation.
- Was appropriate use made of the prescribed forms within the plan, including Appendix C (Crisis Management Team Meeting Log) to record attendance and minutes, Appendix D (Crisis Management Team Decision and Action Log) to document decisions and assigned actions, and the Incident Initial Report (Appendix G)?

EXAMPLE

Objective

For the team to be able to describe how a cyber incident would be managed.

PI

During the exercise, was the following considered, and were the procedures in the plan used?

- Did they make use of the procedures laid out in the Cyber Business Response Plan?
- Was the process flow diagram in the plan used?
- Were additional people invited into the team?
- Was a meeting agenda used?
- Was staff support considered?
- Was confidentiality considered?

- Was there an understanding of how cyber insurance should be used?
- Was critical data pre-identified?
- Was threat intelligence discussed or considered to understand the threat actor?
- Were impacts on the organization understood?
- Were appropriate measures taken to ensure continuity of operations?
- Was third-party support deployed?
- Was the impact on operations, customers and service delivery understood?

PIs help examine the detailed elements of the organization's response and determine whether teams are using the information in the plan to address issues the sponsor wants reviewed, tackle critical factors for a successful response or consider matters specific to the organization or industry. Umpires can use the PIs as focus areas during observation or integrate them into a quantified assessment framework.

Assessing specialist responses

You might conduct an exercise where an element, such as communications, is a key focus. In such cases, it could be helpful to develop specific criteria to assess that part of the framework. The following is an example of an assessment designed specifically to evaluate an organization's communications response to the media and social media aspects of the exercise scenario. As with other evaluation frameworks, this could serve as a simple checklist for umpires to recognize best practice, or a specialist communications umpire might be appointed to assess the communications response in detail. They could utilize this framework and may opt to apply a scoring scale.

- Did the team acknowledge the incident quickly? Was their initial response timely?
- Did the team utilize all the social media platforms used during the exercise?
- Were the content and tone of the posts appropriate given the situation?
- Did the team develop a 'core message' with key themes to be used across all platforms?
- Were the communications put across adapted in style and tone for different audiences, i.e. was the company's statement on their website different from their posts on X?

- Did the team engage with individual posts addressing urgent issues? i.e. 'My mother works in the office affected by the fire, is she safe?!'
- Did the team address/correct rumours or misinformation on social media platforms?
- Did the team release new or updated statements when more information was made available to them?
- Did the team pay particular attention to posts with a lot of attention? (likes/retweets)
- Were all platforms being monitored continuously? Or did the team only respond using one or two?
- Where required, did the team know who was responsible for signing off on communications before they were issued?
- Was the language used by the team clear? Did they use complex or technical terms?
- Did the team follow the procedures outlined in the crisis communications plan (if applicable)?
- Did the team develop an appropriate hashtag and use it on social media posts during the incident?

By clearly defining what 'good looks like' and documenting the criteria for umpires to observe, you create a more holistic view of the team's response and highlight areas for improvement. Involving a subject matter expert, particularly in specialist areas such as communications, cybersecurity or logistics, ensures that the evaluation criteria reflect best practice and the latest thinking in that domain.

Expected response to inject

As outlined in Chapter 14, one of the criteria for writing each inject is to determine the team's expected response. Once an inject is delivered, the role-player responsible should record whether the expected response was received, whether a different response was given or whether no response was received. This information can provide valuable insight into the team's performance and should be taken into account in the overall evaluation of the exercise. It's important to agree with the sponsor whether this feedback should be documented, and if so, whether it should be captured on an inject-by-inject basis or summarized as an overall comment in the post-exercise report.

Quantitative assessments

In my experience, most organizations do not want a formal assessment that provides a quantitative score of their team's response. Exercises are usually viewed as learning experiences, opportunities to make mistakes in a safe environment, and having an exercise score or scoring detracts from this.

In the UK, particularly in the public sector, even mentioning 'assessment' in the context of an exercise can discourage participation. Staff may feel threatened, and trade unions may get involved if they believe the process could be used punitively or to identify underperforming team members. For this reason, many organizations avoid using the word 'assessment' when describing the evaluation process.

However, there is one area where teams are often keen to be assessed: how their incident management team performs compared with peers or an industry benchmark. This type of benchmarking offers valuable insights without the negative connotations of formal scoring.

EXAMPLE

'Incident Team Performance Assessment'

I ran a series of exercises for an insurance company's crisis management team and several of its operational teams. During the first year, their crisis management team's performance was adequate. However, when we were invited back the following year to run another exercise, their response had noticeably deteriorated. Although the team composition remained largely the same their ability to respond to the scenario had worsened. This put us in a dilemma of how to sensitively report this as part of the post-exercise report.

Typically, our post-exercise reports contain 10–15 observations and recommendations, along with an 'exercise director's comment' summarizing the team's overall performance. Regardless of how well or poorly a team performs, they usually receive a similar number of learning points. Therefore, it's this final exercise director's comment that needs to clearly convey whether the team has improved or declined in their response. The issue I faced was that these comments often relied on hearsay or subjective impressions, rather than being grounded in quantifiable or structured assessment. This made it difficult to offer robust, defensible feedback, especially when challenged by the client. To address this, we introduced the 'Incident Team Performance Assessment' (ITPA), an optional add-on for clients that provides a more structured, qualitative assessment of team performance.

This was conducted in two parts:

1 Self-assessment by each participant, completed individually at the end of the exercise.
2 Umpire assessment, focusing on team-wide behaviours and competencies.

The self-assessment helped triangulate the scoring and provided internal validation. When challenged about lower scores, we could point out that the results came from the team itself, not just the umpires. Exercise participants were asked to assess their performance in areas such as leadership, team dynamics, the usefulness of their plans and procedures, and overall teamwork. Each category was scored out of four, with a short descriptor explaining what each score represented. The umpire assessment used the expanded PICTS framework, where each criterion could be scored out of four, with the top score reflecting a 'world-class' response.

To ensure fairness and objectivity, the same assessment framework was not only completed by the umpires but also by the exercise director and the role-player coordinator, allowing us to demonstrate consistency across multiple perspectives. All results were compiled into the post-exercise report, and by applying this evaluation methodology to all crisis team exercises, we could present numerical data to show whether the organization's crisis response capability was improving or regressing. This was based on concrete figures rather than the exercise director's opinions. It also enabled clients to target training in areas where scores were lower.

Once we had developed the ITPA, we gained a tool to evaluate any team and demonstrate whether they were improving or declining in capability. Over time, we accumulated a large number of these assessments and could show organizations how they compared to their peers and whether they were ahead or falling behind. In some cases, participants disputed their scores, claiming they should have received higher ratings. By including both internal and external umpires, along with participant self-assessment, these challenges became easier to manage, as the score reflected a group consensus rather than a single opinion.

If the scoring results are shared only with the sponsor, or if participants are unaware of the assessment's quantitative nature, this can create the perception that something dishonest is occurring. This may cause individuals to be hesitant about taking part in future exercises. This risk should be openly discussed with the sponsor, and a decision should be made on how to communicate and handle the assessment process.

Developing assessment scales

If a quantitative score is required, it's best to use a simple scoring system. The one I usually use is a four-level scale:

- **0 = N/A.** Not applicable in this instance. For this exercise, it is not possible to review the team against this criterion.
- **1 = Little to no evidence.** During the exercise, I did not observe this criterion being met, or up to 20 per cent of the criteria were met.
- **2 = Some evidence.** Around 50 per cent of the criteria were observed during the exercise.
- **3 = Full evidence.** 80 per cent of the criteria were met or were met in full.
- **4 = World / Best in class.** During the exercise, I observed new or not yet seen performance of the criteria. It was carried out in a new, practical way, and this was the best I had ever observed.

It is essential to have a clear scoring criterion so that new umpires, or those you haven't worked with before, can easily understand how to apply the scoring consistently. Using only four scoring levels helps keep the process simple and makes it easier to decide which category best fits the observed performance. In contrast, using a score out of ten often makes the process more subjective.

There is also the option of using a more descriptive approach to scoring team performance. This is particularly useful when asking participants to complete a self-assessment of their team's performance at the end of an exercise. It relies less on reading a detailed scoring scale and more on their own perception of how the team performed. The following are examples where participants choose the most appropriate description. This sheet can be combined with the overall feedback form.

A. Were roles and tasks clear and understood?

1. Clear understanding: The bigger picture was well understood. Tasks were clearly defined with achievable outcomes.
2. Fair understanding: The purpose and role were generally understood, though some clarity or support was lacking.

3 Some understanding: There was poor understanding of roles and tasks, with a lack of definable outcomes.

4 Poor understanding: There was little or no understanding of roles, no direction on tasks and no support.

B. Were communications among the team effective?

1 Effective: Information was quickly disseminated. Communications were clear and well understood.

2 Fairly effective: Information was disseminated, but some communications required clarification.

3 Somewhat effective: Information was eventually shared, but communications often lacked clarity.

4 Ineffective: Information was lost or not passed on. Communications were unclear or did not occur.

C. Did the team run effective meetings?

1 Effective: Meetings had a clear purpose and structure, were well-led, gave clear direction and generated confident action points.

2 Fairly effective: Meetings had a purpose and some structure, and outcomes were understood.

3 Somewhat effective: Meetings had a weak purpose and little structure, but outcomes eventually became clear.

4 Ineffective: The purpose of meetings was unclear, they lacked structure, were confusing and left participants unsure of what to do next.

D. Did the team work well together?

1 Worked well: Communication was strong, tasks were productive, support was mutual and the atmosphere was positive.

2 Fairly well: Communication was adequate, tasks were completed and some support was available.

3 Somewhat well: Communication was difficult, tasks were slow or unfinished and support was limited.

4 Poorly: There was no communication, tasks failed, support was absent and the atmosphere was strained.

Capability assessments

As discussed in Chapter 6, you may wish to undertake a competency assessment to evaluate the capability level of a team. Many of the frameworks outlined in this chapter, particularly the expanded PICTS framework, can be adapted into tools for competency-based assessment. By applying an assessment scale, you can assign a score that can be used over time to monitor whether the team's performance is improving or declining. Alternatively, the score can be used to determine whether the team meets a predefined competency threshold.

ASSESSMENT OVERLOAD?

As shown, there are several ways to evaluate or assess an exercise. It's unlikely that all methods will be used, as this could overwhelm umpires and lead to a large number of assessment forms to complete. You may choose to combine different assessment criteria or focus on a single approach, such as the expanded PICTS framework. The level and type of assessment will depend on factors like the sponsor's preferences, the duration of the exercise, the number of umpires available and the experience level of the team.

Conducting the evaluation or assessment: the umpire's role

The umpire plays a vital role in evaluating team performance during an exercise. Their main duty is to assess the team's response against established criteria, which are developed as part of the exercise design process. When a quantitative or qualitative scoring system is in place, umpires apply it consistently to evaluate specific skills, behaviours, decision-making and adherence to plans and protocols.

To ensure accuracy and fairness, umpires must be well prepared. Ideally, they should be involved in the planning phase of the exercise, or at minimum, review all exercise documentation thoroughly beforehand. This includes understanding the scenario, objectives, team structure and the assessment or evaluation criteria being used. For more complex exercises, such as SIMEX, they should also attend rehearsals to align with the rest of the delivery team and ensure consistency in how the criteria will be applied.

Umpires should observe unobtrusively, noting team dynamics, information flow, decision quality, leadership and the use or non-use of plans. Their evaluation often covers structural elements (e.g. roles and responsibilities), adherence to processes (e.g. incident meeting protocols, logging) and behavioural indicators (e.g. communication clarity, leadership, teamwork). When assessment frameworks include a scoring system, such as a 0–4 scale, umpires must apply these consistently. Clear scoring criteria enable new or less experienced umpires to contribute confidently and help minimize subjectivity.

Interventions during the exercise should be rare and occur only when the exercise deviates from its objectives or the team becomes overwhelmed. In such cases, the umpire may raise this with the exercise director and suggest a recalibration or additional inject to bring the activity back on track. However, intervention should never interfere with the natural flow of the team's decision-making or learning process.

After the exercise, umpires contribute directly to the evaluation phase. They present findings during the hot debrief and input into the post-exercise report. Where assessments were made using structured scoring (such as performance indicators or team self-assessments), umpires can help analyse the results, identify trends and offer recommendations.

Using specialist umpires, such as communications professionals to assess media responses or IT staff for cyber scenarios, adds further depth to the evaluation. These individuals can apply domain-specific criteria to ensure that technical or reputational elements are assessed to a high standard.

Assessment of the delivery of the exercise

While the primary focus of evaluation should be on the participant's performance, it is also advantageous to assess how the exercise is delivered and conducted. This helps ensure that future exercises are well structured, relevant and effectively executed. However, it's important to remember that enjoyment is not the primary goal; participants may find the scenario challenging or uncomfortable, yet still gain valuable learning.

A short, printed feedback form should be used to capture feedback and comments on the exercise. This form provides useful insights into how the exercise was received and identifies areas for improvement. Crucially, feedback should always be collected during the exercise timeframe, ideally during the hot debrief session. If participants are allowed to take the feedback form away, they very rarely return it.

The feedback form typically includes:

1 A simple rating scale for the exercise overall (Excellent, Good, Average, Poor).

2 A section to comment on the conduct of the exercise, allowing views on logistics, delivery, timings and facilitation.

Continual improvement and demonstrating organizational value

While individual exercises provide valuable insights, the real benefit lies in tracking performance across time. Organizations invest considerable time and effort into running exercises, so it's important to ask: Is our incident management capability actually improving?

If an incident team only trains once a year for a few hours, and there's regular staff turnover, it's likely that performance will stay the same or even worsen, unless the exercises are part of a broader programme of ongoing development.

To measure progress over time, a structured approach such as the **Incident Team Performance Assessment (ITPA)**, detailed earlier, can be used. By applying the same assessment framework across multiple exercises, whether through umpire scoring, team self-assessment or feedback forms, it becomes possible to identify trends and benchmark progress. This allows organizations to spot consistent weaknesses, reinforce strengths and target areas for additional training.

One widely recognized tool for evaluating the effectiveness of training and exercises is the **Kirkpatrick Model**, which assesses four key levels:

- **Level 1: Reaction.** Did participants find the exercise useful, engaging and relevant? This is typically captured through immediate post-exercise feedback.
- **Level 2: Learning.** What new knowledge, skills or confidence did participants gain? Umpires can assess this during the exercise by observing behaviours and performance.
- **Level 3: Behaviour.** Are participants applying what they learnt in the exercise to real incidents or in future exercises?
- **Level 4: Results.** Has the exercise led to improved organizational outcomes, such as better incident response, faster recovery or reduced risk exposure?

By applying these levels, organizations can start to evaluate the return on investment (ROI) from their exercise programme, not just in terms of engagement, but also in terms of performance enhancements.

Structured frameworks such as the **expanded PICTS, performance indicators** and **quantified scoring models** can all feed into this broader view of value and effectiveness. When used consistently, they allow for **year-on-year comparison** of the same team's performance, **benchmarking between teams** or across sites, **evidence-based reporting** to sponsors and leadership, and a stronger business case for continued investment in crisis preparedness.

KEY LEARNINGS

- Evaluation must be planned from the outset and agreed with the sponsor.
- The purpose of evaluation is to identify learning and improvement, not to criticize.
- Structured frameworks such as PICTS help ensure consistent, comprehensive assessment.
- Evaluation should focus on meaningful issues rather than a blow-by-blow commentary.
- More complex exercises benefit from detailed criteria, specialist assessment and expanded frameworks.
- Quantitative scoring can support benchmarking and trend analysis when used transparently.
- Umpires must be well briefed, well prepared and consistent in applying the evaluation criteria.
- Feedback should be collected immediately during the exercise time frame, not afterwards.
- Participant reflections such as 'three actions to improve the response' surface valuable insights.
- Consistent evaluation enables year-on-year comparison and demonstrates organizational improvement.

Note

1 HM Government (2024) *Exercising Best Practice Guidance*. UK Resilience Academy, Cabinet Office and Emergency Planning College, Version 1:September 2024. https://assets.publishing.service.gov.uk/media/66f124be69fa2ae94de745c9/24.51_CO_EDS_Exercising_Good_Practice_Guidance.pdf

18

Delivering the exercise

In this chapter, you will learn about:

1. Planning for the delivery of the exercise
2. The week before the exercise
3. The 'dress rehearsal' the day before the exercise
4. Arrive and set-up
5. Exercise briefing
6. Conducting the exercise
7. Hot debrief and feedback

You have agreed on the day and locations of the exercise. The design team has been working hard on the scenario and storyboard; you know who will deliver the exercise and you have a fine set of injects or questions that will drive the scenario forward. Your sponsor has signed off on all of these, and you are almost ready to go. You have some last-minute checks to do, and then it is the day you have been waiting for, probably for a long time: the day for the delivery of the exercise.

Planning for the delivery of the exercise

Several items need to be decided before the delivery of the exercise. These should ideally be agreed upon three to four weeks in advance to allow sufficient time for arrangements to be agreed and implemented.

Room set-up: Decide whether the room should be fully prepared before the exercise with wallboards, printed plans, role cards detailing responsibilities, grab bags and admin support ready, or if the incident management team should be tasked with setting it up themselves. Setting up the room could be one of the exercise objectives.

Exercise staff communication: Determine how the exercise staff will communicate during a SIMEX. Options could include a dedicated WhatsApp group, Microsoft Teams channel or Slack channel, phone calls or even radios with earpieces. Personally, I avoid radios and earpieces as they can come across as unnecessarily theatrical.

Security and confidentiality: If the scenario involves sensitive content (e.g. a ransomware attack), ensure all materials are clearly marked 'For exercise purposes only'. Brief participants on confidentiality and collect all exercise materials at the end for secure shredding. Consider issuing warnings beforehand to prevent confusion with a real incident, especially if a live play element is involved. This also helps raise the exercise's profile within the organization.

Plans access: Decide if participants should bring their own plans or if you will provide them. It is extremely disheartening for the business continuity manager to spend months preparing a plan, only for participants to arrive without it and then make up their responses without even consulting it.

Observer management: If there are observers, decide where they will be placed. Will they be in the incident room or watching remotely via video? While both have benefits, avoid crowding the incident management room with too many non-participants.

Publicity: Consider whether you want post-exercise publicity. Hiring a photographer or journalist to capture and report on the event can raise the profile of business continuity within the organization, particularly in larger exercises involving multiple teams. People generally enjoy seeing photos of themselves in action and reading a positive write-up, and this is a good opportunity to promote the business continuity team's work.

Use of PPE: If the exercise involves a live element requiring personal protective equipment (PPE), all umpires and the exercise director should wear suitable clothing.

Joining instructions: Although the exercise director will present a briefing to participants immediately prior to the exercise starting, it should be decided whether to send out exercise joining instructions beforehand.

The instructions can include the date and time of the exercise, what preparation they should carry out before it and an assurance that it isn't a test but a learning experience.

Feedback forms: Decide whether feedback forms will be used to collect information from participants. What will be asked on the feedback forms? Will they focus on three areas of improvement or three actions they should take in response to the exercise? Should there also be an assessment of the exercise? Consider how online participants will receive the feedback forms.

Post-exercise report. There should be a discussion with the sponsor on the content and style of the post-exercise report and whether there is any particular way they want it set out.

Contingency planning. You might want to carry out some contingency planning and assess the risk that could impact or possibly cancel your exercise. These risks could range from a transport strike preventing participants from reaching the event, to inclement weather stopping a live exercise from taking place. It could also include what should happen if communications go offline during the exercise or if key participants are suddenly unavailable.

EXAMPLE

Mitigating the technology risk

I was asked to plan and deliver a SIMEX exercise for a multinational organization, with most of the crisis team in Bermuda and several others participating online. The exercise control and role-players would run the event from the organization's London office. It was agreed that the exercise would be conducted via Microsoft Teams. During the commercial discussions, it was decided that there was no requirement for someone from the exercise delivery team to be physically present in Bermuda. This was a significant risk for me because if Teams failed or went offline on the day, the exercise would have to be cancelled midway, as we, the exercise directing staff, would be unaware of what was happening. We also needed someone on-site to input the injects.

There was also a challenge with video conferencing: it is very difficult to hear all conversations in the incident room, especially if the team splits into groups with separate discussions. The team was highly senior, and it was crucial for both our and their exercise planners that nothing was left to chance and that their conversations in the incident room were observed.

Due to this risk, it was agreed that a member of the exercise team would fly to Bermuda to act as an umpire and deliver the injects. Although it was a long round trip for a three-hour exercise, in the end it was worth it because the exercise proceeded without any technological issues and the crisis team appreciated having someone from the exercise team on-site to observe and support.

The week before the exercise

The week before the exercise, several checks need to be carried out to determine whether any changes could affect it. These should be reviewed, and the exercise adjusted accordingly. You hope that the changes are not significant enough to affect the delivery of the exercise, but I have seen cases where it nearly requires a complete rewrite just a couple of days in advance. The following needs to be checked:

Participants are all attending. Are the people you have planned to turn up still attending, or have there been any personnel changes? If people have changed, has an alternative been nominated? I have found in the past that when participants learn the CEO is not attending due to availability, others slowly melt away and make excuses not to be there. You then find the deputy's deputy is attending, or some roles are missing entirely. There's no easy solution to this one except to ensure early on that the CEO has mandated the exercise, and that the right people are expected and committed to attend.

Participants attending from another location or going online. Exercises with half the staff in a room and the other half online are challenging but not impossible to run. Online participants often get frustrated; they struggle to hear what is going on in the exercise room and find it hard to contribute effectively. If the exercise was originally planned for everyone to be in one room, and you're told that some will now join from another location, it is preferable to assign an umpire in person to their room so they can be observed. Last minute changes happen occasionally, and you, as the exercise director, need to be flexible, adapt and adjust the exercise accordingly.

Real events. Occasionally, exercises are postponed or cancelled due to real events happening. This can vary from an actual incident, such as a fire, flood or cyber-attack, to a business issue, such as a takeover, loss of a supplier or the resignation or sacking of a senior manager. Almost until you call ENDEX (end of the exercise), you are at the mercy of real-world events. This is just a fact of life. You cannot really do anything about it, and you hope it does not happen.

'Dress rehearsal' if required

When delivering a SIMEX, I almost always conduct a rehearsal the day before the exercise, on-site with the exercise design team and those who will deliver it. Sometimes, this is the first time that all those who have been working on the exercise have met in person, and it is a good opportunity to get to know each other before being thrust into delivering the exercise the next day.

The rehearsal is best conducted the day before the exercise and is usually planned for the late afternoon, so you can use the morning if you are travelling to the exercise site. Allow at least two hours for the rehearsal, as going through all the required actions takes some time.

Especially important is checking that all the technology works for delivering the exercise and that you can connect to the local Wi-Fi if needed, as well as ensuring the screen is working if using slides to deliver or brief the exercise. If the exercise is to be delivered purely online, a dress rehearsal is still required, as the exercise team may be co-located, or it is a good opportunity to brief everyone who will deliver the exercise.

It is important that all those who are going to deliver the exercise attend the rehearsal for the exercise briefing. The following should attend: the exercise director, umpires, role-player coordinator, role-players (design team) and any other staff involved in delivering the exercise.

The following checklists will help the exercise run smoothly.

Venue and room set-up

1. Check whether the room designated for the exercise participants is of a suitable size, has the necessary technology or connectivity for online participants and is set up as agreed in advance. If there are breakout rooms or spaces for the team to split up, are they suitable and within easy access of the main room?
2. Check the role-players' room: is it suitable for the number of people who will be delivering the exercise? Is there suitable connectivity to the

participants' room? Are the rooms close by? It is preferable that the rooms be close by so the exercise director can move between them and have a quick chat with the role-player coordinator. In some organizations, visitors must be escorted, making it difficult for the exercise director to move between rooms.

3. Check the incident room set-up: is it fit for purpose and reflective of a real incident environment?
4. Decide whether the room should be laid out as it would be during a real incident, including placeholders and task lists, support team positions and information boards with incident details ready.
5. Ensure any equipment needed is available and working: whiteboards, flipcharts, stationery for the team to use, as well as having battle boxes/ grab bags delivered.

Technology check

1. Check access to Wi-Fi if required; note that access may need to be set up in advance and passwords requested.
2. Test all telephones you are using; ensure speakerphones are available and functioning if needed.
3. If running a hybrid exercise, check video conferencing links and ensure remote participants can connect.
4. Check that participants or specific roles, such as the communications person, can log in to any exercise software used to deliver the exercise. Check that any other software used to run the exercise can be accessed and isn't blocked by the organization's firewall.
5. Check mobile signals or Wi-Fi in the rooms where the exercise staff will be working on the day.

Exercise briefing run-through with role-players

1. Go through the participants' exercise instruction and highlight any key items.
2. Go through the injects or questions and check that they are still valid and no last-minute changes are needed.

3. Go through who is carrying out each role during the exercise and what their responsibilities are. This should include the exercise director, umpires, role-player coordinator, role-players and any observers.
4. Go through how the exercise will be evaluated and any evaluation sheets or documents.
5. Ensure role-players know how to log communications with exercise participants.
6. Know what will happen at the end of the exercise and details of the hot debrief and any discussion on the exercise by the exercise staff after the participants have left.
7. What activities should take place after the exercise has finished, such as the umpires or role-players debrief?

By the time the rehearsal is finished, all those running the exercise should be clear about their roles and how it will be delivered.

Exercise staff preparation on the day before the exercise

Apart from the rehearsal, if you are conducting one, each individual involved in the exercise delivery should undertake their own personal preparation. This could include re-reading all relevant plans to ensure you understand how the team is supposed to respond and what recovery strategies and solutions they have in place. Review the last post-exercise report to remind yourself of any points from previous reports and check if they are repeated in this exercise. Finally, re-read the exercise instructions to see if anything has been missed or still needs to be prepared.

Arrival and set-up on the day of the exercise

Depending on the level of set-up required for the exercise, arrive 60–90 minutes before the briefing time. The following are the actions to set up before the exercise:

1. Arrange tables and chairs to best suit the style of exercise.
2. Ensure required communications equipment is working.
3. Connect your laptop to the display screen for your briefing (ask for an IT contact to help, if required).

4 Layout exercise documentation and resources (such as telephone directories, response documentation, templates/forms, wallboards, battle box contents) as required.

5 Note if the room set-up is part of the exercise objectives; do not arrange anything other than the documentation that you have developed for delivering the exercise.

6 Make sure that the umpires are briefed:

- They should be close to the team so they can hear and see what they are doing. This could be looking over the team's shoulder if participants are using a laptop.
- They should avoid eye contact with exercise participants, so the participants don't talk to the umpire directly and look for confirmation.
- They should avoid using a laptop because it puts a barrier between them and the team, and should not 'play' with their mobile phone during the exercise.
- They should speak to you, the exercise director, if they feel the exercise needs to be stopped or changed.

7 Update any role-players on changes to participation etc. in case this impacts the scenario.

Exercise briefing

For me, the exercise briefing is essential for the success of the exercise. Once it begins, participants need to be clear on how the exercise will be conducted. The initial briefing is crucial in setting the tone and ensuring everyone understands what is expected of them. This is especially important if many participants are new to exercising or have not taken part in this type of exercise before. If the participants are experienced and familiar with the format, then the briefing can be brief. However, if it is a new team or there is a change in how the exercise is run, then a more detailed briefing is necessary. There is always a balance between providing enough information and not using too much of the exercise time. It is also important to adopt the right tone during the briefing. If participants treat the exercise lightly or do not take it seriously, the value of running it will be diminished.

Typically, you conduct the exercise briefing before the exercise begins. This ensures everyone knows how the exercise will be carried out. There may be situations where you do not deliver the briefing immediately before the exercise and instead do so earlier. These could include no-notice exercises, where participants are already familiar with the format, or instances where you have been asked to start the exercise without a briefing. In such cases, the briefing can be given prior to the exercise. It might be delivered as a short session for all participants beforehand or recorded as a video for them to watch at their convenience. If the exercise is no-notice, the briefing may be provided as soon as participants start taking part, either on a one-to-one basis or in small groups.

Not all the following points may need to be briefed for each exercise, but I believe it is better to overbrief participants than to leave them confused about how the exercise will work.

Senior manager introduction: If possible, have a senior manager open and emphasize the importance of the exercise. This could be a senior manager who is taking part in the exercise, or one can be invited to do the introduction and then leave.

Welcome: Introduce yourselves or the organization running the exercise. If there is time, go around and have all participants introduce themselves. When introducing the exercise delivery team, I tend not to talk about our backgrounds. The emphasis should be on the participants, not on the skills and qualifications of the exercise staff.

Housekeeping: Provide the exercise timings, including start and finish times, as well as any scheduled breaks. Please provide details of any fire alarms, toilet facilities and catering arrangements. Explain that if they have to take real calls during the exercise, they should leave the room and take them outside.

Trigger warnings: If the exercise scenario covers topics that could have an emotional impact on participants, such as a terrorist attack, the death of colleagues or sensitive issues like inappropriate behaviour by senior managers, then this should be flagged during the briefing. Participants should be warned that the exercise may include content they could find distressing. They should be given the option to step out or excuse themselves from the session without needing to give a reason.

Purpose and objectives: It is a good idea to remind people why the exercise is being conducted and what the objectives are that they are meant to be achieving.

Participants: Who is taking part in the exercise and what are their roles? This could include exercise participants, exercise director, umpires, observers, role-player coordinator, role-players, organizations participating for real and simulated organizations.

Scenario details: Exercise participants will need to be briefed on the key details of the scenario. This includes confirming the time and date of the exercise, particularly if they differ from real time. You should also state the location where the exercise is taking place and outline what has happened in the scenario so far. If relevant to the scenario, describe the exercise weather conditions and the share price.

Exercise details: It is essential that participants understand how the exercise will be conducted. If the exercise is a SIMEX, explain how communications will work, how they will receive injects and how they are expected to respond or provide information back. Clarify whether communication will be by phone, email, through an exercise control platform or in person. Participants should also be told how the media and social media will be simulated, and how they are expected to respond to these inputs.

Participant expectations: Depending on the group's experience, you may need to explain what is expected of them during the exercise, what they should do for real and which tasks can be simulated. For example, participants could be instructed to respond as if it were a live incident, mobilize in accordance with the relevant procedure, set up the room and allocate roles as they would in a real event. They should process information, hold team meetings, assign actions, log all relevant details, consult plans as needed and use wallboards, forms and other tools as part of their normal response process. You may also want to reference the objectives, which outline what they should be doing during the exercise. You might also include details of any assessment taking place during the exercise and what the umpires are looking to see demonstrated.

Safety briefing: Depending on the type of exercise, a safety briefing may be needed for participants.

Real events: If a real incident occurs or a casualty or injury necessitates stopping the exercise, it should be paused or terminated immediately. A clear phrase such as 'NO DUFF' should be used to indicate that a real situation is unfolding, and all participants should await further instructions on how to proceed. The term 'No Duff' originates from military training, where 'Duff' referred to something false or fictional. Saying 'No Duff' signals that the event is real and not part of the simulated scenario. It is widely recognized in emergency services and military exercises as a way to quickly distinguish between real and exercise events.

Debrief and reporting: Advise that after the exercise, there will be a debrief (briefly describe how it will be conducted), and the results will be included in an exercise report submitted to your client contact.

'Don't fight the scenario': This is critical to point out, and I always say it as part of the briefing, even in the simplest of exercises. At the beginning of the exercise, it is helpful to remind participants not to challenge the scenario. You want to avoid arguments about whether the scenario could really happen. This is especially common in exercises involving IT failures, where IT staff may insist the scenario is unrealistic because of the controls or backups they have in place. This kind of challenge can derail the exercise and shift the focus away from response. Reassure participants that the scenario is not a reflection on their capability or management of their area, but simply a tool to test the organization's response. Ask them to accept the scenario as given and use it as the context for their decisions and actions during the exercise.

Exercise start: Explain the back story and what has happened to date/what they would know.

Conducting the exercise

The moment you have been planning for weeks, not months, has finally arrived. The exercise begins.

When running the exercise, it is all about managing people. The technical work has been completed during the preparation, and this phase now focuses on delivering what has been planned while ensuring the exercise remains on track and the intended learning takes place.

Avoid eye contact unless it is a walkthrough: Unless the exercise is a plan walkthrough, avoid making eye contact with participants. If you do, they may default to speaking with you instead of discussing the situation with their exercise team colleagues.

Let the exercise flow naturally: Allow the exercise to unfold without unnecessary intervention. Unless the exercise's design requires facilitation or redirection, avoid imposing yourself on the scenario. Let the team work through their response unless it goes off track or requires correction.

Divide responsibilities between the umpires and the exercise director: Umpires should focus on observing participants, while the exercise director should concentrate on the overall delivery of the exercise. In a SIMEX, managing the injects, timings and pace of the exercise can be a full-time job, making it difficult for the exercise director to observe team actions directly.

Be cautious about laptop use: Avoid encouraging participants to use laptops during the exercise unless they are clearly needed to access plans or communication tools. Once participants begin using laptops, there is a risk they will become distracted by day-to-day work and disengage from the exercise.

Take detailed notes: Keep thorough notes during the exercise. If you run multiple exercises, the details can blur together. Your notes will help you recall key moments, behaviours, issues raised and actions taken that should be fed into the debrief or the exercise report.

Recognize when the exercise has reached its conclusion: Watch for the point when the scenario has played out and participants are no longer generating new actions or responses. When energy levels drop and there is little new input, it may be time to draw the exercise to a close.

Stick to your timings and allow for a proper debrief: It is easy to get caught up in the energy of the exercise, especially if participants are fully engaged. However, it is vital to stick to your planned timings and leave enough time for a proper debrief. The debrief is where much of the learning happens, and it should not be rushed.

Be inquisitive about what participants are doing: If someone is referencing a document or an online source, ask what it is. Understanding the tools and resources participants are using gives you insight into how they are making decisions and what assumptions or guidance they are working from.

Ensure coverage when groups split up: When participants break into smaller groups or sub-teams, ensure there are enough umpires to observe each group. Valuable interactions and learning points can be missed if no one is present to observe and record them.

Keep the exercise on course: Monitor whether participants are following the injects and assumptions as planned. Exercises can drift if participants misinterpret injects, go off on tangents or invent their own scenarios. Keep an eye on how the scenario is evolving and be ready to step in to bring it back on track if needed.

Check for active participation: Observe whether participants are actively discussing, reacting and collaborating. If they seem disengaged, consider inserting an additional inject to prompt involvement or engage them directly. Make a note of when and why this occurred, as this can help determine whether the issue stemmed from the exercise design or a personal factor.

Challenge participants to act, not just talk: During the exercise, it is easy for participants to say what they *would* have done rather than actually doing it. When this happens, challenge them, ask them to carry out the action rather than simply describe it. For example, if they say they would issue a holding statement, ask them to write the actual words. If they claim they would contact a stakeholder, ask how and what they would say. Encourage participants to move from theory to action, as this helps reveal gaps in capability and ensures the exercise reflects realistic decision-making and response behaviour.

It is important throughout the exercise to focus on its execution and remain alert for any issues, going off track or silliness creeping in. Full concentration is required from all exercise staff until the hot debrief is complete; then you can relax, hopefully reflecting on a job well done.

Conducting an online only exercise

Running online exercises is not much different from running in-person exercises. I usually give participants the questions or injects and then let them get on with it. The exercise team should switch off their cameras and only turn them back on when they need to interject in the exercise. There may be a temptation to record or transcribe the session, but I would strongly advise against it. You do not want a recording of senior managers responding to an incident to be made available, as it could be used to embarrass them, and participants may not feel comfortable speaking openly if they know they are being recorded.

It is highly likely, especially at the beginning of an incident, that the response will be conducted online, so it is important that this method of incident management is regularly practised.

Native language

If you are conducting an exercise for those whose first language is not yours, you have a dilemma. Do you allow them to discuss in their own language, and you are unable to understand what they are saying, or do you conduct the exercise in your language? Both have their merits; hold a discussion with the participants in advance, and then decide on the most appropriate course.

Ending the exercise

If possible, the exercise should conclude at a natural point. This allows responders to tie up any outstanding issues or actions before the call for 'ENDEX' is made. It is useful to decide in advance when the debrief will start, ideally at least 15 minutes before the scheduled end of the event, and stick to this timing. You can prompt participants to complete any final tasks or hold a quick meeting in order to bring the exercise to a logical close. Natural endpoints can include:

- After a team meeting or briefing to other participating teams, when all responders have concluded telephone calls.
- When the response is clearly winding down with few additional actions identified.
- Following an assessment of long-term impacts.
- Once the objectives have been met.
- Simply, when the CEO says it is time to finish (which has happened to me before).

Hot debrief and feedback

Debriefings are essential to review the response or discussion, give participants the opportunity to provide feedback on their role, the process and the plans, allow the exercise staff to provide observations against best practice and offer improvement tips, review the objectives, and agree on next steps or actions.

Debriefings can be either hot or cold. A hot debrief is conducted immediately after the exercise finishes and usually involves all responders, facilitators, observers and, if applicable, role-players. Cold debriefs are held sometime after the exercise, allowing more time for reflection and analysis.

Immediately following the exercise, feedback forms should be issued to all participants to capture their thoughts and perspectives. These are then included in the post-exercise report.

There are a few effective ways to assess an exercise. One simple method, whether you are the exercise umpire or director, is to write down key points as they arise during the exercise. Later, select the five most important points and share them during the debrief. This ensures that feedback remains focused and manageable.

Another approach is to use an assessment framework. This provides a structured lens through which to evaluate performance across multiple areas. It also allows you to note activities that were expected but not observed, highlighting potential gaps in the response.

Debriefings can be run in a variety of ways, depending on the team and context:

- You can ask each participant to share one key learning point, going around the group. This method is quick, inclusive and often insightful.
- Another useful technique is to have responders write 'what went well' and 'what could be improved' on Post-its, placing them under those headings on flipchart paper or a designated wall. The facilitator can read these out loud and ask for clarification if needed. This method works well for newer, nervous or less vocal teams, particularly when a strong hierarchy is present.
- Finally, feedback forms can be used to capture written reflections. You might ask participants to list three things they learnt from the exercise and three areas to improve the organization's response. This helps capture insights that might not come out during a live discussion.

KEY LEARNINGS

- Plan all logistical elements, room set-up, communication tools and roles, well in advance to avoid last-minute disruptions.
- Confirm participant attendance early, particularly senior leaders, as their absence can reduce the exercise's impact.
- Be prepared for real-world events that may interrupt or postpone the exercise and know how to pause it safely if needed.
- Conduct a rehearsal with the exercise delivery team to align on roles, technology and final adjustments.
- Deliver a clear and thorough briefing that covers objectives, logistics, roles and how the exercise will be run.

- Manage the exercise by observing rather than leading, intervening only when it veers off course or needs support.
- Encourage participants to act rather than discuss hypotheticals, asking them to demonstrate actions where possible.
- Keep detailed notes throughout the exercise to capture observations, behaviours and decisions for the debrief and report.
- Design and deliver online exercises carefully, ensuring remote engagement while respecting privacy and avoiding recordings.
- Prioritize the hot debrief, using a structured approach to review objectives, share insights and agree on improvement actions.

19

Cold debrief and follow-up

In this chapter, you will learn about:

1 What a cold debrief is and when you should conduct one

2 Different methodologies for conducting a cold debrief

3 How to follow up after the exercise

4 Reflection on the exercise

A well-structured and organized hot debrief (a debrief that takes place immediately after the exercise), followed by a short meeting with those who ran the event, is usually sufficient to gather learning points, evaluate the exercise and generate enough material to write the post-exercise report.

However, you might also choose to conduct a cold debrief, which takes place sometime after the exercise has been delivered, usually between one and two weeks later. As it is conducted after the exercise, it gives participants time to reflect on the exercise and the team's performance. There are a number of reasons for conducting a cold debrief:

- If the exercise was particularly complex and requires further evaluation.
- If participants' performance was below expectations and needs deeper analysis and discussion.
- If multiple parties were involved and internal discussion is needed before wider sharing.
- If participants were under pressure and now want to reflect more calmly without the emotional reactions that surfaced during the hot debrief.

- If there was strong push-back against feedback from the umpires or exercise directors.
- If there is likely to be regulatory or external interest in the post-exercise report, making it critical that the content is accurate, balanced and appropriately pitched.
- If the sponsor wants to bring together participants and the exercise delivery team to agree on the key messages and content of the final report through a workshop-style session.

I very rarely conduct a cold debrief, except when the client wants to have a workshop to discuss the content of the post-exercise report. However, there can be many benefits to leaving time between the exercise and the cold debrief, allowing time to reflect on the response, see the exercise in context and give more considered feedback. Cold debriefs should be scheduled in advance and not agreed as an afterthought after the exercise has been conducted.

Conducting a cold debrief

A clear agenda should be prepared for the debrief to ensure that all participants understand how it will be conducted and how long it is expected to last. The attendees will depend on the purpose of the debrief and what it is intended to achieve. Participants may include all or selected exercise participants, the exercise director and umpires and, where appropriate, members of the exercise design team, role-players, the role-player coordinator and observers.

The debrief can be structured in a number of different ways: there could be a straightforward approach, looking at phases of the exercise in turn, or the debrief could focus on specific elements of the exercise. It could also consist of timeline reconstructions or functional breakouts to discuss specific functional areas' issues.

A range of techniques can be used to facilitate the debrief, whether for the entire session or for specific elements of it. These techniques may also be applied during a hot debrief immediately following the exercise, although some may prove too time-consuming unless sufficient time has been allocated (for example, where the exercise runs for a full day with at least an hour set aside for the hot debrief). All of these methods can be adapted for online delivery with only minor adjustments to format.

Structured debriefing

A structured debrief is a practical, inclusive and focused way to gather reflections from an exercise, training, workshop or incident. It employs a consistent four-question format to promote both personal reflection and team development. One key concept is that it is not intended to reach consensus but to provide a variety of ideas or comments. This approach is especially effective in mixed-level groups, particularly when senior managers or strong personalities are involved, as it helps ensure individuals reflect on their own experiences rather than simply aligning with senior or dominant voices. Everyone has their turn to share their views, and since they have written their notes in silence, they are not influenced by others' thoughts.

The questions are grouped into two main parts. The first part looks back on the experience:

Question A1: What three things didn't go so well?

Question A2: What three things went well?

The second part is forward-looking and reflective:

Question B1: What's the most valuable lesson you've learnt, and how will you use it in future?

Question B2: What three actions should be taken to improve the response or the process going forward?

These questions don't need to follow the exact wording given above, but the structure is essential and works well in a variety of situations.

When using the framework to evaluate workshops, training or incidents, follow the same set of questions in the A1/A2 and B1/B2 formats, but tailor them to the activity you are debriefing.

Before the session, you should prepare a visual on a flipchart with key themes (e.g. Team, Leadership, Plan, Communications, Procedures, Training, Equipment) that participants in the debrief may want to comment on.

The participants should be seated in a semi-circle of chairs facing the visual. They should be briefed on what will happen during the debrief and how the answers will be used. They are reminded that the debrief is designed to elicit a range of views and so a consensus is not required. There should be a designated facilitator for each debrief. Their role is to guide the discussion, help participants explore and clarify their feedback, and ensure key points are accurately captured, without imposing their own opinions. Remaining neutral throughout is essential to create a safe and open space for honest reflection.

During the debrief, participants then use sticky notes to write their answers to A1 and A2 in silence, one colour for positives and another for areas that need work. They then, in turn, come up to the visual and place their sticky notes on it while reading them aloud; first, everyone does their A1 answers, then everyone does their A2 answers. This creates a visible cluster of views and helps highlight themes or hot spots for discussion. The facilitator then sums up the findings from this part of the debriefing, and the first part concludes.

For the second part of the debriefing, participants are provided with individual cards (typically postcard-sized) which have the B1 and B2 questions written on them. They then again write their answers in silence. For the feedback, which is the same as in the initial part of the debrief, each person, in turn, stands up and reads their reflections and answers to the B1 and B2 questions. The B1 cards (personal learning) are kept by the participant, while the B2 cards (team actions) are submitted and become part of the output of the debrief.

This approach works well with groups of up to 12 people per facilitator. For larger groups, you can split the participants and run multiple sessions simultaneously. It is equally effective across different levels of seniority or within cross-organizational groups, and it usually takes less than an hour to complete.

If you are short on time, you can focus solely on A1 and A2, or alternatively, run it as a written or online exercise. However, B2 responses often provide the most significant contributions to post-exercise reporting.

This technique can easily be run online, with participants either reading out their A1 and A2 responses or typing them into the chat. The facilitator should track and summarize the key themes or areas that participants' comments relate to, just as they would with a visual in a face-to-face session.

After action review

An after action review (AAR) is a fast, flexible and simple method for reviewing an incident, exercise, workshop or training. Originally developed by the American military in the 1970s to review large-scale training operations, it has since become widely adopted across both military and civilian settings.

The AAR process revolves around three core questions:

1. What was supposed to happen, and what actually happened?

2 What went well, and what didn't? Why?

3 What would you do differently next time?

These questions encourage participants to compare expected outcomes with reality, explore reasons behind successes and challenges, and develop actionable improvements.

You can run an AAR with as few as two people and ideally no more than twelve per group. It can be used with any level of staff and works equally well for workshops, exercises, training days or real incidents.

When running an AAR, start by setting the tone. Make it clear this isn't about blame or fault, it's about learning. Encourage open, honest discussion and stress that every opinion matters, regardless of seniority.

Each question should be asked in turn and fully explored before moving on to the next. Roughly split your time: 25 per cent for Question 1, 25 per cent for Question 2 and 50 per cent for Question 3. Most of the talking should come from the participants; the facilitator's job is to guide, clarify and capture learning points.

If time is tight or the event is straightforward, you can use the AAR framework to review the whole exercise. If it's more complex, you may want to structure the discussion by key themes or walk through it chronologically.

What? So what? Now what?

This is a simple but effective technique that helps shape the content of your post-exercise report. It works in three parts: First, the issues from the exercise are identified during the debrief, which is the 'What?' Next, the team reflects on the significance of the issue, the 'So what?' asking what it means and why it matters. Finally, you move to the 'Now what?' stage, where the specific actions needed to address or build on what was learnt are discussed. The 'what?' and the 'so what?' can be written as observations in the post-exercise report, while the 'now what?' is the recommendation or recommendations.

Stop – Continue – Start

This technique cannot be used to debrief the entire exercise, but it might prove useful for reflecting on the exercise in a different way and could identify points that other techniques may not. It is organized around identifying the activities we want to stop, what went well and should be continued, and the activities we should start.

Using a mix of debriefing techniques can help capture a wide range of views and provide a more detailed evaluation of the response, making it easier to identify lessons learnt from the exercise. That said, time is often limited, so there might not always be the luxury of using more than one method.

Next steps and follow-up

Once the post-exercise report is agreed and signed off, one of the most important steps of the entire exercise process takes place: agreeing who is responsible for carrying out the recommendations, by when they should be completed and, where needed, how they should be implemented.

The exercise output, as documented in the recommendations section of the post-exercise report, will usually include one or more of the following actions:

1. Updates to plans or procedures.
2. Development of new responses or contingencies.
3. Training for individuals or groups; this might include addressing knowledge gaps, providing incident management skills or delivering role-specific training, such as loggist training.
4. Ideas for future exercises or key elements to include within them.
5. Adjustments to team structure, including clarifying roles and responsibilities or changing the composition of the team.
6. Enhancements to technology, tools or supporting systems, or suggestions for the purchasing of additional software.
7. Resource improvements, including equipment, facilities and workspace arrangements.
8. Development of teamworking or leadership skills.

It is essential to record the actions taken in response to the recommendations and to keep a clear audit trail showing how each recommendation was addressed. Recommendations do not always need to be accepted exactly as documented. They may be revised, deferred or even agreed not to be implemented. This could be due to being superseded by other projects, delayed by budget constraints or deemed not cost-effective. Whatever the outcome, all decisions must be documented and formally approved by the exercise sponsor.

If the exercise identified learning points that could benefit different parts of the same organization, the wider industry or local areas, the organization should consider sharing them, whether through presentations, industry forums or by publishing an article in a relevant trade publication.

Reflection on exercise delivery

Once the exercise has concluded, it's important that the exercise delivery team take a moment to reflect on their own performance and the exercise's delivery. I usually do this with the delivery team immediately after the exercise debrief. We talk through learning points and identify what could be improved to make the exercise even better next time. The reflections should consider the following: Did the timings work? Were the injects effective? Was communication smooth behind the scenes? It's useful to capture these insights while everything is still fresh.

Exercise practitioners, in addition to using this book, should keep their own personal record of learning throughout their career, capturing what they've learnt, how their approach has evolved and ways they can continue to improve their exercise delivery skills.

KEY LEARNINGS

- Cold debriefs allow more reflective, in-depth learning than immediate hot debriefs.
- Cold debriefs are most useful after complex exercises or where strong feedback needs further discussion.
- Cold debriefs should ideally be scheduled in advance and held within two weeks of the exercise.
- Structured debriefs use a four-question format to capture balanced and diverse insights.
- After action reviews (AARs) are flexible, quick methods focused on what happened and how to improve.
- Techniques like 'What? So what? Now what?' and 'Stop – Continue – Start' help turn feedback into clear actions.

- Cold debriefs should be supported by agendas, visuals and skilled facilitation to ensure psychological safety.
- The post-exercise report should include clear actions, deadlines and owners for each recommendation.
- Follow-up should include tracking implementation and justifying any changes or non-adoption of recommendations.
- Exercise delivery teams should also reflect on their own performance to improve future exercises.

20

Exercise documentation

In this chapter, you will learn about:

1 Writing the exercise instruction

2 Writing the post-exercise report

Documenting your exercise is a crucial part of its development and delivery. There should be a single central document that records all information related to the exercise's design and development. This serves as the source of truth for everyone involved and helps avoid confusion caused by scattered notes or multiple versions of working documents. It is particularly important when several people are contributing to the exercise, ensuring consistency and coordination across the team.

There is often a temptation to jump straight into developing slides if the exercise will be delivered using a slide deck. However, slides usually contain only headline points and minimal information. Without an exercise instruction, key details, such as inject timings, facilitator prompts and communication plans, can be lost or unclear. If you revisit the slides later, it may not be easy to understand how the exercise was actually run. The exercise instructions should contain much more detail and always accompany the slides.

Throughout the development process, the exercise instruction should be shared regularly with the sponsor and those involved in designing the exercise. This ensures alignment, transparency and that, on the day of the exercise, there are no surprises about how the exercise will be delivered. It also supports continuity: if the exercise lead becomes unavailable, someone else can pick up the document and continue with minimal disruption.

As a minimum, all exercises should produce two key documents:

1. An **exercise instruction** that captures everything needed to run the exercise.
2. A **post-exercise report** that records the outcomes, learning points and any recommendations.

Writing the exercise instruction

It is preferable to have a standard exercise instruction template that includes the basic heading required for all exercises, with additional headings added as needed for different types of exercises. It is important that the exercise instruction is a living document and is updated whenever an element is agreed or changed. Document control is crucial to achieving this. The document may be updated up to the day of the exercise, with last-minute changes captured in it.

The following are the standard headings which should be in the instruction:

1. **Exercise name:** This should be clearly visible on the front cover of the exercise instruction document. Make sure that version control is also evident on the cover. If the document versions become out of sync, it can be very difficult to consolidate all the information into a single document during a complex exercise.
2. **Purpose of this exercise instruction document:** This section explains the purpose of the document. For example, you might use: 'This planning document holds all the information required for the running of [Exercise Name]. It will be updated as planning develops in consultation with [Client] and published prior to the commencement of the exercise'.
3. **Exercise purpose:** A short statement describing the overall purpose of the exercise.
4. **Exercise objectives:** A list of specific objectives the exercise aims to achieve.
5. **Scope:** This outlines which people, departments or teams are involved, and what plans are being tested as part of the exercise.
6. **Reference documents:** Include any documents that were reviewed or referred to during the planning phase of the exercise and which plans are being exercised.

7. **Exercise style:** Describe the type of exercise being run, such as a tabletop exercise, wargame, SIMEX or another format.
8. **Location, date and timings:** Specify whether the exercise will be held in-person or online, where it will take place and when it will run.
9. **Overview of the scenario:** Provide a brief description of the exercise scenario. More detailed scenario information should be included as an appendix.
10. **Software:** Include details of any software required for the exercise. Additional information, such as login details and user instructions, can be included in an appendix.
11. **Deliverable tracker / project plan:** Include a tracker within the document to show tasks that need to be completed prior to the exercise, or lay out a project plan with deadlines and detail the activities for delivering the exercise.
12. **Participants:** List all participants, along with their normal job roles and the roles they will play during the exercise (e.g. team leader, loggist, human resources coordinator). This list can also be reused in the post-exercise report.
13. **Delivery of the exercise:** Include a list of those responsible for planning and delivering the exercise. If any of them are unfamiliar with their assigned roles, a short description of those roles and their responsibilities should be included.
14. **Running order of the exercise:** Include a detailed timeline showing the estimated duration of each segment of the exercise. Add notes on how each part will be introduced, including the initial briefing and exercise 'rules'. This should also cover how and when the exercise will end. Ensure you document who will deliver each speaking part. If a senior manager is scheduled to give opening remarks, include this in the schedule. You should also document how the hot debrief will take place at ENDEX.
15. **Feedback forms:** Include details about the feedback forms.

Additional information

Additional information which could be added within the exercise instruction, depending on the type of exercise being conducted, includes:

1. **Reference to other documents:** Where there are standard documents such as umpire assessments or inject lists, which are usually developed

in a spreadsheet, they can be referenced in the document. A SIMEX can include several other documents required for the running of the exercise, so these can be referenced.

2. **Joining instructions:** If there are joining instructions to be sent out to all participants, they can be included within the document.
3. **Printing list:** List of documents and the number of documents to be printed for use during the exercise.
4. **Packing list:** List of equipment and props which are needed for the delivery of the exercise and need to be taken to the exercise.
5. **Communications plan:** Include how the exercise team will communicate during the event, such as WhatsApp, Teams, radios and contact details for key exercise staff.
6. **Real-world incident protocols:** Outline what to do if a real incident occurs during the exercise. Include the 'NO DUFF' signal, and who has the authority to pause / terminate the exercise.
7. **Evaluation framework:** Mention the criteria or documents that umpires will use to assess performance.
8. **Risk assessment / safety considerations:** Note any safety-related considerations (e.g. physical risks in a LIVEX, emotional impact of distressing scenarios) and how they are mitigated.
9. **Lessons capture method:** Describe how lessons learnt will be gathered, such as structured debrief, feedback forms or a digital online survey.
10. **Media / photography plan:** If exercise publicity is expected, outline who will manage it, what photos or coverage will be taken and where it will be used.

The post-exercise report

Producing a post-exercise report is one of the most important parts of the exercise, and every exercise should result in the writing of one. Even if you're conducting training rather than a complete exercise, you should still consider producing a post-training report. There are always observations and issues that arise during training, which can improve the organization's response. If these points aren't documented, valuable learning is lost.

The post-exercise report should be a stand-alone document. If it is shared with a client, regulator or senior manager, they should be able to clearly see the key elements of the exercise, when it took place, how long it lasted, what the purpose and objectives were, who took part, what the scenario was and what the key learning points were.

EXAMPLE

Missing information

When conducting an exercise, I always try to obtain previous post-exercise reports to identify learning points from earlier exercises and, admittedly, out of curiosity to see how others write their reports. I once ran a cyber exercise for a large multinational company and, as usual, asked for a copy of their previous post-exercise reports. The report I received was well constructed and included clear, well-written recommendations.

However, as I read through it, I suddenly realized it was missing two key pieces of information: **what the scenario was** and **who attended the exercise**. While the front cover stated that it was a cyber exercise, this could mean anything from a ransomware attack to insider data exfiltration or website defacement, each of which would require a very different response.

If you don't record who attended the exercise, the organization has no way of knowing who was trained and exercised. It's a fundamental piece of information that you would expect to see in any post-exercise report.

Agreeing the content of the post-exercise report

In Chapter 10 we have seen that you should discuss the structure of the post-exercise report prior to the exercise. Depending on how the report will be used and who is going to read it, its content and the style in which it is written may be determined. There are several questions that can be asked to determine the report's content and format.

Is there any particular style they would like the report written in? The organization may have an in-house template that previous reports have followed, and they may want to keep the format consistent.

Do they want the report writer to suggest the urgency and relative importance of each recommendation or do they prefer to consider this after the report has been produced?

Do they prefer a large number of recommendations (15–30), or would they rather have a smaller number of more focused ones?

Where there is a qualitative assessment of the team, would they like this included in the report, or should it be provided as a stand-alone document?

Post-exercise report contents

The layout and content of a post-exercise report will vary depending on the writer's preference, the organization it is prepared for and the intended audience. This could include whether they want a short report with just the key details or a longer report with an executive summary. There are several key points which should be included in all post-exercise reports:

Exercise background: Provide a brief context of the exercise, including who it involved and why it was conducted.

Exercise purpose: State the purpose of the exercise, copied from the exercise instruction document.

Exercise objectives: List the specific objectives as agreed in the planning phase. The exercise objectives could be listed in a table, with a column indicating whether they were achieved, or this could be written in the director's comment.

Exercise style, location, date and time: Describe what type of exercise it was, how and where it was delivered and when.

Scenario overview: Summarize the key elements of the scenario used in the exercise.

Exercise participants: List all exercise participants with their names, job titles and exercise roles.

Exercise delivery team: List directing staff and their responsibilities (e.g. exercise director, umpires, role-players).

Exercise timeline: Include an outline timetable of the exercise.

Observations and recommendations: These are the key elements of the report. These should be presented in a table and grouped around the PICTS framework. The table may include the observation and recommendations, or it may include further information on how the recommendation should be implemented, who is responsible and by when it should be completed.

Performance assessment: Include scoring or commentary from umpire assessments or evaluation frameworks used.

Exercise director's comment: Include a short reflection from the exercise director on the overall delivery and outcome.

Participant feedback: Present feedback collected through forms or surveys and summarize the overall satisfaction with the exercise delivery.

Writing observations and recommendations

When writing observations and recommendations in a post-exercise report, it's important to focus on what actually happened during the exercise rather than what should have happened. Observations should be factual and evidence-based, drawn from umpire and exercise directors' observations, role-player feedback, feedback forms or points raised during the debrief. Avoid judgemental or overly critical language; instead, describe the issue and the impact it had on the ability of the team to operate or to respond to the scenario given. Each observation should be followed by a clear, actionable recommendation that suggests how the issue can be addressed. It should be clear from the observation why the recommendation should be actioned, and there shouldn't be any need to justify why it was included. Where possible, link the observation back to the exercise objectives or plans being tested, so the learning is grounded in the exercise context.

Recommendations should focus on structural or systemic issues, not individual actions. They should be repeatable: if the same exercise, or a similar one, were run again, the issue should likely arise again unless addressed. For example, if the team ignored the plan and created their own response from scratch, the recommendation should be to deliver training or a walkthrough of the plan, so the team is more familiar with the documented procedures. That training could then become an objective for the next exercise, where you test whether the team uses the plan properly. The observations and recommendations section should not be a running commentary of how the team responded to each inject and element of the exercises, as responses can vary depending on who is in the room or how they interpret the scenario. However, if the team made a major error, such as disregarding the agreed recovery strategy and inventing one that wouldn't meet the RTO or other requirements, that should definitely be noted. Overall, recommendations should focus on recurring or systemic gaps, not on one-off decisions that may not recur.

When writing observations and recommendations as a framework, use the PICTS framework, grouping the observations around the organization's plans and procedures, incident management skills that are not demonstrated, communication, teamwork and leadership, and responses to and understanding of the scenarios they face.

The exercise director's comment

Writing an exercise director's comment is not required in every post-exercise report, but it is a valuable opportunity for exercise planners to provide commentary on the team's performance without making explicit recommendations. The director's comment can cover a number of areas. It might include the overall impression of the exercise delivery team of its performance. The director could compare this performance with other exercises the team has taken part in or with other teams, both within and outside the organization. The comment may also address whether the exercise's objectives were met or exceeded. Did the team demonstrate learning from previous exercises, or were the points raised in this report similar to those highlighted in earlier ones? Finally, this section provides an opportunity to praise the team and thank them, as well as the planners, for their support in planning, delivering and participating in the exercise.

KEY LEARNINGS

- Every exercise should be documented in a single, central instruction document to serve as the source of truth for planning, delivery and continuity.
- Exercise instructions must be developed alongside slide decks, not replaced by them, as slides often lack the detail required to fully understand and replicate an exercise.
- Regularly sharing exercise instructions with sponsors and designers ensures alignment and transparency, reducing surprises on the day of the exercise.
- A minimum of two documents should be produced for every exercise: the **exercise instruction** and the **post-exercise report**.
- The exercise instruction should include standardized headings covering purpose, objectives, scope, scenario, logistics, delivery team and key operational details.

- Additional elements, such as packing lists, real-incident protocols and evaluation frameworks, may be added depending on the type of exercise.
- Post-exercise reports are essential, even for training events, as they preserve learning that might otherwise be lost.
- Reports must include key facts such as the scenario, objectives, participants, timeline and observed outcomes.
- Agreeing on the format and expectations of the post-exercise report in advance helps shape relevant and usable outputs.
- Observations should be factual and evidence-based, avoiding unnecessary critique, and recommendations must be actionable, systemic and linked to objectives.
- The **exercise director's comment** offers a space for overall reflection, comparisons to other teams or exercises and an opportunity to thank participants.

APPENDIX

Guidance on conducting cyber incident management exercises

In this appendix you will learn about:

1 The difference between a cyber and a 'normal' incident

2 Planning a cyber exercise

3 Defining objectives

4 Potential cyber scenarios

5 Possible element to be included within the scenario

6 Ransomware notes

This appendix provides guidance on designing and developing cyber incident management exercises.

What is cyber incident management and how does it differ from cyber incident response?

Cyber incident management is the non-technical response to a cyber incident. It includes managing an organization's reputation, developing and implementing a crisis communications strategy, ensuring continuity of operations impacted by the cyber incident if service delivery to customers has been disrupted, and coordinating statutory and regulatory communications reporting, Decisions such as whether to pay a ransom, when to communicate with stakeholders and when to engage third-party support also fall under cyber incident management.

Cyber incident response focuses on the technical actions taken to contain, investigate and mitigate an active cyber-attack. This includes system isolation, forensic analysis and the restoration of compromised data.

There is a crossover between incident management and incident response. For example, the technical team may consult the crisis team on whether to isolate systems, take down networks as a precaution, prioritize recovery steps, or rebuild systems as they were or use the opportunity to improve and build back better.

Why conduct a cyber incident management exercise?

While the technical response to a cyber incident is essential for restoring operations, it is the management of the incident and the accompanying communications that often define whether the overall response is seen as a success or failure. A cyber-attack almost always damages an organization's reputation, but that damage can be significantly worsened by a poor crisis response, such as being slow to notify affected parties, failing to provide timely updates to regulators or appearing dishonest about the impact.

All these elements can be practised during an exercise. The decision of whether to pay a ransom is complex and highly context-dependent, making it an ideal topic to explore during an exercise, where decisions can be tested without the pressure of a real event. Exercises also help senior leaders better understand the actual impact and pressure of responding to a cyber incident, far more effectively than a slide deck presentation ever could.

Is there a difference between planning cyber as compared with 'normal' exercises?

There are several aspects of a cyber incident that, while not entirely unique compared to conventional incidents, can combine in ways that make them particularly difficult to manage. These include the potential for rapid, complex and widespread impact across an organization. Unlike physical or operational disruptions, which are often contained within specific departments or locations, a cyber incident can affect multiple sites and business functions simultaneously, sometimes across global operations. This broad scope requires organizations to coordinate responses across diverse teams, geographic regions and even time zones, all while navigating regulatory, legal, professional and reputational challenges.

Cyber-attacks are often highly technical, with multiple impacts that may not be immediately apparent. Threat actors may also react unpredictably to the organization's actions, further complicating response efforts. The source of the attack may be unclear, involving state-sponsored actors, cybercriminal groups or even insiders, each requiring different response strategies.

Although cyber exercises present specific challenges, they should be planned and developed using the same structure and process as any other exercise.

Planning a cyber exercise

To run realistic cyber incident management exercises, the exercise director and design team need a basic understanding of how cyber-attacks typically unfold. This includes awareness of the technical aspects involved in detecting the attack, containing it and eventually removing the threat. They also need to be familiar with the broader issues, such as whether or not to pay a ransom, government and other organizations' guidance on the subject, and the implications of that decision.

It is important that the team has up-to-date knowledge of the current cyber threat landscape so they can reflect the ways in which contemporary attacks are carried out. The more the design team understands the nature of cyber threats, the more effectively these elements can be built into the exercise. This helps participants learn about the most likely way a cyber incident may develop. To develop an effective exercise, you should align the explanation's complexity with participants' knowledge of the cyber incident. It is also best to involve subject-matter experts to help develop scenario tasks, especially those that require technical accuracy. Their input ensures the exercise is both realistic and aligned with current cyber threats and response practices.

A briefing from the silver team or cyber incident response team (CIRT) to the crisis team can be a highly effective element of the exercise, providing crucial technical insights and helping decision-makers understand the evolving situation. They should present the crisis teams with key decisions rather than open-ended questions, as the crisis team may not have the technical expertise to provide precise answers.

In planning a cyber exercise it is important to reassure people within IT and IT security that the purpose of the exercise isn't to catch anyone out or question the effectiveness of current security measures. When planning the exercise, the design team should focus on the impact of the cyber-attack rather than on how the attacker gained access to the organization's systems. This is realistic as it can take several days, weeks or even never for the organization to piece together how the attack was executed.

Defining the cyber exercise objectives

The following are areas which could be developed into objectives:

1. Build awareness of the unique challenges and organizational risks associated with responding to cyber incidents.

   Category: Know / Feel

2. Explore how the crisis management team coordinates with technical responders, including CIRTs, SOCs and third-party cyber experts.

   Category: Work / Do

3. Verify the effectiveness and usability of existing cyber incident response plans and identify any gaps or areas for improvement.

   Category: Check

4. Make informed strategic decisions on containment, ransom payments and system recovery priorities with limited, evolving information.

   Category: Do / Work

5. Develop and deliver external communications in response to media coverage and social media commentary on the incident.

   Category: Do / Work

6. Communicate with key external stakeholders, including regulators, law enforcement, partners and customers, in line with established protocols.

   Category: Do / Check

7. Manage the organizational response to a supplier-related cyber incident, including coordination of communications, roles and responsibilities.

   Category: Work / Check

8. Develop a strategy to maintain critical customer services and initiate recovery of disrupted operations during a cyber incident.

   Category: Do / Check

9. Assess the effectiveness of internal communications and coordination across departments during a cyber incident, including how information is shared between IT, operations, HR, legal, communications and senior leadership.

   Category: Work / Do

Duration of cyber exercises

Cyber exercises can involve a significant amount of content, but it is possible to conduct a meaningful exercise within a typical timeframe of 2–3 hours. However, given the many different elements involved, it is worth considering a longer exercise, up to a full day, to allow for a more comprehensive exploration of all elements of a cyber incident. One challenge I have often encountered when conducting exercises is the lack of time to properly test the recovery phase of a cyber incident. Understanding the recovery phase is vitally important for the crisis team, as they need a clear idea of how quickly operations can be restored and when system functionality will be restored.

Potential cyber incident management scenarios

The following are a number of different cyber scenarios:

1 **'Standard' ransomware attack:** This scenario can involve either a complete lockout of all systems or selective access restrictions to specific systems. If the organization has Microsoft 365 or other cloud-based services, participants may be able to access these systems directly through bring your own devices (BYOD), making coordination easier. However, a ransomware attack is also likely to involve a data breach, meaning that the crisis team must be aware that sensitive data has likely been exfiltrated. As part of the exercise, details of the exfiltrated data can either be provided in the ransom note or left ambiguous to test the team's assumptions and response strategies. Additionally, continuity of operations and the implementation of business continuity plans should be key focuses, requiring participants to assess the impact on their systems and explore how they would maintain critical business functions during the incident.

2 **Data breach without encrypted data:** In this type of attack, only data is stolen, without any encryption or system lockout, meaning that business continuity does not need to be tested. The scenario can include a ransom note to explore the pay-or-not-pay debate, or proceed without one to focus on regulatory and statutory notifications. A possible exercise set-up could involve a third party discovering the organization's data on the dark web or on publicly available document dump sites like Pastebin. This scenario allows the crisis team to understand which data has been exposed and how to respond, including notifying regulators, affected

individuals and key stakeholders. The exercise could also explore offering credit monitoring to those impacted, how to communicate with customers and how to inform internal staff if their data is compromised. The data breach could be accidental or could be carried out by an insider.

3 **Website defacement:** In this scenario, an attacker has defaced the organization's website, potentially posting illegal content such as the glorification of a terrorist organization or links to illegal materials (e.g. child exploitation content). If the website is managed by a third party, the exercise can test the organization's ability to coordinate with external providers and assess their response capabilities. Additionally, the exercise could include the website owner being locked out, highlighting the challenges of regaining control or taking the site offline quickly. This scenario helps test legal, technical and reputational response strategies, including engagement with law enforcement, public relations teams and web service providers.

4 **Ransomware attack on a SaaS provider to the organization:** This scenario could involve a third-party SaaS provider being breached, leading to the exfiltration of your organization's data. This adds complexity as you must coordinate incident response with the third party, which may have different priorities, legal obligations and response strategies. The exercise can help your organization understand which services the provider delivers, their backup policies and which of your clients they hold data of. If the provider is a large, powerful company, the response dynamics will differ from those of a small, niche provider with limited response capabilities. Additionally, the exercise should consider the risk that the provider will go bankrupt or shut down services, leading to the permanent loss of data.

5 **A supply chain attack, zero-day exploit or unpatched vulnerability is discovered where you do not know if your organization has been compromised:** This scenario involves a known vulnerability being publicly disclosed or a supply chain attack from a third party, such as the Kaseya or SolarWinds incidents, where it is announced that hackers or nation-states are actively exploiting it. Your organization must determine whether it has been compromised. Customers may begin asking whether their data, held by your organization, is affected, even though you do not yet have confirmation of whether your systems have been exploited. A key focus of this exercise could be developing clear communications and key messaging while navigating the uncertainty of the situation.

6 **Doxxing of a senior manager's details:** Doxxing involves the leaking of private information about a senior executive, such as their phone number, home address, family members' details or personal photographs. The exercise would focus on how the organization responds to this threat and what protective measures are implemented. The exercise could incorporate an investigation into who was responsible, how the data was exposed and how to remove the information from public sources to mitigate the risk.

7 **Cyber-attack on OT (operational technology):** OT refers to hardware and software systems that monitor and control industrial equipment, processes and infrastructure. It is commonly used in manufacturing, energy, utilities, transportation and critical infrastructure, where real-time system control and automation are essential. A cyber-attack on OT could render key parts of an organization unable to operate or operate safely. The attack could be an attack by malware or a distributed denial of service (DDoS) attack. If the organization is part of critical national infrastructure, it would need to coordinate an incident response exercise with national cybersecurity agencies and law enforcement. The exercise could focus on how an OT incident would be managed and escalated, what external support is available and how decision-making processes would unfold in a high-stakes scenario.

8 **Data destruction:** The scenario could involve critical data being destroyed, with backups either unavailable or also compromised. This would test how the organization maintains continuity of operations without access to its core systems. It could also explore whether the business can operate using alternative data sources from elsewhere in the organization, and how quickly those workarounds can be implemented.

9 **DDoS attack taking down external-facing systems and websites:** This scenario involves a DDoS attack that overwhelms the organization's public-facing systems, websites or customer portals, rendering them inaccessible. The attack could be financially motivated, such as cyber extortion demanding payment to stop the disruption, or politically driven by hacktivist groups targeting the organization's reputation. The exercise can test the technical response of IT teams in mitigating the attack, including working with internet service providers (ISPs) and cloud security vendors to implement countermeasures. It can provide an opportunity to evaluate crisis communication strategies, ensuring that customers, stakeholders and regulators are informed without escalating panic. The scenario may also explore alternative business continuity

measures, such as redirecting traffic, activating backup websites or temporarily suspending certain online services.

10 **Cyber-attack on a supplier, partner or managed service provider (MSP) requiring a joint response:** This scenario involves a cyber-attack on a key third-party provider, such as an IT managed services provider, cloud provider or supply chain partner, that has direct access to your organization's systems or data. The attack could involve ransomware, data exfiltration or a zero-day exploit affecting multiple clients, requiring a coordinated response between your organization and the affected supplier or partner. A major challenge is navigating different priorities, levels of transparency and response capabilities between organizations. The exercise can test how well contractual agreements, incident response playbooks and escalation procedures align between parties. It also provides an opportunity to assess communication strategies, including how and when to inform regulators, customers and other stakeholders. The scenario could introduce complications such as the provider going offline, being legally restricted in what they can disclose or suffering reputational damage that impacts your organization.

Elements which can be included within the exercise scenario

The following lists detail a large number of different issues an organization may face when responding to a cyber incident. These lists could be shared with the design team or sponsor, who could then be asked which ones they would like incorporated into their exercise. Depending on when the exercise starts and ends, some issues may not be relevant, so the 'initial response' may not be included in the exercise if it occurred before the exercise begins or if there may not be enough time to address the 'recovery issues' before the exercise ends.

Initial response

1 **Initial response and upward reporting:** Testing how quickly an incident is detected, escalated and communicated to key stakeholders. This could come from several entities, including third-party notifications (e.g. suppliers, law enforcement), security operations centre (SOC) alerts, help desk reports from users and automated system alarms.

2 **Detecting an attacker within your network and deciding how to respond:** Assessing the organization's ability to identify a live threat, evaluate risks and determine whether to contain, monitor or remove the attacker.

3 **Assessment of the event:** Evaluating the organization's ability to accurately assess the scope, impact and severity of a cyber incident.

4 **Call-out procedures:** Testing how effectively internal and external teams are notified and mobilized during a cyber incident. This could include disconnecting, capability assessments and external integrations.

5 **Incident prioritization:** Triaging the incident, classifying it, prioritizing the response and assigning tasks. Utilize threat intelligence to understand the malware used. Note that these are technical activities, but the cyber incident response team (CIRT) could brief the crisis team on what action they are carrying out.

6 **Containment activities:** Choosing a containment strategy that ensures teams can swiftly isolate affected systems and prevent further spread of an attack. This may also involve examining the authorities and responsibilities for containment.

7 **Law enforcement notification:** Practising the process of reporting cyber incidents to relevant law enforcement or regulatory bodies.

8 **Working with boards, owner organizations and higher-level organizations:** Include a component to test how these are informed, consulted or approve actions (e.g. ransom payments or public statements).

9 **Working with an SOC:** How the initial notifications from an SOC to the organization will occur, along with the information requirements of both the SOC and the organization. It also explores how they will collaborate and how decision-making will be conducted.

10 **Cyber insurance:** Assessing when and how to engage cyber insurance providers and understanding policy coverage. Practise notifications and call-outs. Practise the ongoing work with insurance and look at how much the insurance company is involved in the response.

11 **Third-party support call-out:** Testing the coordination and response time of external cybersecurity partners, MSPs or forensic investigators. This could also include the use of professional ransomware negotiations.

Management

1. **Conducting the first incident team meeting:** Testing the efficiency of initial coordination, role assignment and decision-making in response to an incident.
2. **Practise working with other internal response teams:** This could include the CIRT and a communications team. Either team may request that the crisis team make decisions.
3. **Threat intelligence:** Evaluating the use of internal and external intelligence sources to understand the nature and origin of the attack. I have, in a number of exercises, produced a threat intelligence brief so that those taking part can get more detailed information on their attackers and take into account their motivation and ways of working.
4. **Legal:** Incorporating advice from legal professionals within the response.
5. **Pay or not pay:** Assessing the decision-making process around ransom demands, including legal, ethical and financial considerations. The authority to pay and the method of payment should also be considered. Whether to contact the attackers to negotiate or even to waste time could be considered. Working with professional cyber ransomware negotiators could also be included within the exercise.
6. **Breaking story:** Simulating media discovery of the incident and testing the organization's ability to control the narrative. This could include customers finding out about the incident before being formally told and then being angry about this.
7. **Secrecy:** Testing how sensitive information is controlled, determining who needs to know what and managing internal leaks.
8. **Regulatory and statutory reporting:** Ensuring compliance with legal requirements by practising timely and accurate reporting to regulators and authorities in all the jurisdictions the organization operates in, including the text for speaking to the ICO.
9. **Frauds and threats from attackers:** Assessing how the organization handles phishing attempts, extortion threats and fraudulent activities following an attack as well as informing staff of these possible threats.
10. **Taking into account staff welfare:** Ensuring the well-being of employees during and after a cyber incident by managing stress, preventing burnout and providing necessary support for affected individuals.

11 **Writing strategic intent:** What are we trying to achieve with a response? What must we do to survive and also take advantage of any opportunities?

12 **Working strategy:** How are we going to continue working in the short, medium and long term? What are our priorities? How do we continue to deliver service and to whom?

13 **Monitoring dark web activity:** Appointing a suitable organization whose role would to be to identify if company data appears for sale or is made available on the dark web.

Communications

1 **Writing communications:** Practising the creation of clear, accurate and timely messages for internal and external stakeholders. This could include writing information for the organization's website.

2 **Lines to take:** Developing key messages and consistent responses to media, customers and regulators to manage reputational impact.

3 **Media and social media:** Testing the organization's ability to manage public messaging, respond to press inquiries and monitor social media narratives.

4 **Internal communications:** Evaluating how effectively employees are informed, reassured and provided with guidance during a cyber incident.

5 **Identifying stakeholders:** Ensuring all affected parties, including customers, regulators and internal teams, are recognized and considered in the response.

6 **Communications strategies:** Developing an overall strategy for engaging with the press and stakeholders and controlling the narrative. This could include being very open about the attack or playing a more low-profile strategy.

7 **Informing stakeholders in a structured manner:** Prioritizing key stakeholders when disclosing information. This can include statutory notifications, deciding which channels to use and fulfilling their information requirements.

8 **Communicating with customers if systems are down:** Ensuring alternative communication channels are in place.

9 **Developing questions and answers (Q&As):** Creating standardized responses for customer-facing staff and publishing FAQs on the organization's website to ensure consistent messaging.

10 **Notifying people of data breaches:** Practising how to inform affected individuals and organizations in compliance with legal and ethical obligations. Deciding whether they will be offered credit monitoring. Considering what reassurance can be provided to them that it will not happen again.

11 **Attribution of the attack:** If the attacks are known, then should this be made public?

12 **Guidance for people whose data has been breached:** Ensuring clear, supportive and actionable advice is provided to impacted individuals.

Recovery

1 **Eradication:** Ensuring recovery can occur only after eradication is complete, including addressing how attackers gained access to the organization.

2 **Technical recovery:** Testing the organization's ability to restore systems, data and services following a cyber incident. Deciding whether the systems will be rebuilt as is or built back better.

3 **Working with third parties:** Assessing coordination with external vendors, partners and service providers during incident response and recovery.

4 **System recovery priorities:** Determining which systems and services should be restored first based on business impact.

5 **Recovery timelines:** Evaluating realistic expectations for system restoration and ensuring alignment with business continuity plans.

6 **Continuity of operations and manual workarounds:** Testing the organization's ability to maintain essential functions when key systems are unavailable.

7 **Lessons learnt:** Discussion on how lessons learnt would be conducted and when they should be conducted.

The use of ransom notes in cyber exercises

Ransom notes are a critical element in cyber exercises simulating ransomware attacks, providing participants with a realistic challenge in decision-making, incident response and crisis communication. These notes typically mimic real-world attacker tactics, demanding payment in exchange for data decryption or to prevent data leaks. The benefit of including ransom notes in an exercise is that they force organizations to confront the pressure and urgency of a ransomware incident and provide a time and an amount of money on which they can decide whether to pay. They also help gauge an organization's preparedness in terms of backup recovery and response strategy and this can be played into the discussion on whether to pay the ransom. If the note is unrealistic, it can diminish the effectiveness of the exercise, leading to a lack of engagement or a misrepresentation of the complexity of real-world ransomware scenarios.

Elements of a ransomware note

A well-crafted ransomware note in an exercise should include multiple elements to enhance realism and test an organization's response capabilities. Key components include:

1. **Demand for payment:** The note should specify a ransom amount, often in cryptocurrency, along with instructions for making the payment. Putting the amount in a cryptocurrency can help the crisis team determine the exact ransom demand. It also aids discussions about whether the crisis team has the authority to pay the ransom and how they would acquire large amounts of cryptocurrency if needed.
2. **Details of the attacker:** If the attacker's name is included in the note, those responding can use threat intelligence to identify the attackers and their motives. Use of real attackers can add to this realism. The crisis team should respond differently to a hacktivist than to a nation state attack.
3. **Deadline for payment:** Cybercriminals frequently impose a deadline, after which the ransom increases or data is permanently deleted. This puts pressure on the team responding.
4. **Threat of consequences:** The note may warn of data destruction, public release of sensitive information or business disruption if demands are not met.
5. **Contact information:** Attackers often provide email addresses, dark web portals or chat-based contact methods for negotiations. Putting this in can be useful, so that the crisis team can debate whether they would contact the attackers, even if it was to waste their time.
6. **Proof of encryption:** Some ransom notes include a sample of encrypted files or a demonstration of decryption to prove they control the data. This

makes the point that data which has been encrypted, takes time to decrypt and is a laborious task.

7 **Instructions for decryption:** Attackers typically outline the steps to obtain the decryption key upon payment.
8 **Psychological manipulation:** The note may use fear tactics, urgency or even attempt to sound 'helpful' to pressure victims into compliance.

A well-planned and delivered cyber exercise can go a long way to ensure that an organization is aware of some of the issues, actions and pressures they might face during a cyber incident. Once an organization has completed one scenario, as seen in this appendix, there are a number of other different attacks that could also have a major impact on the organization.

GLOSSARY

AIG	American International Group
BC	Business Continuity
BCP	Business Continuity Plan
BIA	Business Impact Analysis
BYOD	Bring Your Own Device
CBRN	Chemical Biological Radiological Nuclear
CIRT	Computer Incident Response Team
CMT	Crisis Management Team
COMAH	Control of Major Accident Hazards
DDoS	Distributed Denial of Service
DORA	Digital Operational Resilience Act
DR	Disaster Recovery
ENDEX	End of the exercise
FCA	Financial Conduct Authority
FEMA	Federal Emergency Management Agency
ICAO	International Civil Aviation Organization
ICT	Information and Communications Technology
ISP	Internet Service Provider
IT	Information Technology
JESIP	Joint Emergency Services Interoperability Principles
KS&B	Knowledge, Skills and Behaviours
LIVEX	Live Exercise
MSP	Managed Service Provider
OT	Operational Technology
PICTS	Plans, Incident Management, Communications, Teamwork and Leadership, Scenario Response and Recovery
PRA	Prudential Regulation Authority
QMS	Quality Management System
RTO	Recovery Time Objective
SIMEX	Simulation Exercise
SITREP	Situation Report
URL	Uniform Resource Locator

INDEX

Page numbers in *italic* refer to information within figures or tables.

More from Kogan Page

ISBN: 9781398614871

ISBN: 9781398609754

ISBN: 9781398613492

ISBN: 9781789661842

www.koganpage.com